Interesting Times

Interesting Times
Some New Zealanders in Republican China

Chris Elder

TE HERENGA WAKA UNIVERSITY PRESS

Te Herenga Waka University Press
Victoria University of Wellington
PO Box 600 Wellington
teherengawakapress.co.nz

First published 2024

ISBN 9781776921416

A catalogue record is available from the National Library of New Zealand

Printed in Aotearoa New Zealand by Ligare

Remembering Michael Green
1947–2012

Contents

Illustrations

Maps

0
300
600 miles
0
500
1,000 kilometres
Tunhuang
(Dunhuang)
Sandan
(Shandan)
Hwang Ho
Yenan
(Yan'an)
Lanchow
(Lanzhou)
Sian
(Xi'an)
Shuangshipu
(Feng Xian)
CHINA
Tatsienlu
(Kangding)
Chengtu
(Chengdu)
Batang
Ya-an
Minya Konka
(Gongga Shan)
Chungking
(Chongqing)
Yang Tze
INDIA
Kweiyang
(Guiyang)
Burma Road
Yunnanfu
(Kunming)
Kweilin
(Guilin)
Xi Jiang
Lashio
Mekong
BURMA
(Myanmar)
Hanoi
Haiphong
FRENCH
INDOCHINA
Vietnam, Cambodia, Laos)
Hainan
SIAM
(Thailand)
Rangoon
(Yangon)

Peking
(Beijing)
Tientsin
(Tianjin)
An Guo
(Anguo)
Chefoo
(Yantai)
KOREA
Tsinan
(Jinan)
Tsingtao
(Qingdao)
JAPAN
Hsuchowfu
(Suzhou)
Nanking
(Nanjing)
Shanghai
Wuchang/Hankow/Hanyang
Kiukiang (Jiujiang)
Kuling (Guling)
Yochow
(Yueyang)
Changsha
Kienning
(Jianning)
Hengyang
Foochow (Fuzhou)
Formosa
(Taiwan)
Kong Chuen (Jiangdu)
Canton (Guangzhou)
Hong Kong

Preface

This book had its beginnings in a series of interviews carried out by my friend Michael Green and myself in 1985–86. We had both served in the New Zealand Embassy in Peking, before it became Beijing, and we shared an interest in earlier contacts between New Zealand and China. We set out to meet and record the personal accounts of New Zealanders who had lived in China in the first half of the twentieth century.

At the time we had a vague idea that we might publish something on the basis of what people had to say, but circumstances intervened. In the way of our shared profession we were dispatched to different parts of the world, and when we did find ourselves together in Wellington, leisure time was not easy to come by. Then, sadly, Michael died in 2012. His legacy to me was a big cardboard box of books, notes and cassette tapes, on which I have drawn extensively in carrying forward our joint project.

Our interviews of 38 years ago have shaped the content of this book but they have not entirely determined it. Some whose names came up only fleetingly in the course of our discussions, and even some whose names did not come up at all, had too much to offer to be left out. Conversely, some others who might have been expected to find a place have not. As is implied in the book's subtitle, 'Some New Zealanders in Republican China', this is not a comprehensive account, although it may perhaps fairly claim to be a representative one.

To the extent possible, I have tried to present the actors and their experiences in historical sequence. To provide context, I have from time to time included a brief account of political and military developments at different points over the Republican years. Rather than burden the text with source notes, I have provided the origins of quotes used in an appendix at the back of the book.

My thanks are due first of all to those who gave their time to talk to Michael and me about pre-revolutionary China, in terms of either their own experience or that of friends or relations. I owe a deep debt of gratitude to Karen Evans, another old Peking hand, who transcribed with rare accuracy the often imperfect recordings of those conversations. I am grateful also to all the people who offered comments or otherwise contributed to the work in progress, including Jean and John Brouwer, Duncan Campbell, Sharon Crosbie, Michael Crozier, Barbara Francis, Mary Hall, Pauline Keating, James Kember, Elspeth Paine, Merle Ryburn and Philippa Wood. Rachel Hurd at Dunedin's Presbyterian Research Centre and staff members at the Alexander Turnbull Library have been extremely helpful in locating relevant illustrations.

Finally, I owe a very large debt of gratitude to Fergus Barrowman and the team at Te Herenga Waka University Press. In particular, the skilled editorial guidance of Rachel Scott has been central to producing a text that may hope to do some justice to the resourcefulness, the dedication, and occasionally the humour of New Zealanders who travelled to China before 1949.

In rendering the names of Chinese people and places, I have most often chosen to use the forms current during the Republican era of which I am writing. Where that seems likely to give rise to misunderstanding, I have included in brackets at first mention the current Pinyin romanisation. Where there is no obvious romanisation deriving from the Republican era, I have fallen back on Pinyin. This is a thoroughly unsatisfactory approach, but so are all the alternatives.

Introduction

'May you live in interesting times' is often touted as an ancient Chinese curse. In reality, it is not clear that the expression has ever had a place in spoken or written Chinese, except perhaps in translation from English. Nevertheless, it captures an underlying truth as applicable in China as anywhere else. 'Interesting times' – times marked by constant change and often-conflicting demands – present a particular challenge for human resilience and adaptability.

The era of Republican China began with the fall of the Qing (Manchu) Dynasty in 1912, and came to an end in 1949, when Mao Tse-tung declared the People's Republic of China. The 37 years in between were marked by power struggles between competing warlords, anti-foreign riots, floods and widespread famine, an eight-year conflict with Japan, and the depredations of an ongoing civil war. For the Chinese people, and for foreigners living in China, these were indeed interesting times.

The end of the Republican era saw also the end of a period of over a century during which China was subject to often humiliating demands and constraints imposed by foreign powers. One aspect of that foreign involvement was an influx of people from other countries – not just citizens of the states that had entered into formal treaties with China, but nationals from around the globe. There were few restrictions at China's borders, nor were there significant constraints on how foreign nationals lived and worked within the country.

The motives of those who chose to establish themselves in China were many and varied. They tended, however, to fall within two main streams – those who sought to change China by exposing it to different (mainly Western) practices, values and belief systems, and those who were there to pursue commercial interests. The first stream was exemplified by the influx of missionaries representing the various branches of Christianity; the second by the many foreign companies established in commercial centres such as Shanghai, to buy, sell and manufacture in the Chinese market.

New Zealand came late to this descent upon China. Although two New Zealand insurance companies set up offices in Shanghai in the 1880s, and the first missionary travelled from New Zealand to China in 1891, New Zealand's focus over the last years of the Qing was primarily on promoting, and responding to, the process of colonisation in New Zealand itself. By early in the Republican years, however, New Zealand entities such as the Presbyterian Church and others who were prepared to look beyond the country's established links with the outside world had begun to consider what China might have to offer. Over time, some among their number travelled there to find out.

The range of interests and motives that drew New Zealanders to China was by and large a subset of those applying to the foreign community more generally, although commercial interests were less obviously to the fore. Many travelled under the auspices of missionary groups, whether the various British organisations such as the Society for the Propagation of the Gospel and the Church Missionary Society, the Shanghai-based China Inland Mission, or the uniquely New Zealand Canton Villages Mission. It was not uncommon for a commitment to missionary work to become a gateway to more broadly based activities, such as George Shepherd's work towards rural reform or, earlier, James Houston Edgar's forays into geographical description, anthropological research and exploration pure and simple.

For many, a significant inducement was the fact that China could offer an experience vastly different to life in post-World War I New Zealand. Even Rewi Alley, who came to devote his life to humanitarian causes, was drawn initially by an appetite for risk. 'At that time he was interested primarily in adventure,' J.B. Condliffe reported after a meeting on the eve of Alley's departure, 'and there was a war in China.' Not infrequently, the impulse to seek out new and different experiences preceded a decision to opt for China. Alice Cook was training with an eye to India before she was diverted to deal with a sudden and pressing vacancy at Kong Chuen. The men who accepted positions in the Friends Ambulance Unit were chosen from a roll of conscientious objectors willing to serve anywhere overseas in a humanitarian capacity.

For others, it was China itself that provided the focus. Agnes Moncrieff's first experience, as a delegate to a 1922 World Student Christian Federation conference in Peking, captured her imagination and left her determined to return (and not as a missionary: 'I knew I'd be absolutely no good in some out-of-the-way place, tucked away by myself.') James Bertram was dispatched precisely because there was a perceived need for Britain's colonies to build greater understanding of events in the then Far East. New Zealand economists saw China's case as offering a unique opportunity to study the challenges an emerging power faced in its pursuit of economic growth.

It is hard to tell to what extent, if at all, those who travelled to China from New Zealand were distinguished from those who came from other countries. In Chinese eyes they would have come under the general rubric 'foreigner', without much perceived need for further enquiry (although Alice Cook believed that under the special circumstances of the Canton Villages Mission there was some recognition of New Zealand origins – 'I don't know if they ever knew how many sheep we had, or anything, but they trusted us.') If New Zealanders had passports at all they would have been British passports. In fact James Bertram is identified in Mao's collected works as a 'British journalist'. The British Embassy felt it was within its rights to expel New Zealander Kathleen Hall when the Japanese complained about her conduct.

Within the foreign community there was perhaps greater differentiation between New Zealanders and other foreigners. In Bertram's eyes there existed 'a representative colonial type – the [W.H.] Donald, the Alley'. If for no better reason than that in a pioneer society such as New Zealand tradesmen or service facilities were not always readily to hand, those who emerged from a practical background tended to display qualities of self-reliance and a willingness to improvise. When the truck Rewi Alley was travelling in blew a gasket, he replaced the failed part by hammering flat his aluminium soap-dish, and when that in turn gave way he cemented together two layers of canvas from his kitbag.

Nurse Kathleen Hall, lacking instrument trays, sterilised her medical equipment in bamboo dumpling steamers. Lindsay Crozier, 'a very handy man', brought electricity to his hospital by coupling an old 500-cycle generator to a Chevrolet engine driven by charcoal gas. Marjorie Monaghan's readiness to take up a spade and work on her school's vegetable plot was a matter for wonder to onlookers. 'This kind of add-mix of theory and practice is so much part of our nature,'

Courtney Archer said of his China experience. (Although he himself was not the best example – when asked at his recruitment interview if he could change the back axle of a truck halfway up a hill in pouring rain he replied, 'My god, I wouldn't know where to begin.')

Arguably, there was also a greater readiness among New Zealanders to accept and work alongside their Chinese counterparts. Many in the foreign community brought to their dealings with the Chinese people an attitude of superiority that stemmed from perceived technical advantage, and a sense of moral rectitude rooted in the Christian religion. Dr H.B. Turbott showed no such inclination in his dealings with his two Chinese medical colleagues – 'they were very competent men . . . fully trained . . . they really ran the hospital'. Nor did Agnes Moncrieff, working under the aegis of the YWCA of China, who found 'the finest group of women you could possibly imagine'.

The relative absence of social stratification in colonial society perhaps carried over into a greater willingness to meet the people of their adopted country on their own terms. In Alice Cook's experience, people from the United States tended to be 'a bit bossier', and those from Britain more class conscious (an observation that one British missionary group's requirement that any New Zealand candidates for recruitment be drawn from the 'the "higher" social classes' does nothing to disprove).

While the presence of New Zealanders in China over the period of the Republic did little to raise awareness of New Zealand as a country among the Chinese, the same cannot be said in reverse. From the time James Houston Edgar began contributing stirring accounts of his Tibetan adventures in the China Inland Mission journal *China's Millions* through to more prosaic reporting in later missionary publications and elsewhere, New Zealand readers were constantly introduced to new aspects of China and Chinese society. Often they took a proprietorial interest because such reporting tended to be linked to fundraising for China-related causes, both spiritual and secular. YWCA members 'put a penny in the tin' to help finance Agnes Moncrieff's work; Alley support groups came up with funding and equipment for the Sandan Bailie School; the Presbyterian Church's Busy Bees children's groups provided Annie James with a Ford V-8 motorcar, and a porcelain bath as well.

When those resident in China returned to New Zealand for a break it was common for them to spend part of their time at home undertaking 'deputation work' – travelling around the country addressing meetings and giving interviews about circumstances in the Chinese Republic. These were often undertaken with serious political purpose rather than simply as an adjunct to fundraising. In 1934 Rev. George McNeur startled a reporter from the *Otago Daily Times* by assuring him that 'Many very fine young men and women had given their lives for communism.' Later in the 1930s Bill Holland barnstormed the country inveighing against Japan for its aggression in China, and against the US for facilitating that aggression through its exports of petrol and aviation fuel.

These were not just voices in the wilderness. Holland was able to reach out to his uncle, Sid Holland, already a political figure and later to become prime minister. On the other side of the political spectrum, Agnes Moncrieff found herself being tracked from meeting to meeting by Janet Fraser, wife of Prime Minister Peter Fraser. She showed herself 'extraordinarily interested' in China, and knowledgeable to the point where Moncrieff once told her, 'Well, Mrs Fraser, I think you could make my speech even better than I could.'

Perhaps Janet Fraser spoke to her husband. It was to him that another returnee, Rev. McNeur, by that time retired and living in New Zealand, addressed representations about the plight of Chinese families separated by the war in south China from husbands and fathers in New Zealand. His words fell on sympathetic ears. The government's decision to allow family reunification, at first on a temporary basis and later permanently, laid the foundation for a stable Chinese community in New Zealand.

The New Zealanders who travelled to live and work in China varied in their assessment of what they hoped to achieve. Agnes Moncrieff was realistic: 'When you think of the influence of a mission or anything else in China, it's just a drop in the ocean, isn't it?' George Shepherd had a considerably more all-encompassing vision. Deliberating whether he should devote himself to Chiang Kai-shek's programme of social reform (he did), he burst out, 'What would Borodin do with a chance like this?' Rewi Alley's goals were less lofty. As a factory inspector, as a promoter of cooperatives, and at the Sandan Bailie School his focus was on doing what he could to better the lot of ordinary Chinese – a drop in the ocean perhaps, but nonetheless worth the effort.

History is divided on how much China's long-term development was affected by the Western presence over the 'interesting times' of the Republican period. Less, perhaps, than the protagonists thought at the time, bearing in mind the sober assessment of R.H. Tawney, who concluded in *Land and Labour in China* that 'Salvation could not be imported from the West, even if the West possessed it; it is not an article of commerce. It must come from China herself, if it is to come at all.'

It is hard to argue that the undertakings associated with New Zealand fall outside this dictum. Alley's wartime cooperative movement, Shepherd's programme of rural reform, McNeur's Canton Villages Mission all in the end fell by the wayside, or were swept away on a tide of revolutionary fervour. Left to plot its own course after 1949, China set about working towards Chinese solutions to Chinese problems.

Republican China: A Brief Account

Towards the Republic

By 1912 the mandate of China's Qing Dynasty had run its course. Riven by internal divisions, incapable of meaningful reform, humiliated by the incursions of foreign powers, the court that had ruled China for 268 years could no longer command authority. On 12 February 1912 the child emperor Pu Yi abdicated the throne, ceding power to a provisional revolutionary government. For a short time that government was headed by Sun Yat-sen, until he stepped aside in favour of Yuan Shikai, the strongman thought most likely to be able to impose unity on a fragmented country.

Before taking office, Yuan Shikai had pledged his support for the republican ideals of Sun Yat-sen, but once installed he set about reducing the influence of the revolutionaries. The parties supporting revolutionary reform, brought together into the Kuomintang (Nationalist Party – KMT), found themselves at odds with Yuan and his supporters. Boosted by a massive loan from foreign powers, Yuan dismissed Parliament, marshalled his well-drilled troops to quell opposition, and by 1914 had established himself as a dictator, effectively an emperor in waiting.

Nearby Japan had no wish to see a strong new dynasty emerge in China. In January 1915 it presented Yuan with a list of demands (the 'Twenty-one Demands'), acceptance of which would have reduced China to little more than a vassal of Japan. Yuan nevertheless did agree to many of Japan's requirements, in the belief that doing so would secure Japan's support for his imperial ambitions. As it turned out, not only did he fail to placate the Japanese, he also lost the respect of a number of the military commanders who had provided his power base. Deprived of their support, and in the face of active Japanese opposition, Yuan's pretensions to imperial status came to nothing. A disappointed man, he died on 6 June 1916.

The warlord period

In the absence of a single obvious successor to Yuan, China descended into a chaotic time of competing regimes, the 'warlord period'. The government in Peking was at the behest of whichever military leader held sway for the time being in northern China. In the south the Nationalist Party, now run by Sun Yat-sen, established a rival government in Canton (Guangzhou), which was equally dependent on the goodwill of local warlords. Throughout the country those with the military power to impose control over particular regions continued to exercise that control to enrich themselves and their followers.

Through a series of treaties imposed upon China by force of arms, foreign powers had acquired the right to establish concessions or settlements in the main commercial centres – self-governing enclaves beyond the reach of Chinese law. The shifting tides of government after 1912 did not materially alter the operation of this treaty port system. In these enclaves foreigners enjoyed extraterritoriality – the right to be governed by the laws of their own country. The foreign powers continued to deal with the Peking-based government, not least because doing so offered the best guarantee of a continuation of the their extraterritorial rights.

China was inveigled into declaring war on Germany late in World War I, then denied the fruits of that commitment when the Treaty of Versailles allocated the German concessions in Shandong to Japan. This prompted the first real manifestation of national feeling, with student demonstrations in Peking on 4 May 1919 sparking parallel expressions of outrage widely across the country. Shocked by the strength of popular dissent, the Peking government endorsed its delegation's refusal to sign the Versailles treaty.

In July 1921 the first plenary meeting of a new political party, the Chinese Communist Party (CCP), was held in Shanghai. Among the 13 delegates was a young writer and labour leader from Hunan, Mao Tse-tung. A central topic of discussion was the possibility of forming an alliance with Sun Yat-sen, and such an alliance became an unlikely reality later the same year. Never particularly well defined, this First United Front saw government firmly in the hands of the Nationalist Party, with increasing Communist Party influence in mass propaganda and military affairs.

Sun Yat-sen died in March 1925, his vision of a united republican China never realised. Later the same year long-bubbling anti-foreign sentiment came violently to the surface after Shanghai police fired upon a student demonstration, inflicting fatal casualties. The nationwide reaction saw boycotts of British and Japanese commercial enterprises, and further violence, most notably in Canton, amid a growing sense that foreign interference was the source of China's woes.

In Hong Kong, a mass withdrawal of labour brought the colony almost to a standstill. Foreigners in China's interior, including missionaries, were forced to retreat to the coast, or even leave China altogether.

What became known as the '30 May Incident', in which the British municipal police opened fire and killed 13 demonstrators in Shanghai and wounded many more, galvanised anti-imperialist sentiment. With it came widespread resentment towards the Peking government and the coterie of warlords who were essentially acquiescent in perpetuating foreign nations' extraterritorial rights and privileges.

1. The Explorer

James Huston Edgar approaches Tibet

For one New Zealander at least, the fall of the Qing Dynasty in 1911 was a distinctly unwelcome development, as it imposed severe constraints on his travel within Sino–Tibetan borderlands. James Huston Edgar would spend the remaining 25 years of his life in remote, difficult and often dangerous parts of China's hinterlands, but he was never able to attain the goal to which he most aspired: life on the high plateau of Tibet.

In the final years of the Qing, China had moved aggressively to assert its presence in Tibet. This came in response to the 1904 Younghusband Expedition, which saw a British expeditionary force enter Tibet from India and take Lhasa by force of arms. The British did in time withdraw, but the military adventure left China acutely aware of the vulnerability of its western borders, and no less of the opportunity to strengthen them afforded by the disorder in Lhasa following the British incursion. Chinese forces led by the uncompromising Chao Erfeng, 'the Butcher of Kham', pushed into eastern Tibet, sacking monasteries, breaking the power of the lamas, and establishing effective Chinese suzerainty over the Tibetan marches (as the border areas were known).

By 1910 Chao had established Chinese control over much of Tibet, extending to a military presence in Lhasa itself. That control could not, however, survive the collapse of the ruling dynasty and in December 1911 revolutionary forces in Chengdu seized and executed Chao Erfeng.* Lacking clear lines of authority, starved of pay and rations, soldiers drifted away from their posts, or mutinied, or were forcibly expelled.

Over the period of Chinese dominance, James Huston Edgar, a missionary with the China Inland Mission (CIM), had established himself in the Szechuan border town of Tatsienlu (now Kangding), and from there had struck out progressively further west. His journeys took him over the high mountain passes to Litang (afterwards memorialised in an article entitled 'The Highest Town on Earth, *and* the Dirtiest')

* By popular account he was beheaded standing up, because he refused to kneel to a social inferior.

and on to the major religious centre of Batang.

On Edgar's first visit to Batang he found the town dominated by 'a magnificent Lamasery . . . with gold or guilded roofs and spires, [which] contains 1,500 lamas, who pay little attention to either Peking or Lhassa'. When he returned four years later the monastery was 'a mass of ruins' following the attentions of Chao Erfeng. Cheered by the opportunities for mission work the Chinese intervention appeared to offer, in 1909 Edgar removed his household from Tatsienlu to Batang, further removed from his support base but, importantly, 650 kilometres closer to Lhasa.

It was in Batang that Edgar was based at the onset of the Republican era, and it was from that remote outpost that he was forced to beat a retreat to the security of the coast when the collapse of imperial authority made his position no longer tenable. The journey was not an easy one: revolutionary tumult in Szechuan had cut off the most direct line of retreat so he and his family had to follow an unfamiliar and difficult route south across Yunnan, through the gorges of the upper Mekong River and down to the Gulf of Tonkin, then by sea to Shanghai.

In 1911 Edgar was 39 years old and the CIM was the largest Protestant mission society in China. Throughout his career he was assiduous in carrying out the mission's core function, the distribution of biblical texts, if somewhat cavalier in his approach. 'Bible distribution is like shelling a fortified area,' he informed readers of the CIM's journal, *China's Millions*. 'Put in enough missiles, and vital damage will be done.' In 1920, a reasonably typical year, Edgar travelled 3400 kilometres at altitudes of up to 16,000 feet (488 metres), visited 65 towns and villages and five lamaseries, and distributed a total of 37,594 books and tracts. He could, he said, have achieved much more had it not been for political unrest and a shortage of funds.

Interviewed in Dunedin in 1986, Ron Malcolm, Edgar's nephew and himself the son of a CIM missionary, recalled the meticulous accounting that went into reports for CIM publications, and his uncle's reservations about their real worth:

> Your reports only included the number of people you'd baptised because that was the only way they had of judging your success or otherwise, and he [Edgar] said he'd put them under – a lot of them hadn't enough

> sense to understand what it was all about. But as he said, a lot of the missionaries, he felt, were really trying to paint a picture to satisfy their homeland, because . . . *China's Millions* came to their supporters in the churches at home, and the supporters [would think] oh, he's baptised 20 people, or whatever. You think, oh, he's doing great, [so I'll] send out another ten dollars or pounds or whatever it was. And he saw through all that. Poor chap, he said they never kept a list of all the people who defected or left them . . .

'Putting them under' was Edgar's term for the ceremony of baptism. As with the distribution of texts, his approach to this aspect of missionary work was a liberal one. In a letter to Anna Malcolm, Ron's mother, he announced the baptism of 14 new members, followed by the comment that 'the new members were stupid as a rule, but as no effort could get any definitions into their poor old heads I hoped for the realities and put them under . . .'

Work as a colporteur slid easily across into journeys of exploration, justified in the missioner's eyes as seeking out new areas for evangelical outreach, but probably owing at least as much to his innate spirit of inquiry. In Ron Malcolm's view,

> He was basically an explorer. He was a Fellow of the Royal Geographical Society, not just a member. And he had this capacity to get facts. He would go into far greater detail than the average person, and this is what made him of value to the mission. That kind of thing thoroughly enticed him.

Edgar himself attributed what became an enduring commitment to exploration and inquiry to his early upbringing. Born in Victoria in 1872, he and his family moved to New Zealand when he was four years old to take up land near Tapanui in west Otago. Writing in a penny notebook 50 years later, he recalled the impact of the adopted frontier society he was later to exchange for another.

> The ravine and part of the campaign country were robed with grand and sombre forests and the plateaux beyond with trackless open wastes of towering birch. Wild pigs in great numbers were found in the rolling tussock clad downs and wild cattle in the plateaux of the Hinterland

> . . . Tapanui in many [ways] was a very romantic outpost of British civilisation. The Blue mountain with its deep sombre clefts, tundra wastes and open birch forests were to most realms of mystery and away beyond to the west were snowcapped Southern Alps and unexplored Takitimus. The call to explore came early and the cause is not far to seek.

A romantic outpost Tapanui may have been, but it had little to offer someone of Edgar's ambition. He came to refer to it dismissively as 'Happy Valley', after the vale of facile pleasures in Samuel Johnson's novel *Rasselas*.

Before he was 14 years old Edgar had left the local school to work variously as a farmhand, a rabbiter and a bushman. Later he spent time as a swagman, travelling around the country, and for a time living in a Māori settlement at Tolaga Bay. Over these years he became increasingly attracted to the idea of working as a missionary. Whether propelled more by evangelical zeal or a zest for travel is a question he sometimes pondered in later life, without ever arriving at a final answer. Either way, in 1895 James Huston Edgar applied to the newly formed Dunedin CIM Council to be accepted for missionary work in China. The application was unsuccessful, it seems because of his limited formal education.

Bitterly disappointed, Edgar decided to leave New Zealand for Australia in order to study at Adelaide's Belair Bible Institute. It was an unhappy parting: even 40 years later he remembered it, writing to his sister-in-law and confidante Anna Malcolm that 'the cold blustery spring night at Rattray St. wharf as an ambitious but forlorn youth left his home for the unknown, unblessed and unsung, still sends a chill down the spine of one who claims its shores no more'.

Australia treated him more kindly. In 1898 a renewed application to the China Inland Mission, this time in Melbourne, met with success. In 1899 Edgar took ship for the CIM headquarters in Shanghai to begin 37 years' endeavour as a missionary and explorer in China's borderlands.

The town of Tatsienlu provided an early setting-off point for his activities, and it was there that he came to establish his base after the fall of the Manchus had rendered the Tibetan marches unsafe. At 8600 feet (2621 metres) above sea level, the town lies at the centre of a region that includes some of the most broken country on earth, characterised by Britain's naval intelligence in a wartime geographical handbook as 'a mass of sawtooth peaks, precipices, box canyons, sombre forests and pounding streams'.*

Edgar set out to explore and give some account of this difficult landscape. He edged his way through 'suicidal lateral canyons . . . where dogs and goats, if required, are carried in when young'. He is credited with having been the first Westerner to see a giant panda in the wild. He described, and sketched, Mt Minya Konka (Gongga Shan), at 24,906 feet (7556 metres) the highest peak in 'China Proper', although he did not at the time publish his description 'owing to an idea that description of scenery without exact measurements was poor geography'. (A successor, Joseph Rock, was not so inhibited, in 1930 providing *National Geographic* with an account of his exploits among 'the vast mountain systems wholly unknown not only to the western world, but to the Chinese themselves'. He set Minya Konka's height at 30,200 feet (9205 metres), higher than any other mountain in the world, and had to be talked down by his editors.)

A steady flow of reports and articles drawing upon his travels, together with the publication of his first book, *The Marches of Mantze*, saw Edgar elected a Fellow of the Royal Geographical Society. The accolade clearly meant a great deal to him, not least because it served as a riposte to those in New Zealand who had, he considered, failed to recognise his worth. He conveyed the news forthwith to friends in Dunedin, and the *Otago Daily Times* obligingly brought it to wider notice in an entry headlined 'From Tapanui to Thibet'.

Edgar undertook his explorations sometimes on foot, sometimes on horseback, sometimes alone, sometimes in the company of other missionaries, but most commonly with a small team of Chinese support staff. Occasionally the support crew tried his patience, as when he came upon his cook using biblical texts as firelighters, but by and large he was generous in his appreciation of their contribution. As he put it in concluding an article, 'Pioneering Among the Kin Ch'wan Hordes', written for *China's Millions* in 1916:

* No one in British naval intelligence, of course, had ever been anywhere near Tatsienlu. The description was lifted in its entirety from a paper Edgar contributed to the *Journal of the West China Border Research Society* in 1926.

> My thanks are due to . . . my patient, toiling coolies who never murmured in the worst places, who were always willing to share with me the last scraps of their maize scones, and whose kind-hearts prompted their vile tongues to curse impudent youngsters and insinuating imposters of all races and creeds.

The CIM compound in Tatsienlu became a stopping point for foreign expeditions of various sorts. One early traveller to the region was Lt-Col Frederick M. Bailey, whose appetite for exploration had been whetted by participation in the Younghusband Expedition of 1904. His goal was to trace the course of the Tsangpo River, which he ultimately established flowed into the Bay of Bengal as the Brahmaputra, almost 4000 kilometres from its origins in Tibet.

Bailey and Edgar set out together, travelling down the Yangtze River in hide coracles before leaving the western bank to make their way over high passes to the valley of the Mekong. They crossed the Mekong hanging from a single-strand rope bridge, clutching a 'saddle' and letting gravity take them to the far side. Their blindfolded horses followed by the same route. Continuing southwest through Tibet, they passed through a series of high mountain ranges into the valley of the Salween, where the two parted company.

Bailey recognised in Edgar a kindred spirit. His account of his travels, *China – Tibet – Assam: A Journey, 1911*, described his travelling companion as

> . . . typical of the best class of missionary for Tibetan work, not fanatical and prepared to work more by example than by actual teaching in the first instance. I later accompanied him into country where no missionary had ever been, where one mistake or any indiscreet excess of zeal would have done immense harm; in the country through which we travelled he left behind a multitude of friends and the very best impression . . . He was always ready to place his vast knowledge at the disposal of travellers, and I was by no means the only one who had used him to further their plans. He delighted in leaving his home at a moment's notice and travelling with some perfect stranger for days with the idea both of helping him and of obtaining information for his mission.

Another visitor who called on Edgar's services was the pre-eminent botanist and plant collector Ernest Henry Wilson, who, over the course of three expeditions, identified and introduced to European cultivation many new plant varieties, among them *Actinidia chinensis* (Chinese gooseberry, now kiwifruit). The preface to Wilson's major work, *A Naturalist in Western China, with Vasculum, Camera and Gun*, acknowledges his debt to Edgar: 'to another friend, J. Hutson [sic] Edgar, I am indebted for much information concerning the peculiar customs of the Tibetans and other non-Chinese races'.

'The peculiar customs' of the people he lived among were just one of Edgar's areas of inquiry. The broad scope of his interests is reflected in the articles that increasingly found a place in learned journals. The meticulously detailed accounts of particular journeys give way to notes on the coiffure of the women of one tribe, the stone implements used by another, the physical peculiarities of a dwarf race, the equally peculiar lolus or 'human unicorns', the rites of Lamaism, life in a Tibetan nunnery, the topography of mountains as yet unclimbed, even a clinical analysis of the physiological and mental effects of life at high altitudes.

Such knowledge was not always easily won. Following the advent of the Republic and the collapse of Chinese authority, the Tibetan border areas descended into petty warlordism and brigandry, and mission workers often went in fear of their lives. On a visit to New Zealand, Edgar recounted to his awestruck nephew how he had once escaped harm by performing a haka.

> Here he was, going along this high pass, and there were bushes all the way down and so on, and in the moonlight he suddenly noticed figures running between the different trees coming up the path. And when they were getting towards the path all of a sudden he realised they were ambushing him, you see. So he just thought of a Maori haka and he suddenly danced down and charged down the hill – kamati kamati, you know – and did this Maori haka and he said there was just an explosion as they tore down the bank – they thought they'd struck a real devil.

On another occasion, having stumbled into a brigands' camp, he extricated himself by offering Bible tracts for sale – and insisting on

At Tatsienlu, 'The CIM compound came to be a necessary stopping point for foreign expeditions.' In this case, that of Joseph Rock in 1932.

'Their blindfolded horses followed by the same route' – crossing the Yalung River.

payment. Once, travelling by river, he was forced to shelter below the gunwales while his boat was raked by the machine-gun fire of discontented soldiery.

By the time of China's reunification in 1928, Edgar had published a second book, *The Land of Mystery: Tibet*, and the first (and perhaps still the only) dictionary of the language of the Kiating, a little-known people based north of Tatsienlu. His articles had appeared in a range of scholarly publications. To his fellowship of the Royal Geographical Society had been added fellowships of the Royal Anthropological Institute and the Asiatic Society. He was the founder, honorary president of the Chengdu-based West China Border Research Society, and a frequent contributor to its journal.

The Land of Mystery was based on a series of lectures Edgar delivered in Australia and New Zealand in 1926, during his last visit on furlough. In Dunedin he spent time with Ron Malcolm's family: 'Whenever he came to stay with us he'd walk up and down while he was drying the dishes or anything – he'd be talking the whole time, just going flat out.' As a speaker, 'He had this characteristic of Coleridge's mariner – you know, he could fix you with his beady eye. He was just terrific. When he sat in front of a crowd, or in a room, he had to be the centre of attention.' To help ensure he was, Edgar frequently took the stage wearing the thick fur-lined coat he favoured in Tibet.

The missionary returned to New Zealand three times on furlough. As well as addressing meetings he spoke to newspapers, not always in flattering terms. 'Were I asked . . . what is a Tibetan noted for, I should unhesitatingly reply, his smell!', he told the *Otago Daily Times*.

Edgar's visits took him to the main centres on both sides of the Tasman, and to the small towns of his youth – Tapanui (where his family still lived), Owaka, Balclutha. In 1918 he travelled to the Chatham Islands, where he walked the length of the main island and abstracted two Moriori skulls. These became a point of contention when the authorities refused to let him keep them for scientific study – another instance, in his view, of the country in which he grew up failing to recognise his true worth.

Chiang Kai-shek's nominal reunification of China in 1928 did not greatly change the state of affairs in the country's far west, where warlords continued to vie for influence. In 1935, however, events on the national stage did have repercussions for the area surrounding Edgar's chosen base at Tatsienlu.

The path selected for the Communist army's forced retreat, the Long March, took the Red forces through Sichuan and the Lolo borderlands to the Dadu River. There, just 70 kilometres from Tatsienlu, they fought the battle of Liuding Bridge (Liuding Qiao), described by Edgar Snow in *Red Star Over China* as 'the most critical incident of the Long March'. By Snow's account, Red Army soldiers countered the removal of decking planks from the iron-chain suspension bridge by swinging hand over hand along the chains, in the face of sniping and withering machine-gun fire, to win the far bank and clear the way for their comrades to cross.*

Edgar, who had already evacuated his wife and other mission staff, thought it prudent to absent himself from the Red Army's line of advance. He and a companion removed themselves to an abandoned fortification in an area known as Lower Bogland, 13,000 feet (3962 metres) above sea level. After 25 days they made their way cautiously back down to Tatsienlu, 'like the good old Duke of York'. They found the Communist forces had bypassed the town, although they had justified the missionaries' caution by carrying off two priests from a nearby mission station.

James Huston Edgar was by now 63 years old, and in poor health. He was strongly resistant to suggestions that he might take another furlough outside China, or even consider retirement. Indeed, he had for some years sought an opportunity to remove himself from Tatsienlu to somewhere even more remote – Lop Nor, say, far to the west in Xinjiang's Tarim Basin. 'If I have to die soon', he wrote to Will and Anna Malcolm in Dunedin, 'why not die in a fine way? A lasting advertisement is better than a funeral at home. And a mound – unknown – near Lop Nor better than a tombstone in "Happy Valley" (Tapanui).'

In May 1936 *China's Millions* published a letter from Edgar headlined 'Surrounded by Reds', telling of his time as an 'absentee landlord' in Lower Bogland. It went on to give a cheerful account of his activities since:

* Snow's account may be overstated. Many years later Deng Xiaoping told US National Security Advisor Zbigniew Brzezinski that the opposing forces had been limited to some of the local warlord's troops armed with muskets, but the action had been elevated for propaganda purposes.

> Every day I am on the street for three or four hours. The camps are visited early in the morning, and later, at some strategic point, the Pentecostal-like masses are dealt with as they swing and saunter to and fro in the city. In this way thousands of contacts are made with picturesque men from the geographical 'nowheres'. Sometimes, if they are outlandishly wild, we take them inside and treat them to the gramophone.

The letter is prefaced by an editorial comment: 'This letter from Mr J.H. Edgar has a pathetic interest in the fact that it was received by us after the news of his home call.'

Edgar died in Tatsienlu on 23 March 1936, following a bout of influenza. The *Otago Daily Times* reported soberly on his death so far away from home. From the report, it is clear that other members of the family did not share his wanderlust. His father and three brothers lived still in Tapanui. A sister had married and moved as far afield as Dunedin.

2. The Medical Man

H.B. Turbott in south China

Towards the end of the time when Edgar was coping with life under the various warlords in the Szechuan border regions, another New Zealander arrived to confront an equally disturbed situation in southern China. Like Edgar, Dr H.B. Turbott travelled to China as a missionary; again like Edgar, his motives extended some way beyond the purely evangelical. Indeed, in Turbott's case, the missionary impulse seems to have been almost entirely absent.

> You thought you were going to do some good, and so on. But I really wanted to be a surgeon and the proper thing to do in those days was to go home and sit the exam in England. We [New Zealand] didn't have one in those days and everybody went home to sit the exam. I was going to do the same thing but I happened to top the group in the final exam in Dunedin, and the professor invited me home and said, 'What are you going to do with yourself now you've passed?' I said, 'Well, I've got a house surgeoncy in Waikato Hospital and I'm going there now.' 'Oh,' he said, 'what do you want to be?' And I said, 'I want to be a surgeon.' 'Well,' he said, 'if you want to be a surgeon the best thing to do is to go to either India or China.' I said, 'Why?' And he said, 'Well, because you get there the experience in a few months you wouldn't get for years in New Zealand, and a very varied one too.' So that's how I originated the idea of going to China.

In China, Turbott was part of the Canton Villages Mission run by the Presbyterian Church of New Zealand. It had its beginnings in the work of Rev. Alexander Don, who from 1882 had undertaken missionary work in New Zealand itself, ministering to Chinese miners in the goldfields. Few miners stayed in the New Zealand long term – after they had accumulated a sufficient stake they returned to their home villages about the Guangdong provincial capital of Canton. Why not, Don suggested, follow them there and establish a mission that could build upon that basis of familiarity?

Spurred by the vision of becoming 'the first church in the Southern Hemisphere to open in China', in 1902 the Presbyterian Synod of Otago and Southland laid the foundation for such a mission. It was under the stewardship of Rev. George Hunter McNeur, a minister from south Otago, who coincidentally had studied, like Edgar, at the Belair Bible Institute in Adelaide. In time, McNeur was able to acquire land for a mission compound at Kong Chuen (now Jiangcun), about 20 kilometres north of Canton.

It was to Alexander Don that Turbott directed his application to take up a position at Kong Chuen. The interview that followed does not seem to have generated much enthusiasm on either side. Turbott recalled, 'He was a sour customer if you don't mind me saying so . . . If you hadn't been keen to go you wouldn't have gone.' Don had by then completed 18 tours of the goldfields and may have thought he had a right to be sour. His 53,000 kilometres of hard travel, half of it on foot, over 28 years had produced only a small handful of enquirers whom he thought worthy of baptism.*

By the time the newly qualified Dr Turbott and his wife arrived at Kong Chuen in 1923 the CVM compound housed missionary residences, a 100-bed hospital with an associated nurses' training school, a girls' boarding school and a conference centre. About 20 New Zealanders were on the staff – as missionaries, teachers and nursing and medical support. Among their number was Annie James, trained as a midwife and remembered by Turbott as 'a very pleasant person, full up of her objective'. Single-minded in the pursuit of that objective, James was to become the face of the CVM in later years, and, after imprisonment by the Communist regime, the last New Zealand missionary to leave China.

In the short time the hospital had been operating, two New Zealand doctors had already fallen victim to the unhealthy local conditions, one dying before he had even begun work. Two Scottish brothers, John and Edward Kirk, were now providing medical care on a part-time basis, with the burden of the day-to-day work falling on two Chinese graduates. Turbott found himself dealing with illnesses for which his New Zealand training had scarcely prepared him – malaria, leprosy,

* This was a very Presbyterian approach to conversion. The CIM was much more forgiving, as J.H. Edgar's cheerful willingness to 'put them under' attests.

Party of Outgoing CVM Missionaries, September 1923. From left: Mrs McKenzie, 1923; Rev J.M. McKenzie, 1923; Rev H. Davies, 1909; Miss M. Findlay, 1923; Mrs Turbott, 1923; Mrs Davies, 1904; Nurse Park, 1923; Master Jock Davies.

Annie James, left, soon after she arrived in China in 1912; with Annie McEwan and Annie Hancock. (Presbyterian Research Centre Archives) typhoid, snake bites, even wounds inflicted by grasshooks (sickles) and muskets in inter-village disputes.

> While we were operating one day a bullet or two came through the window of the surgical room. We sent a messenger running to say, 'Here, you're shooting at us.' Back came the messenger to say, 'No, it wasn't them. It was the other people the other way.' They stopped shooting at us, just the same . . .

Turbott had in fact chosen one of the most turbulent periods in the consistently turbulent warlord period to take up residence in the environs of Canton. The dispute in question had arisen from one peasant's water buffalo grazing upon grass growing on another's boundary strip, and came to involve 35 villages. To such disputes between clans were added incursions by the various politicians' private armies and straight-out banditry. In the New Zealand doctor's (not entirely reliable) recollection, there was often enough little to distinguish between the last two.

> Canton city, all the time I was living in that area, was under the charge of Sun Yat-sen. He went away sometimes to England, to confer with his British friends, and while he was away Chiang Kai-shek used to come down and levy a toll on the city. The method was to put his troops in, block a street, both ends, with his troops, and then go from shop to shop demanding ransom . . . If the first one or two objected they were just shot, and then the rest of the street . . . gave whatever money the soldiers demanded. There was a sort of warlord inter-warfare which went on all the [almost three] years I was in Canton.*

The nature of the country surrounding the hospital at Kong Chuen could hardly have been more different from the precipitous and sparsely populated environs of James Edgar's base in Tatsienlu. The mission lay on the plain that extended for many miles north of Canton. It was surrounded by broad expanses of rice paddies, crisscrossed by waterways and narrow roads. Villages and market towns dotted the landscape, their buildings clustered closely together to free more land for cultivation.

* This is a little unfair to Chiang Kai-shek, as activities of this sort were being pursued well before he came onto the scene. At that time some banks in Canton declined to deal in cash at all, on the grounds that to do so only invited robberies.

Many of the villages were surrounded by high walls as a protection against intruders.

Most medical services were offered at the base hospital, but there were times when Turbott was called upon to travel to his patient. He came to learn that his medical bag was not always a guarantee of personal safety.

> It was purely hospital work with priority calls from the villagers for urgent help. For example, I was called out one night at 10 o'clock to a woman who couldn't deliver a baby, which was very rare in China. And I sent a message down to say, 'I'm coming down – don't shoot.' Because they had a wall around all the villages, they were all walled in, with night guards walking around with muzzle-loaders – that's really what they were – against robbers. Anyhow, when I got within [about] 200 yards they started popping at me. Didn't make any difference if you sent a message. Anyhow, they were no good at shooting so I got past in the end. I got to the hut through the spirit door – it was just a simple little hut of sun-burned bricks, with a trestle bed on one side and a trestle bed on the other side. The woman was in trouble on one, and underneath were two or three pigs and half a dozen fowls and so on . . . And she was completely helpless. I said, 'No, I'll have to take you to the hospital . . .'

During his time at Kong Chuen, Turbott had his first taste of public health work. He became involved in an American research project into the incidence and the severity of hookworm (schistosomiasis), a parasitic disease then widespread in southern China. It leads to severe illness and often death. Johns Hopkins University professor W.W. Cort, who recruited Turbott, was an early contributor to the body of knowledge that ultimately saw the disease largely eradicated. Turbott reported:

> The only other volunteer [to do Cort's fieldwork] was a woman, a Canadian from the Canadian hospital in Canton, and the pair of us worked like slaves for this damn fellow for three months analysing all of the field stuff we gathered from various farms and all around the place to find out just what kind of hookworm was there and how much there was etc. He enjoyed all our work . . . but he never mentioned or gave us credit in his book which he wrote afterwards.

Ungenerous though he may have been in acknowledging others' contribution to his research, Cort was apparently not entirely without gratitude. He recommended Turbott for a tuberculosis research position in the United States. Turbott declined, but countered with a request to be given a course of training in the use of X-rays, a technology not then available at the Kong Chuen hospital. To his surprise the response was favourable, and he found himself enrolled in a three-month course at the Peking Union Medical College. Funded by the Rockefeller Foundation, the College was intended to provide China with a stream of able doctors trained in Western medicine. In Turbott's estimate, the scheme was only too successful – '100 [students] a year with 200 professors teaching them to be very good doctors. They taught so damn well that most of them got jobs overseas.'*

At the end of the three-month course students sat a final exam, including a practical test: 'Go to the laboratory, get the gear you require, build your X-ray machine, take a picture of your hand, present it to the examiner . . . I've still got the picture I took of my hand, and it was a bloody clear one, a good one.'

Regrettably, Turbott was never able to apply his newfound knowledge at Kong Chuen. On the very day he received his certificate of competence in radiography, the anti-British riots of 1926 broke out. There was no question of returning to Canton – the only safe course was to leave China for the time being. He set out for Hong Kong to join his wife and other CVM colleagues, who were evacuated from Kong Chuen.

> We were hurried out [of Peking] the next morning on the Blue Express, which was a beautiful British train . . . When we got to Nanking you stopped at the other side of the river and crossed in a boat, and the first thing I knew when we landed was my suitcase was torn from me, I was thrown into the gutter, and a couple of coolies were pounding me. Then there was a tall Chinese in a beautiful silk cheongsam screeching at these coolies and hitting them with his stick and driving them away. I got up and recovered my suitcase . . . and he said, 'Now, you come with me. You are going to . . .?' I said, 'Shanghai.' 'Right. You come with me and I'll take you to the station,' which he did. And put me into the

* According to Jonathan Spence (*The Search for Modern China*, 1991, p. 384), a staff of 123 foreigners and 23 Chinese at the Peking Union Medical College oversaw the graduation of 64 Chinese medical students between 1924 and 1930.

> train and said, 'Now, you stay there and don't get out until you reach Shanghai.' When I reached Shanghai the city was being rampaged through by armed people, who if they saw a foreigner would take a potshot at him. I kept below the windows because they had potshots at my hotel at times, and round about midnight I was smuggled out into a big American ship and landed in Hong Kong.

As a British colony, Hong Kong offered a safe haven from the violence that engulfed much of southern China that year. In the colony, however, Chinese discontent was translated into a general strike.

> Hong Kong was under martial law. The governor had declared that every white person in the place must take a job which had been abandoned by the Chinese people in the anti-British riots. There were nearly 2 million there in those days in Hong Kong. Some were apportioned to milk the few cows that were used to give milk for the foreign children, others to do this or that – collect the rubbish. I was, shortly after landing, booked to learn to drive a tramcar . . . So in half a day I learned to drive a train car, and drove it for six weeks in Hong Kong city.
>
> The first month [it was] empty – the Chinese wouldn't use it. It was an indefinite strike and then gradually it began to break. One day I had a Chinese conductor on my tram; before that I'd had another European. The Chinese conductor came dashing through on the first or second day and said, 'There's a bomb! There's a bomb!' I went to the back of the car and there *was* a bomb – it was smoking under the back seat. So I threw it in the gutter and got the car going again, and before we'd gone about 20 yards the bomb blew up, so we dodged that. But gradually in the next fortnight the Chinese came back and I lost my job. I have a certificate saying that I'm a licensed driver of the Hong Kong and Shanghai Corporation.

Sixty years later Turbott could still produce both the X-ray photograph of his hand and his certificate as a licensed motorman. Neither proved of lasting use. Faced with the prospect of an extended period of idleness in Hong Kong, with no guarantee that it would ever be possible to resume medical work in China, the doctor decided to return to New Zealand. He did so with regret, because his work had left him with a high regard for the Chinese people, and a wealth of useful experience.

> My time in China was invaluable to me all the rest of my life. Because not only did I get in touch with all the possibilities in tropical medicine, but I got the – what would you call it? – consciousness and the ability to take on anything that came along. Because I never knew what was going to come along in China – I mean I was dealing with various quite tropical things including some leprosy and so on, and I took it all in my stride . . . You had a sort of wider vision of things, you didn't worry about things, you were there to do what you could with whatever turned up.

That Turbott chose to return to New Zealand, rather than pursuing his original intention of going on to London and a career in surgery, was a consequence of his China experience. The widespread incidence of preventable disease, and his hookworm research, took him in another direction: 'I decided I wanted to be a Health Man.'

The decision was a happy one for New Zealand. From pioneering work among predominantly Māori populations on the East Cape, Turbott rose to become director-general of health from 1959 to 1964, a constant advocate of improved public health practices and a thorn in the side of successive administrations. He is remembered still as 'the Radio Doctor'. For more than 30 years his was a constant voice, dispensing practical health advice on the National Programme every Saturday morning.

Republican China: A Brief Account

The Northern Expedition

After the death of Sun Yat-sen in 1925 the Kuomintang, still based in Canton, abandoned efforts towards peaceful reunification. Chiang Kai-shek, commander of the military training college at Whampoa, drew together a disciplined and well-trained military force. In early 1926 he launched the Northern Expedition, with the objective of subduing the northern warlords, combating foreign influence, and achieving a united China.

The Northern Expedition met with rapid success and provincial warlords hastily sought ways to conciliate the revolutionary forces. By mid-1926 the expedition had taken the key Yangtze Valley urban base of Wuhan, and from there moved on to occupy Nanking (Nanjing). The Canton government, which was coming to reflect more and more the views of its Communist elements, re-established itself in Wuhan.*

Chiang Kai-shek, once in control of Shanghai, decided the uneasy alliance could not last. On 12 April 1927 he launched a pre-emptive strike, killing the Communist leaders within his reach, and setting about a widespread purge of Communist cells, destroying the CCP's infrastructure. Within months he had brought the Wuhan administration to heel, and established a reunited Nationalist government in Nanking with himself at its head. By the end of 1928 a renewed drive north had seen the northern capital, Peking (for much of this period named Peiping), fall to KMT forces, and a new capital for all China established in Nanking.

The Long March

The national unity achieved following Chiang Kai-shek's Northern Expedition was fragile at best. Most of the warlords had been forced into an accommodation but they had not been defeated militarily.

* Wuhan is made up of what were previously three separate cities situated at the confluence of the Yangtze and Han rivers: Hankow (Hankou), Hanyang and Wuchang. The foreign concessions were situated in Hankow.

They maintained control of their armies, and siphoned off resources for their own use at the expense of the wider population. While Communist attempts to foment urban discontent met with no great success, a separate group led by Mao Tse-tung, Chu Teh and others made progress in organising the peasants in rural areas of Hunan and Kiangsi (Jiangxi), while successfully repulsing Nationalist 'bandit extermination' campaigns.

In 1934 Chiang Kai-shek launched a campaign against the Communist forces that finally succeeded in dislodging them from their rural stronghold. Threatened with encirclement, on 16 October 1934 about 80,000 Communist troops broke through the KMT lines and set out on what would become the Long March.

The Long March was a tactical retreat that took more than a year and covered a distance of more than 8000 kilometres. It crossed 12 provinces in the face of frequent attack and extreme privation. In October 1935 the remnants of the original force arrived in northern Shensi, to join forces with an existing base of Communist guerrilla fighters.

The following year the Communists, under the leadership of Mao Tse-tung, established their headquarters further east, in Yenan (Yan'an), and set about the process of rebuilding. While their ultimate aim was to continue class struggle in China, they had acquired another, more immediate objective – to counter Japan's increasingly bold incursions into Chinese territory. Mao called on the Nationalist forces to form a renewed united front to this end.

3. The Humanitarian

Rewi Alley and the cooperative movement

Rewi Alley arrived in China in 1927. His intention, he said, was 'to have a bit of a look around'. Apart from brief periods of travel outside the country, he remained in China for the rest of his life. When he died in Beijing in 1987 he was honoured as 'a great internationalist fighter and a true friend of the Chinese people'.

Alley was born in 1897 at Springfield, near Christchurch. His first experience of life beyond New Zealand was on the battlefields of northern France, where he served with the New Zealand Expeditionary Force and was twice wounded. On his return to New Zealand he set about the task of converting an area of scrub and bush in back-blocks Taranaki to productive farmland. The venture failed – 'the scenery was great but you can't eat scenery,' he recalled late in life. Restless and impoverished, Alley decided to seek opportunities beyond his native country.

For anyone who was white and moderately presentable, 1920s Shanghai offered many such opportunities. The city was the fullest embodiment of the treaty port system, with its attendant expatriate privileges. Its two foreign enclaves, the International Settlement and the French Concession, were quite independent of the long-established Chinese City to their south, and equally independent of Chinese legal authority. Many foreigners chose to work in the International Settlement, where tall office buildings lined the riverside bund, while making their homes in the tree-lined avenues of the more fashionable French Concession. Few found much occasion to spend time in the crowded Chinese City.

Within the self-governing foreign enclaves it fell to expatriate administrative bodies to set in place regulatory systems and make them work. Alley swiftly found himself installed in a position of responsibility as a sub-officer in the International Settlement's Fire Department – part of a polyglot brigade of foreigners who directed the city's firefighting resources and, at least in theory, implemented regulations designed to prevent the outbreak of fire.

Fire prevention carried with it a responsibility for the inspection of factories and workshops. Alley was increasingly drawn to this aspect of his work, which in time led to his appointment as the department's inspection officer, engaged full time on oversight of working premises. To facilitate his work he applied himself to serious study of Chinese, focusing on the Shanghai dialect. Such efforts set him apart from his colleagues in the Fire Department mess, whose inclination was to pass their leisure time in the more congenial pursuits readily on offer in the city that had come to be known as 'the Paris of the Orient'.*

The impression that Alley was, measured by expatriate norms, a queer fish, was compounded when he chose to spend his annual leave in 1929 working on famine relief in Suiyuan Province (now part of Inner Mongolia). It was in the course of the four-day train journey to Salaqi, where the China International Famine Relief Commission had set up its headquarters, that Alley met for the first time the American journalist Edgar Snow. Snow was later to write the groundbreaking account of Mao Tse-tung and the Communist campaigns, *Red Star Over China*. This was the book that told of the crossing of the Liuding Bridge, an event that had caused J.H. Edgar to beat a hasty retreat. In the years ahead, Alley and Snow were to work closely together on projects in support of China. Of this first chance meeting on a north China railway platform, Snow recorded:

> He was a strangely out-of-place figure in that dark, sickly crowd, his sunburned face covered with dust beneath a fiery bush of upstanding hair. He was of only medium height, but he had tremendous rugged arms and legs. When he stood with those giant legs spread apart in a characteristic attitude, he seemed somehow rooted to earth. But it was the man's great head, with a profile like something carved from Stone Mountain, that struck me.

Snow invited Alley to join him in his 'special car', but the Chinese politician with whom he was travelling vetoed the proposal and Alley returned cheerfully to his fourth-class carriage. 'He was quite happy

* Anne-Marie Brady suggests that in his early years in Shanghai, Alley's views did not differ greatly from those of his expatriate colleagues. She bases this on comments in letters to his family at the time. The letters were destroyed at Alley's request in 1968.

where he was. He had better company than mine, at that.'

In 1932 Alley left the Fire Department to take up a newly created position as chief factory inspector within Shanghai's International Settlement. He had no illusions about his role – 'What the old Shanghai Municipal Council wanted of their factory inspectors was to keep the city tidy, make things easy and pleasant for big business, and silence criticism.' Nonetheless, he set to work to challenge the often appalling working conditions that prevailed in the factories of Shanghai's industrial districts.

Once more he found himself at odds with Western managers operating under the principle of extraterritoriality, which freed them – and those to whom they delegated power – from the application of Chinese law. 'A woman who beat her apprentices while they worked, screamed with rage when made to effect a simple improvement, and to emphasise her words, snatched up a live chicken, tore it to bits with her hands, and stamped on it.'

Many of those who worked in the factories were children, brought in from the countryside and easily replaced when of no further use. Alley worked to set in place regulations to better their lot, and to provide practical help. Writing later of that time, he recalled 'the irrepressible gaiety of dying apprentices in lead battery factories when I would go to take urine from them for testing for lead content – "What, you're not going to drink all of that in one day are you?"'

Rewi Alley did not start out as a disciple of the left. He owed his Fire Department job to his background as a second lieutenant in the New Zealand Territorial Force. Over time, however, the humanitarian impulse that underlay his commitment to workplace reform and relief efforts came more and more to be framed in a political context. He was introduced to the works of Marx and Lenin, and became part of a floating discussion group of foreigners who applied Marxist ideology to consideration of events in China. The group included American-born Agnes Smedley, the left-wing journalist and writer, who became one of Alley's closest friends and confidantes. Smedley in turn introduced Alley to Soong Chingling, the widow of China's first president, Sun Yat-sen, who drew Alley into the network that sheltered and facilitated 'progressives' in 1930s Shanghai. Later, she would be instrumental in supporting his work in China's interior.

In 1932, and again in 1937, Rewi Alley travelled back to New Zealand on leave. In China, too, he built links with the not inconsiderable New Zealand community. Agnes (Nessie) Moncrieff, who had been sent from Wellington to serve as a 'foreign secretary' in support of the Shanghai YWCA, was a friend. When New Zealand economist J.B. Condliffe travelled to China under the auspices of the Institute of Pacific Relations, Alley was on hand to meet him on the Shanghai docks. Successors to Condliffe, Bill Holland and Brian Low, like him graduates of Canterbury University College, sought Alley out when they arrived to begin work in China. Later he served as a guide and would-be mentor to poet and writer Iris Wilkinson, who wrote under the pen-name Robin Hyde. In her account of her foray into China, *Dragon Rampant*, he appears as Caley.

Alley's 1937 leave was linked to a study tour of industrial safety practice in the US and the United Kingdom. By the time he returned to Shanghai late that year, Japanese attacks on the city were well under way. Chinese industrial production was a key target, with factories being destroyed or looted to provide scrap metal for the Japanese war effort. Thought was turning to the possibility of relocating China's industrial capacity away from the coast and into inland provinces beyond the reach of Japan's military.

In Shanghai, Alley was reunited with Edgar Snow, there to cover the war. Snow was accompanied by his wife, Helen Foster (Peg) Snow, like him a journalist, and later, writing as Nym Wales, the author of several books on China. Peg Snow was instantly attracted to Alley: 'He had sandy hair and blue eyes as deep as the ocean off the continental shelf . . . God's angry man, volcanically alive with all kinds of frustrated indignation.' Alley was apparently less smitten. In later years he caustically recalled her demanding levels of comfort and indulgence. alien to both Alley and her husband.*

It was out of discussions between these three that a concrete plan evolved to promote industrial production in unoccupied China, named the Gung Ho industrial cooperatives. Peg Snow saw the project as one 'that I would be able to look back on as my small but long-term

* It is easy to see how he might have formed that impression. Peg Snow eventually exited war-torn Shanghai with 40 boxes of personal effects and two large bamboo carrying-cabinets full of miniature trees.

contribution to history'. Both she and Alley have laid claim to penning the pamphlet that first commanded wider attention. According to James Bertram, the original concept was Peg's: 'She was a scatty, crazy woman, but this was her best invention.'

Edgar Snow, introducing the scheme to an American audience in the *Saturday Evening Post*, was coy about its provenance: 'Right after the Shanghai war a New Zealander named Rewi Alley and two Americans worked out a plan which they called the Chinese Industrial Cooperatives.' The two Americans were of course Edgar himself and his wife Peg, but journalistic neutrality would not have been well served by acknowledging this. From early on, Snow chose to focus on the role and personality of Rewi Alley as the best approach to building international support for the movement.

The concept of cooperative production was not in itself new – there were many precedents. As Alley himself commented: 'The old Chinese guild was a kind of cooperative . . . The Chinese family itself is a kind of cooperative.' What set apart the CIC movement (later referred to as Indusco) was its combination of cooperative principles and measures to effect the removal of production beyond the reach of the Japanese. Searching for a snappy title to represent what the movement stood for, Alley came up with a simple two-character phrase: 'Gung Ho' – Work Together.

The Gung Ho movement acquired real momentum through the intervention of the British ambassador, Sir Archibald Clark-Kerr, 'a good Scotchman fallen along diplomats',* according to Agnes Smedley, who had arrived in China not long before. He brought with him a liberal outlook and a distaste for appeasement. On the basis of reading the Snow/Alley pamphlet and a discussion with Edgar Snow, Clark-Kerr undertook to try to sell the Indusco plan to key decision-makers in Hankow. (Hankow was at that time the seat of the Nationalist government, following its retreat from Nanking.) As Snow reported it, the discussion went like this:

* Archibald Clark-Kerr was appointed ambassador after his predecessor, Sir Hughe Knatchbull-Hugessen, was badly injured when a Japanese plane mistakenly machine-gunned his car. A Japanese emissary sent to convey a formal apology to his family the following day remained only a short time before excusing himself, explaining that the plane which had brought him was needed to bomb Nanking that afternoon.

'Suppose I did agree. Have you got me a leader I can pull out of my hat? And has he got the Chinese staff we need?'

'I'm glad to hear that "we", Sir Archibald. Yes, I think we have a leader. His name is Rewi Alley.'

Those on whom the decision rested in Hankow were in essence three: W.H. Donald, Australian advisor to the inner circle of Chiang Kai-shek (known as the Generalissimo); H.H. Kung, Premier and Minister of Finance; and, crucially, the Generalissimo's wife, Soong Meiling. Soong Meiling was the youngest of the three Soong sisters, all American educated, who achieved prominence in various ways over the Republican years. The eldest, Soong Ailing, became the wife of H.H. Kung, while the middle sister, Soong Chingling, married Sun Yat-sen and became Rewi Alley's friend and mentor in Shanghai. Their brother, T.V. Soong, was a banker and politician who served for a time as China's premier.

Soong Chingling was already supportive of the Indusco proposal, but given the state of familial relations that would not necessarily have recommended it to her younger sister. In the event Meiling did come down in favour of the plan, Donald agreed, and H.H. Kung, who would have to find the money to finance it, grudgingly came on board. In May 1938 Alley was summoned to Hankow and set to work.

In China's very temporary capital, Gung Ho was allocated space on the top floor of the building that had housed the Yokohama Specie Bank (over the protests of Minister of Defence He Yingqin, who feared it might attract Japanese bombs to the district in which he lived).

Alley worked to build a good relationship with Soong Meiling, who brought to the venture the authority of Chiang Kai-shek. He also met for the first time Chou Enlai, then the CCP representative to the United Front of opposition to the Japanese. While control of the cooperative effort was vested firmly in the KMT administration, Chou and the CCP supported it as something that would help to keep Chiang Kai-shek focused on opposition to the Japanese, rather than allowing himself to be diverted into efforts to crush the Communist forces with which he was nominally allied.

With the establishment of the Association of Chinese Industrial Cooperatives in August 1938, Rewi Alley was appointed chief technical

Sinza Fire Station HQ staff, August 1931, Rewi Alley on the right.

The Soong sisters inspect bomb damage in Chungking, 1940. From left: Soong Chingling, Soong Ailing, Soong Meiling.

advisor responsible for the promotion and organisation of cooperatives – the only non-Chinese within the organisation. He threw himself into the task of evacuating factories from Wuhan to areas more remote from Japanese attack, and setting up cooperative production units as widely as possible within unoccupied China.

The alarm which Alley's devotion to Chinese causes had earlier generated within the expatriate community in Shanghai followed him inland. According to Edgar Snow, 'Old China Hands considered Alley a crackpot and a dreamer.' A Belgian journalist, Jacques Marcuse, noted with scorn in his 1967 book *The Peking Papers* that 'Rewi Alley was already known in Chungking in 1940 as "Screwy' Alley"'. Meeting him at that time, Marcuse thought Alley

> a very active sort of fellow, fresh from his native New Zealand, bustling about in khaki shorts and shirt, physically the very prototype of the scoutmaster, oozing cheerfulness yet lofty thought, sublimating China of which he knew little, with already something about him of the promising evangelist who has had the call without quite managing to identify the voice.*

The early successes of the Gung Ho movement belied such criticism. Incomplete wartime statistics can only be indicative, but according to Edgar Snow's 1941 assessment:

> In two years Indusco set up a record in China for the shortest distance between paper planning and action . . . Industrial Cooperatives were growing so fast that yesterday's data was stale before it was printed. Early in October of 1940 there were over 2,300 of these vest-pocket factories spread across 16 provinces and under the technical direction of seventy branch headquarters. A much later Chinese assessment suggests that in the peak year of 1941 there were around 3,000 cooperatives in operation, with a total of some 30,000 members.

Rewi Alley was indefatigable in his efforts to establish the structures, the know-how and the funding that would allow Indusco cooperatives

* From the dustcover photograph of Marcuse, complete with monocle and meerschaum pipe, it is possible to surmise that he was someone with whom Alley might not, under any circumstances, have struck an easy rapport.

to thrive. In the first two years of the movement he travelled 30,000 kilometres throughout war-torn China. In Peg Snow's view he was 'the indispensible man. He went out into the villages and got the work moving by sheer force of effort and personality, though constantly harassed and sabotaged by the opposition. The creation of these cooperative industries is one of the most astounding accomplishments in any pre-industrial country.'

Few other foreigners could have brought to the movement the knowledge of industrial practice, the familiarity with the local people and the language skills Alley had at his disposal. Beyond his personal contribution, in fact, the extent of external involvement was much less than is often supposed. The task of establishing industrial cooperatives in the hinterland fell to a great extent to Chinese activists who had built up expertise and experience over earlier years of working towards rural reform. The extent of their 'astounding accomplishment' is most usefully measured in terms of the obstacles they had to overcome along the way, including rampant inflation, widespread corruption, and all the logistical and other difficulties of operating in a war-torn country.

Edgar Snow worked to good effect to build international support for the CIC, particularly through the articles he wrote for the *Saturday Evening Post*. Inevitably, a primary focus was on the character and achievements of the foreigner at the fore of the Gung Ho process. He was 'the most extraordinary man I know', a 'world war hero', 'Marco Polo in reverse', a 'perpetual motion machine' – even, in words attributed to a visiting doctor, 'a saint'. The opening paragraph of the most ebullient article to appear in the *Post*, 'China's Blitzbuilder, Rewi Alley', compares the New Zealander favourably with T.E. Lawrence – Lawrence of Arabia. 'He means to China today at least as much as Colonel Lawrence meant to the Arabs, and perhaps more. Where Lawrence brought to Arabia the destructive technique of guerrilla warfare, Alley is teaching China the constructive organisation of guerrilla industry.'

The Lawrence comparison is in one sense closer to the mark than Snow may have intended. It has been said of Lawrence that he was given to backing shyly into the limelight. Rewi Alley was not immune from the same tendency, as indeed the 'Blitzbuilder' article itself illustrates. It is prefaced by a page-high reproduction of a heroic bronze bust of

Alley,* and includes a lot of commendatory material that gives every evidence of having been sourced from Alley himself.

Alley's close colleagues were inclined to look beyond the myth. 'That man Rewi Alley is here,' Englishman George Hogg reported in a letter to his mother. 'He is the so-called father of our Gung Ho and much played up in American magazines to that effect. His chief merit so far as I'm concerned just at present is that he can make plum puddings out of persimmon.'

Hogg in fact seems to have dedicated himself to keeping Alley grounded. After the 'Blitzbuilder' article, a consensus arose that 'Rewi Alley had been getting too much fan mail'. In Hogg's account, he and others 'Carved the text of HE IS ALTOGETHER LOVELY from a piece of pink paper. The odd letters that dropped out fell naturally into an unrepeatedly rude epithet. Text and epithet were pinned up together over Rewi's bed one morning before he climbed out of his mosquito net.' The target of the prank 'sulked for two or three days on end'.

In the end, it had to be accepted that overseas publicity needed to be built around a striking personality, and Alley was best suited to the role. His prominence did little to endear him to H.H. Kung and the central bureaucracy of the KMT, coming as it did to be associated with fundraising from overseas sources. From early on, the CIC became in effect two separate movements: the CIC central headquarters in Chungking, and the International Committee for the Promotion of Chinese Industrial Cooperatives (ICCIC), established in Hong Kong in July 1939 under the chairmanship of Bishop Ronald Hall and subsequently removed to Chengdu. The main issue at stake was whether international contributions should be transferred to and administered by the central CIC office or allocated directly to fieldwork. The latter course was open to the criticism that the administration would be in foreign hands, redolent of paternalism and imperialism. The former option, in Alley's view, was a sure recipe for inefficiency, featherbedding and corruption.

Alley's personal relationship with the Generalissimo's wife, Soong Meiling, entered stormy waters when a writer for the *New Yorker*, Emily

* The work of New Zealand sculptor Francis Shurrock, the bust was exhibited in 1939 at London's Royal Academy. The original was lost at sea on its way back to New Zealand during World War II; a replacement, cast in 1958, is now in Canterbury Museum.

(Micky) Hahn, linked the two in a way to which Meiling took exception. The vivacious Emily Hahn, then based in Shanghai, shared her small flat in the International Settlement with a gibbon called Mr Mills, who accompanied her to cocktail parties and wore a fur coat in winter. She had established herself as the secondary wife of a Shanghainese poet and publisher, Sinmay Zau (Shao Xunmei), and through Sinmay had secured permission to write a biography of the three Soong sisters, with the proviso that the text should be cleared with them before publication.*

Now Alley, who was recovering from illness in Canton, received an urgent summons to make himself available to Mme Chiang (Meiling) in Chungking. He hastened by bus, train and air, to be told on arrival that the Generalissimo's wife had taken violent exception to an assertion in Hahn's book, then in proof form, that she had called him 'Darling Rewi'. That her displeasure was real became abundantly evident when they met. 'I did not even know that your name was Rewi!' she stormed, somewhat implausibly. Alley disclaimed contact with Emily Hahn, and added that the suggestion that he was her 'Darling Rewi' was 'hard on us both'. The matter was eventually smoothed over, leaving Alley with the sense that travelling halfway across China for such an encounter had not been the best use of his time.

Mme Chiang was peculiarly sensitive about her personal prestige. She had already dispensed with the services of another New Zealander, George Shepherd, for, as she saw it, presuming to speak with her authority in making representations in the United States. When she learned that another foreign helper, Ralf Sues, had invoked her name (albeit positively) in a private conversation, she never spoke to Sues again. Whatever the facts behind the 'Darling Rewi' allegation, it is hard to imagine that it enhanced her support for the movement that Alley represented. Nor is it likely that she was impressed by his disinclination to dress formally for his meetings with her, even to the extent of putting on long trousers.

In the end, those within the KMT administration who had sought unsuccessfully to profit from the CIC, or for other reasons had no interest in seeing industrial reform of this sort go forward, largely succeeded in

* Such a condition might seem conducive to a work of pure hagiography, and so it proved. Emily Hahn did, however, redeem herself in her next book, *China to Me*, which was as frank and full of indiscreet revelations as anyone could wish.

undermining the Gung Ho experiment. Even those who had backed it initially, including Mme Chiang, lost their enthusiasm. 'The brakes were put on,' Alley lamented later, 'and the thing was gradually stifled, the worthy Madame and the fat old Dr Kung getting what they could out of the patient before it was murdered.'

In truth, it was not simply a lack of enthusiasm at the political level that saw the CIC movement lose its way. Its enterprises generally relied upon the energies and skills of refugee workers, and had little connection with established rural communities. The goods they produced were not always of particularly high quality. Many cooperatives fell victim to corruption and financial speculation on the part of their leaders, particularly those with links to existing communities and power structures.

Side by side with his work on the industrial cooperatives, Alley lent support to the establishment of Bailie schools, so named in honour of Joseph Bailie, a veteran American missionary who had devoted his life to relief work, and to the promotion of education in China. It was Bailie who pointed Alley towards famine relief in the northeast soon after he first arrived in Shanghai. Bailie schools were intended to buttress cooperative endeavours by combining classroom learning with work experience, preparing their pupils to engage in collective production as part of the cooperative movement.

More than one factor caused Alley to direct his attention increasingly to the Bailie schools and approaches to education. One was that in September 1942 his appointment as 'technical advisor' to the CIC was terminated, ostensibly because he had had secret dealings with the Communists. This did not greatly distress Alley: 'As salary and allowances were never paid, I suffered no financial loss.') He fell back on his role as field secretary of the International Committee, avoided showing his face in Chungking, and for the time being carried on much as before.

A second factor was his growing disillusionment about what could realistically be achieved against KMT opposition. In this, Alley was influenced by the views of George Hogg, who had by this time taken up the headmastership of a small Bailie school in Shuangshipu (Fengxian), a village in the Qinglin mountains in southern Shansi (Shanxi). Alley wrote:

> George had become convinced that a successful cooperative system could not be built in the KMT area. In his opinion, the idea of expanding Gung Ho on any large scale would have to be temporarily abandoned, as it would only lead to the endowment of small capitalists calling themselves 'cooperatives' and factory managers using the Gung Ho name to avoid taxation.

George Hogg was to be an increasingly important friend and collaborator for Alley from this time on. An unlikely product of the British public school system and Oxford University, Hogg had first been introduced to Alley by Agnes Smedley in the summer of 1938, when Smedley and Hogg were both based in Hankow. After the fall of Hankow, Hogg travelled widely in the guerrilla areas of northern China.

When he suffered a near-fatal attack of typhus fever, he was saved by the coincidental presence of a New Zealand missionary nurse, Kathleen Hall. He went on to spend time with the Communist Eighth Route Army, and finally gravitated to work as a cooperative inspector and publicist for Gung Ho. When he and Alley met for a second time, at the Gung Ho regional HQ in the town of Paochi, Hogg was just 24 years old.

Shuangshipu had from the early days of the anti-Japanese war provided a staging point for Rewi Alley's journeyings in support of the industrial cooperatives, and later the Bailie schools also. Initially he set out to build a small cottage on the hill above the village. When it was decided to establish a Bailie school there, the three-roomed structure was converted into classrooms and student accommodation. Excavation in the loess cliff face above created what travellers came to know as 'Rewi Alley's cave' – a dwelling dug into the hillside, with a wooden frontage incorporating paper windows to light the interior. By Hogg's account, the structure evoked differing reactions among foreigners who learned of its existence.

> Some speak of it with sentimental affection.
>
> 'Very primitive, my dear,' they write to their friends back in comparative civilisation. 'Of course there's no doorbell or knocker. The Chinese just walk in and out as though they own the place.'

> Certain other quarters have held it to be a splendid country mansion, built out of 'squeeze money' and hired out at fantastic rentals to rich Americans. The only possible basis for this last rumour was Graham Peck, who was at that time almost penniless; Graham filled the cave's then-empty bookcase with a row of attractively done wooden blocks entitled *From Blind Alley to Cooperative*, *Up Your Alley* and so on, but he certainly paid no rent.
>
> Various well-meaning friends dispatch equally well-meaning emissaries to 'reform' Rewi's household ménage, and restore the man himself to at least a semiforeign shadow of his respectable Shanghai Municipal Council days. These people usually go away saddened. Some of them have even stopped coming up to look – instead they walk about the village picking up stories while their truck fills up with gas. 'The people up there live just like the Chinese. Their cook can't even make the simplest semiforeign dishes.' Such stories ripen alarmingly with age, so that in some places 'that poor man Alley' is considered to have already degenerated past help into a piece of Oriental 'poor white trash'.

An advantage of a cave dwelling is that there is always scope for further embellishment. Alley and Hogg (who took up residence there when he became headmaster of the Shuangshipu school) whitewashed the walls and papered them with an eclectic range of photographs of friends and pictures cut from magazines. They set in the light of the paper window

> a large, amply robed Buddha with folded hands, who in case of extreme need could be conjured into a frock-coated butler bringing in a tray of drinks. To add a further touch of culture, we dug niches in the walls in the shape of cathedral windows, and filled them with high-nosed, bearded statues of hitherto unsung contemporaries of Marco Polo, unearthed from the new city moat being dug around Loyang.

The Shuangshipu Bailie school did not have an auspicious beginning. There were nine separate appointments to the post of headmaster in one year before the baton was passed to George Hogg. Under his tutelage, and with Alley's support, student numbers grew, machinery became available for student training, and food production was increased to a level that approached self-sufficiency. It became possible to recruit additional teachers, and for the first time the school became imbued with a sense of common purpose, winning the support of the local community.

It seemed too good to last, and so it was. To a degree the school was a victim of its own success. The CIC bureaucracy questioned whether it would not be a good idea to re-establish it closer to the headquarters in Paochi, where it could serve as an exemplar for important visitors. As well, the senior boys became targets for conscription by the KMT armed forces. While Hogg was inclined to meet these challenges on the ground, Alley was less sanguine that it would be possible to do so. His preferred solution, as Hogg recorded in a letter to his family, was to find a new site for the school, removed as far as possible from the twin scourges of bureaucracy and militarism.

> He isn't exactly a pessimist, but he is taking a very firmly prophetic view. Consequently my peace of mind is constantly being disturbed by such remarks as 'Don't forget the apple tree when we go, George; they have to be taken up carefully, roots wrapped in straw,' or 'I wonder how the goats will stand the trip?' The trouble is we have about fifteen tons of essential machinery apart from other things, and no trucks – only two carts and not enough mules to go round. So I sometimes feel like bashing him. But of course it wouldn't do any good. His mind just works that way – in a sort of continuous non-stop stream of ideas which are seized upon and brought to the surface in a very loosely associative way. This is really a very useful kind of mind to have, as in thinking over one problem it brings up everything remotely connected – things that ordinary people wouldn't think of, or would overlook – often vital details. It is also a very accommodating mind; when it hits a rock, like 'no trucks', it flows all around it and goes on it and goes onto apple trees and goats. Meanwhile it would appear to have forgotten all about the rock, but actually (I hope anyway) it is still setting about the rock with a swirling undertow like that on the beach at Newquay, and will eventually spring a surprise on you, such as 'we don't need trucks, anyway, I've got six army transport planes coming along tomorrow.'

4. The Humanitarian – Sandan

Rewi Alley turns teacher

As 1943 progressed, Rewi Alley became increasingly preoccupied with the need to seek out a new site for the Shuangshipu Bailie school. In August the opportunity arrived when Joseph Needham made a forced stopover in the town. Needham was in the early stages of research towards what would become the most all-encompassing (and certainly the most voluminous) Western description of Chinese scientific and technological achievements. His magisterial study, *Science and Civilisation in China*, had by the time of his death reached 24 volumes. Ranging back more than 3000 years, it set the bar for all subsequent inquiry in the West.

Needham had arrived in China the year before to take charge of a newly created body called the Sino–British Scientific Cooperation Office, attached to the British Embassy in Chungking. His mission was to identify opportunities for scientific cooperation with Republican China, and to do what he could to facilitate such cooperation. That he was prepared to give this brief a liberal interpretation is demonstrated by visiting Shuangshipu, in the course of the first of 11 expeditions that took him into China's hinterlands. His goal on this expedition was the desert town of Dunhuang, and more specifically the Buddhist caves nearby, where archaeologist Aurel Stein had found (and carried off) some of the world's earliest printed texts.*

Needham spent two nights in Shuangshipu while the CIC machine shop repaired a broken spring on his two-and-a-half ton Chevrolet truck (converted from an ambulance for the journey). Knowing that the expedition's route led up the Kansu (Gansu) Corridor, away from potential Japanese advances, and towards sparsely populated settlements bordering the Gobi Desert, Rewi Alley arranged to travel on with them. 'As things afterwards turned out,' Needham noted in a letter, 'it was a blessing that he did.'

* Small, energetic and autocratic, Stein travelled extensively in the Gobi Desert regions in the early 1900s. Even when dining on his own in the middle of the desert he made it a point to dress for dinner.

The two men struck an early rapport. 'I never met a better friend and a more reliable colleague,' Needham wrote home. Two years later he contributed a foreword to Alley's first book, *Yo Banfa!*: 'When after five decades one can begin to see one's life in perspective, it is possible to pick out perhaps half a dozen men who have not only been cardinal influences, but in whom it has been possible to see and touch what constitutes human greatness . . . Rewi Alley I admit unhesitatingly among my half-dozen immortals.'

There is no reason to believe that this was a more demanding journey than many others Alley made in those years, but it is better documented, thanks to Needham's letters and diary. What the British scientist had set out to accomplish in one month fact took four. The broken spring repaired at Shuangshipu was only the beginning of a series of mechanical mishaps, compounded by an absence of replacement parts. A blown cylinder-head gasket was replaced first by hammering flat Rewi's aluminium soap-dish, and, when that failed, by cementing together two layers of canvas from his kitbag. The resources of another CIC workshop had to be called upon to deal with failed main bearings and a bent crankshaft. Ignition failure called for desperate measures ('made all 6 cyls. fire by arranging a spark gap outside the plugs, very queer').

Miraculously, it proved possible, by one means and another, to keep the truck going until it reached its destination, Chienfotung (Caves of the Thousand Buddhas), 25 kilometres beyond Dunhuang. There it broke down irretrievably. 'Wrote telegram to Embassy asking for a salvage truck,' Needham recorded unhappily in his diary. 'Might as well have asked for the moon.'

The solution finally adopted was to remove the engine and have it transported to the nearby Yumen oilfield for repairs. The three weeks spent stranded at the tiny oasis was not time wasted – Alley and Needham explored and documented the 400 man-made caves that dotted the adjacent cliffs. When at last the recalcitrant engine was reunited with the truck, 'practically the whole population of the Chienfotung oasis spent practically the whole day pushing it round and round the little parade ground' before it spluttered into life. The next day the party was at last able to progress to the rather larger oasis of Dunhuang on the first stage of the return journey. 'As we were on our way into the city, bumping up and down the wildly rutted track, Rewi, who was riding on the running board of the cab, stuck his head inside and said (American accent), "Now we're going to taste Big City Life."'

Retracing the steps from oasis to oasis along the Kansu Corridor brought Alley back to the desert town of Sandan, which he had earmarked on the outward journey as a likely new site for the Bailie school. The original town had a long history as a forward trading centre for those entering China from the northeast (in Tang times a prince was stationed there to deal with incoming traders, leading Arab merchants to mistake it for China's capital).

Over the centuries the town had lost its strategic significance and suffered the depredations of warfare and frequent earthquakes. Deforestation of the mountains flanking the desert plain had contributed to erosion of the soil. Many buildings had been abandoned: by the time the science expedition passed through, the population had declined from 240,000 just 200 years earlier to some 30,000. From Alley's point of view this was all to the good, as it meant accommodation could be obtained at a little cost.

Sandan was a long way from anywhere – 450 kilometres from Lanchow (Lanzhou), 660 kilometres from Dunhuang. Again, this was not, for Alley, a disadvantage: 'It was a place where city officials of the KMT would not be likely to come, where cooperative training and production could be gone ahead with quietly, and even expanded, without exciting too much suspicion or envy.' He admired the natural resources available – coal, clay for pottery, paper-making materials. He even admired the desert – Needham noted that 'According to Rewi, this country is like that near Otago, New Zealand, and would support millions of sheep, if the oases would grow the winter feed, roots or ensilage.' This was, later experience demonstrated, an estimate that erred on the side of optimism.

Having secured the somewhat bemused acquiescence of Gung Ho headquarters (the very people they wished to distance themselves from), Alley and Hogg set about moving the school. Lacking any more recent guides, Rewi drew upon the *Travels* of Marco Polo, who had covered the same ground some centuries earlier, to prepare George Hogg for the journey:

> 'When you are marching through the sands at night, George,' he says, 'don't be afraid when you hear bells and gongs and weeping and gnashings. Everyone will say it's ghosts. But it is really the hot surface of the sands contracting in the night – they make that noise when they are disturbed by people kicking up the surface.' 'Thanks, Rewi, I'll remember, old boy.'

Alley went ahead to Sandan and rented some houses for temporary accommodation, and the premises of a disused temple to form a longer-term base for classrooms and industrial production. The first tranche of 33 students, at this time all boys, arrived on Christmas Eve 1944. With scant regard for Western religious festivals, they were set to work the very next day on refurbishing the temple. Two months later the main body of students arrived in Sandan, led by George Hogg, now firmly established in his role as headmaster. The journey was of epic proportions – almost 1000 kilometres of very bad road in icy winter conditions, bearing with them more than 12 tons of machinery and other equipment salvaged from the Shuangshipo site.

Alley was present in Sandan only intermittently over the time of the school's establishment there. He still had responsibilities to the cooperative movement, and he remained in dispute with the movement's HQ in Chungking over the appropriate funding model for paying out overseas contributions – an issue that would affect directly what funds might be available to the new school.

On the ground, Hogg led the boys in restoring the temple complex (retaining, as local authorities required, three of the largest Buddhas), building classrooms and a sports field, and installing industrial plant – a boiler, a cotton mill, looms, a machine shop. When Alley made a return visit in July, the school was well on the way to realising his vision. Classroom instruction and industrial production were both going forward, senior students were increasingly taking responsibility, new students were being recruited locally.

Towards the end of that month the school suffered a crippling blow. Playing basketball with the boys, headmaster Hogg stubbed his toe. From that trifling wound an infection developed. By the time tetanus was diagnosed the illness was beyond treatment, and within three days George Hogg had died. He was just 30 years old.

Up to that time Alley had had no ambition to become greatly involved in the affairs of the new Sandan school. His contribution at Shuangshipo had been limited to taking an occasional benevolent interest in the success of Hogg's efforts. With Hogg's death, however, he saw himself faced with a clear choice: to step in himself and continue the work Hogg had begun, or to allow the venture to fail. So stated, he saw no option. He plunged wholeheartedly into making the school a success, 'an adventure in creative education'. Not until 1947 did he again leave Sandan, and then only to travel to Shanghai to take up once more the vexed question of funding.

At the time of George Hogg's death the school roll numbered about 100. Over the next five years Alley built it up to 400 students and 200 workers and staff. The 'workers' were mainly engaged to work full-time in coalmining and agriculture, which required more input than the students could provide. The grounds of the school had extended a good way beyond the confines of the original temple complex, and included access to coalmine shafts and land for grazing.

Over time a variety of training sections were established to provide students with work experience. In his book *Sandan: An Adventure in Creative Education*, Alley listed sections dealing with textiles, electricity and welding, transport, chemicals, leather, papermaking, pottery, glass, agriculture, mining, surveying, accountancy and medicine. Classwork was designed to give access to information and theoretical concepts relevant to the different areas of work. Broader educational goals were not despised, but neither did they take up much space in a regime intended to fit students to address in a practical way rural China's most basic needs.

Sandan Bailie School aimed as far as possible to be self-sufficient. The paper-making section produced school writing pads, locally made textiles became school uniforms, the school farms provided food. As well, output from the various production units was sold to provide about a third of the school's operating budget. The remainder was sourced from overseas donors, who channelled their donations through the International Committee for Chinese Industrial Cooperatives.

In 1947 Colin Morrison, dominion secretary-general of the new New Zealand umbrella charity organisation Corso (Council of Organisations for Relief Service Overseas), travelled to China 'to see how best Corso,

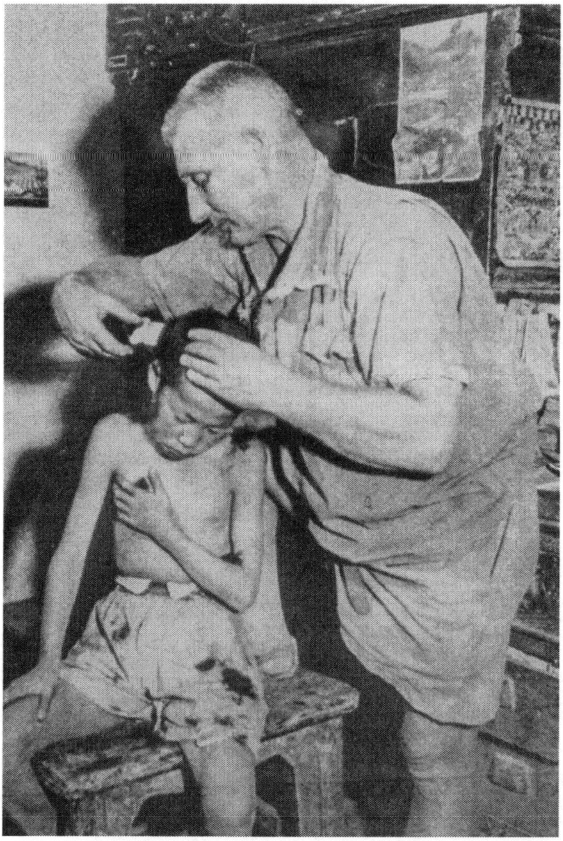

Rewi Alley welcomes a new student to Sandan.

Max Wilkinson with a student and stud sheep from New Zealand.

and through Corso the public of New Zealand, might aid China in relief and rehabilitation'. The idea of an exploratory mission to China was put forward by James Bertram, himself a China veteran, who had taken up a role as dominion appeals organiser.

Morrison spent seven days at Sandan with Rewi Alley. He was impressed by the educational experiment, and by the existing New Zealand connections (Alley had been energetic in soliciting support in cash and kind from individuals and organisations in his home country). Following receipt of Morrison's favourable report, Corso's contribution came to make up about 40 per cent of the shortfall in the school's finances. In Alley, Morrison saw 'a man doing his job under extremely primitive conditions, looking and hoping for the material help this, his native country, among others, might send him. New Zealand must not let him down.'

The visit happened to coincide with the arrival in China of a milestone New Zealand contribution to the Sandan project – 25 Corriedale sheep donated by New Zealand breeders. Morrison helped facilitate the shipment. An earlier effort to introduce New Zealand sheep to Kansu had not ended well: 100 sheep provided on a commercial basis in 1941 had been forced by the war to enter China via Calcutta, and were lost to human knowledge somewhere on the Tibetan plateau.

The Sandan consignment was shipped safely to Shanghai, but still faced a difficult journey to reach China's far northwest. After due consideration, Morrison concluded that the only possible option was transport by air. It was a bold call, for it was without precedent in China, except for a small number of mules conveyed by General Chennault's 'Flying Tigers', the First American Volunteer Group of the Republic of China Air Force, some years earlier.

In 1947 postwar relief operations in China were in the hands of the United Nations Relief and Rehabilitation Administration (UNRRA), in cooperation with its Chinese counterpart, the Chinese National Relief and Rehabilitation Administration (CNRRA). (The sheep destined for Sandan were in fact part of a larger shipment of New Zealand sheep and cattle organised by UNRRA.) Morrison set himself to argue that the two relief organisations should between them assume financial and organisational responsibility for airlifting his charges to Sandan.

Central to his argument was the contention that the eyes of New

Zealand's donor community were firmly fixed on a successful outcome for Rewi Alley and Sandan. In the end he carried the day, but not without difficulty, as he noted in his report: 'I feel it only right to record that the fact I succeeded in having the sheep flown to Kansu and the freight met by CNRRA was not as a result of any co-operation on the part of the Australians in the Agricultural Section of the China Office of the UNRRA,' adding darkly, 'More of this I could say.'

Happily, Colin Morrison was able to turn to a New Zealander, Max Bickerton, to facilitate the transfer. Bickerton was at the time acting executive secretary to the ICCIC, based in Shanghai. He supported Morrison in his representations, and subsequently volunteered to accompany the sheep on their onward journey.

Bickerton was a colourful part of New Zealand's postwar presence in Shanghai. He was a grandson of Alexander William Bickerton, the notoriously eccentric founding professor of chemistry at Canterbury University College, who had combined his academic duties with the establishment of a socialist commune, later transformed into an amusement park. The Wainoni Pleasure Garden boasted a zoo, fireworks, puppet shows and mock naval battles. Max was heir to both his grandfather's eccentricity and his notoriety. He lived and studied for 10 years in Japan before being arrested under anti-communist legislation, subjected to brutal interrogation, and deported. Caught in Hong Kong at the time of the Japanese invasion, he was interned in Stanley Camp, where he served as an interpreter and translator for the prisoners.

After the war Bickerton made his way to Shanghai and a position with the Chinese industrial cooperatives. He was, it appears, thoroughly at home in the libertine atmosphere of pre-revolutionary Shanghai, although a Shanghai contemporary's recollection of him as belonging to 'a whole group of European homosexuals who used to have the most incredible orgies along with the Twenty-first Parachute Division of the Kuomindang army' probably overstates the reality.

Morrison and Bickerton were not successful in persuading either of China's national airlines to fly the sheep so they turned instead to the civilian reincarnation of General Chennault's Flying Tigers, Civil Air Transport (CAT). CAT was at that time occupied in ventures such as flying arms to Muslim warlords inland, paid for by high-value commodities destined for resale in Shanghai. Towards the end of the civil war it moved into immensely profitable 'rescue missions', whereby CAT planes would fly into areas blockaded by Communist forces and conduct bidding wars for seats among senior KMT officials desperate to get out. Reminded of Chennault's earlier success transporting mules, CAT agreed to undertake a flight to Lanchow, capital of Kansu Province.

The airlift of the New Zealand sheep aroused considerable interest within the Shanghai media. Commonplace now, transporting stock by air was then a novel concept. The plan attracted headlines such as 'Operation Bopeep', and 'Airlifting New Zealand Sheep Causes Shanghai Sensation'. Max Bickerton ensured that it did not escape notice in New Zealand, contributing to the *New Zealand Listener* an article describing the transfer, 'They Went for a Ride in a Tiger'. The sheep emerge as the heroes of the journey:

> The sheep were exemplary passengers. Nuzzling together, steaming, palpitating in four pens made of bamboo poles banked with bales of hay, whenever the journey got a little bumpy, they just looked at me with patient eyes and chewed off another wisp of hay. I wanted to convey to them the historic nature of their flight and describe some of the beauty of the rugged country over which we were passing, but I was not successful.

The article describes the stages of the flight – three hours to Hankow, then a further three hours to Lanchow. The following day the sheep completed their odyssey with a 450-kilometre journey by truck along the old Silk Road to Sandan. Rewi Alley was there to welcome them, and to be photographed for the *Listener* with his arm around one of the pedigree rams. The difference between the newly arrived Corriedales and the native sheep was apparent to Colin Morrison, also part of the welcoming committee: 'The native sheep look so much like goats and actually shear only 1½–2 lbs of wool per clip.'

As an unfortunate codicil to the episode of the flying sheep, it became apparent over time that the native sheep looked like goats for a reason. Max Wilkinson, who travelled from New Zealand to take charge of animal husbandry at Sandan, recalled later that the Corriedales were not well suited to grazing in Sandan's near-desert conditions. Whereas the long-legged native sheep stayed on the move all day, feeding on such tufts of vegetation as they could find, the New Zealand sheep could not keep up, and required a laborious process of hand feeding. They needed shelter through winter, and generated an ongoing dependence on New Zealand for items such as sheep dip. In Wilkinson's view, it had been a worthwhile experiment, but not a successful one.

The less than successful outcome would not have come as a revelation to Rewi Alley. In his correspondence with his brother, G.T. (Geoffrey) Alley, then director of the Country Library Service, whom he had recruited to carry the project forward from the New Zealand end, he presented the shipment as a gamble.

> It would do the average New Zealand farmer good, and make for an interest in this country, if he put a bet on Gansu sheep and their betterment, at the same time as he puts his bets on the tote in Riccarton. A sporting chance. Would the sheep get through, would they be cared for, would they stand this climate, would they help a lot of farmers such as they themselves are, to pull themselves up by their own bootstraps?
>
> Sure, the whole thing is a gamble. But it is a gamble that would be good for us here and for people in New Zealand to play, for the sake of the good of their own souls. Here, we should never cease trying to abolish this poverty which, if it stays, will be the breeding ground of so many new wars, so much human distress. There, you have to realise that there are other countries in the world besides New Zealand and its Commonwealth neighbours.

By this time Alley was heavily involved in soliciting assistance from New Zealand for his Sandan project. The sheep were the largest single gift, but West Coast miners donated mining equipment, the stock and station firms sent sheep-shears, Girl Guides and Brownies gave 500 parcels as part of an International Friendship Project. Contributions frequently came as a result of direct appeals from Alley, and inevitably the aid provided came to be seen as much as a donation to him personally as a contribution towards China's relief and rehabilitation. 'Rewi Alley groups' sprang up in centres including Auckland, Christchurch, Waimate and Dunedin. Corso set up a Committee for Chinese Industrial Cooperatives, with a particular concern for the Sandan school.

Morrison's convinction that Alley's experimental school was a worthy focus for Corso's relief efforts was reinforced by advice he received from diplomatic and foreign aid administrators in China. It made sense, they counselled, for a relatively small donor such as New Zealand to concentrate its effort on a single area of need, the more so if that area of need already had a clear point of association with New Zealand. Morrison returned to New Zealand bearing a grocery list of supplies needed for Sandan. Of the 22 aid positions throughout China he recommended Corso should seek to fill, six were at the school.* By 1949 Corso was supplying and funding seven teaching and technical staff, with experienced helpers such as Courtney Archer transferring from the Friends Ambulance Unit and additional foreign staff drawn from other countries: the UK, Canada, the US.

One of the requests made of Corso was the provision of medical staff. Despite the disarmingly frank position description ('An interpreter will be provided, but not a very good one'), a well-suited couple was found willing to take the job on: Dr Bob Spencer, a recent medical graduate, and his wife Barbara, a nurse. The two arrived in Sandan in 1947 to find themselves faced with the need to establish a hospital literally from the ground up. The first task was to design and then to supervise the building of a mud-brick complex. On top of the mud walls, roofs were made of more mud plastered over straw mats.

While the completed building fell some way short of the standard of hygiene required in New Zealand medical facilities, it exceeded by far anything previously existing in that part of northwest China. Spencer found himself in charge of the only hospital open to the ordinary people over an area more than twice the size of New Zealand.

The flow of patients began as soon as the building was complete, and well before the medical equipment shipped from New Zealand had made an appearance. Early on, Alley mentioned apologetically that he had found it necessary to accede to the demands of the reigning prince of the Alashan Banner in Inner Mongolia to provide medical services to his son. 'Bring your prince to our school in two months' time and we will have a wise man here who will most certainly cure his disease,' Alley had pledged. The prince, who proved to have a large growth on

* Morrison also recommended that New Zealand should establish official representation in China. It did not do so at that time, although it did provide someone to head up the Australian Legation in the person of Prof. Douglas Copland, a Timaru boy and a graduate of Canterbury University College.

one eyelid totally blocking his vision, became the hospital's first surgical patient.

> We began a frantic search around the school to find a few instruments suitable for the operation. Bob soon discovered he had brought a pair of small scissors he had once used for dissecting dogfish during his student days, and we also had two pairs of artery forceps he had collected from the reject pile of one of the hospitals at home. One needle, one operating knife which had definitely seen better days, and two pairs of nail tweezers, one borrowed from a member of the foreign staff . . . These were the sum total of our instruments.

Happily, the operation was a success, much to the joy and gratitude of the young prince: 'I must ask my father to give you a camel.' To the relief of his benefactors, the camel was commuted to six curly-horned sheep, which were added to the school's flock.

The Mongolian sheep were only the first contributions in what developed into an extensive system of barter as impoverished peasants flocked to seek medical help.

> Small packages of a few potatoes, a little wheat, chickens, ducks, or a sheep from the wealthier patients were brought along as payment for major operations or medical treatment. Indeed, at clinic time, our hospital courtyard often assumed quite the appearance of a farmyard with animals and poultry in all directions, but trouble really started when grateful patients tried to usher their livestock into our consulting room, and one day in particular when one patient was too smart for us we had a terrible time before we rescued two ducks and a lamb from among the dispensary bottles. We never quite knew what might be handed to us, but even so I was not really prepared to have one of our peasant patients thrust two snarling baby foxes into my arms one day after clinic. The foxes caused a lot of excitement as they were only a month old and very wild . . .

Bob and Barbara Spencer came to realise early on that between the school students, the wider Sandan community and associated calls on their services (by now including veterinary and dental work), their time was more than fully occupied. Nonetheless, they recognised a need to provide a training programme for the student assistants, fearing (as it turned out, correctly) that it would not be possible to recruit suitably qualified replacements when their term came to an end.

The medical section, no less than the other sections of the school, provided hands-on experience, backed up by evening lectures. By the time the Spencers had completed an extended term in 1950, they left their 20-year-old senior assistant able to perform major operations such as Caesarean sections, the amputation of limbs and appendicectomies 'with great ease and skill'.

The Spencers were present to see the town of Sandan, and with it the school, fall to Communist forces in late 1949. Although there was great anxiety beforehand, particularly about likely depredations by retreating KMT forces (Alley had in place a contingency plan that involved keeping the troops at bay with the help of the school's three rifles and a commandeered machine-gun), in the event it was a peaceful transition. To support the Communist forces, or perhaps bowing to the inevitable, the school relinquished to the People's Liberation Army all the trucks the transport section had available. The PLA continued west towards the Yumen oilfields without making further demands on the school or its students.

In the army's wake, however, there arrived a group of CCP cadres to make their own assessment of the school and the foreigners associated with it. The investigation was thorough and wide-ranging, according to Max Wilkinson, who was involved in the proceedings. It took place in an atmosphere of dissonance within the student body. Some were unhappy about disciplinary measures – Rewi Alley had been subjected to harsh physical discipline as a child, and continued the tradition at Sandan.* Other students resented the favouritism shown to 'old students' – those whose time at the school dated back to Shuangshipo. Nonetheless, no matters of serious concern were placed before the investigating group.

After a week of inquiry, the cadres expressed themselves satisfied and went on their way. That no allegations of impropriety were brought forward was for Max Wilkinson the surest guarantee that there existed no grounds for such allegations. There is some evidence that Rewi Alley

* In a letter written soon after liberation, Alley renounced corporal punishment as something made necessary by the Nationalist regime, but no longer required in a Communist state.

was homosexual, but nothing to suggest that this carried over into his relations with the boys in his care.

In assessing the operation and objectives of the Sandan experiment, the Communist authorities can only have taken heart from the broad endorsement accorded to the school by a newly minted outside authority, the Food and Agriculture Organization of the United Nations. A 1949 FAO study, *Training Rural Leaders*, gave a cautious tick to the results achieved by that point.

> The work at the Shandan school is a pioneer attack on the old and long neglected problem of human misery. Perhaps only time can show the true significance of the school or of the movement from which it has grown. But what has already been accomplished, despite manifold difficulties, suggests that in the long run the Shandan experiment may prove to be the most worthwhile project in rural reconstruction yet undertaken in China.

The Sandan Bailie School did not in the long run have an opportunity to build on its credentials as an experiment in rural reconstruction. The vision of China's post-revolutionary government did not include reliance on foreign advisors and external funding to buttress the country's development. In 1951 the ICCIC was wound up in Peking.

As workers' contracts at Sandan ended, Corso directed its funding elsewhere.* Later in 1951 the Chinese authorities took the school over to serve as a training base for the oil industry. Rewi Alley and Courtney Archer were summoned to Peking, to help present the New China to the world. There Alley remained until his death, 36 years later.

* This was a pragmatic decision, according to Colin Morrison, and not the result of pressure from the New Zealand government, despite the absence of diplomatic relations between New Zealand and the People's Republic of China.

Republican China: A Brief Account

The war against Japan

Japan's 'China Incident' had its beginnings in 1931, when Japan assumed control of Manchuria, establishing a puppet regime under former emperor Pu Yi. (Even after the conflict in China developed into a full-blown war, Japan continued to term it an 'incident', in order to avoid triggering the constraints the United States Neutrality Act imposed on dealings with countries at war. As Japan's spokesman in Peking at one point explained to a questioner, 'You know, this is a special undeclared war.' Some diplomats came to talk of World War I as 'the Great Incident'.)

The following year Japan launched an attack on Chinese districts of Shanghai, forcing an acceptance of a neutral zone around the city. In 1933 Japanese forces moved into the provinces immediately south of Manchuria, Jehol and Hebei. The Nationalist government was forced to declare northeast China a demilitarised zone. Despite these humiliations, Chiang Kai-shek continued to place a higher priority on countering the Communist threat than opposing the Japanese.

Matters came to a head in December 1936 with the 'Sian Incident'. On an inspection visit to Sian (Xian), Chiang found himself confronted by a mutiny of troops persuaded of the need to combine with the Communist forces to oppose Japan. He was held hostage until he made a somewhat equivocal undertaking to set aside his anti-Communist drive in favour of forming a united front against the Japanese. As a consequence, the Red Army was renamed the Eighth Route Army, while companion forces in the south became the New Fourth Army. Both were placed under the strategic direction of the Generalissimo.

On 7 July 1937 a minor incident near the Marco Polo bridge (Lukouchiao), some 16 kilometres outside Peking, triggered clashes between Chinese and Japanese forces. Full-scale warfare followed. Before the end of the month Japan had consolidated its hold on the entire Peking/Tientsin region, and from there it extended its grip over northern and central China. Shanghai fell towards the end of

1937, after three months of bitter fighting. On 12 December 1937 the Japanese army entered China's capital, Nanking. The 'Rape of Nanking' saw an orgy of violence and killing that continued for some weeks. The Nationalist government retreated 500 kilometres up the Yangtze to a temporary capital in Hankow.

Fighting continued in central China through most of 1938. In the south, Canton was seized by Japanese naval units in mid-October. Hankow, which had been subjected to heavy Japanese bombing, fell a few days later. The Generalissimo had prepared a new wartime capital in Chungking, above the Yangtze gorges. There he retreated, and there he remained until the end of the war. Japan was left in control of Manchuria, all China's coastal provinces, the north China plain, and the land about the middle reaches of the Yangtze River.

5. The Reformer

George Shepherd and rural reform

Rewi Alley had an alter ego. Like Alley, he was born and grew up in a country town in southern New Zealand. Like Alley, he gravitated to China, and became proficient in the Chinese language. Like Alley, he relied on practical experience rather than book learning. Like Alley, he took charge of an important project for the Nationalist government. His name was George Shepherd, and Rewi regarded him with deep suspicion.

George William Shepherd was born at Mataura, in eastern Southland, in 1894. He left school at 13 and for seven years worked in a Dunedin hardware store, Paterson & Barr. At the age of 21 Shepherd attracted the attention of a group of Dunedin businessmen (initially impressed, it appears, by his willingness to sacrifice Saturday afternoon rugby for Bible study). The businessmen sponsored him to travel to Chicago and enrol in the Moody Bible Institute, a fundamentalist Christian college. From there it was a short step to his chosen vocation as an evangelistic missionary. 'I commenced my first term of service in China equipped with an active mind, a business training, and a Bible course.'

Shepherd travelled to China in 1917 as a missionary of the Plymouth Brethren, with the support of his Dunedin sponsors. The Plymouth Brethren were at that time active in missionary outreach from New Zealand. In China they had chosen to focus their efforts in Jehol (Chengde), north of the Great Wall, the stronghold of the warlord Chang Tso-lin (Zhang Zholin). There Shepherd joined forces with other New Zealand Brethren missionaries and applied himself to study of the Chinese language. When later congratulated on the facility with which he had 'picked up' Chinese, he was more honest than many other students of the language, then or now. 'Let me say right here, that there was no picking up about it. I studied five hours every day for five years.'

As well as setting aside those five hours, and meeting the heavy demands of missionary work, Shepherd found time for an extensive programme of reading. In setting out to remedy what he perceived as gaps in his education up to that point, he pursued a programme that was as extensive as it was eclectic.

> I visited Shanghai and purchased standard textbooks on Geology, Economics, Biology, Anthropology, Psychology, Evolution, Philosophy of Religion, Introductions to the Literature of the Old and New Testament, Church History, History of Egypt, History of Greece, History of Rome, Europe in the Middle Ages, Introduction to English Literature, Modern Essays, Tolstoi, not to mention all I had access to on Buddhism, Taoism, Confucius, and the Chinese Philosophers. Besides going carefully through these I read full editions of the life of [American clergyman] Phillips Brooks, and Robert Louis Stevenson, not to mention Shakespeare, Milton, Browning, Macauley, Burns, Goldsmith, Dickens, Longfellow, Everson, George Eliot and others . . . In fact, to be honest, I cannot now remember all that I did devour in my eagerness to measure up to the standard required of a modern missionary.

Shepherd's remarkable programme of self-study led him away from the conservative approach of his Plymouth Brethren colleagues. A broader perspective was reinforced by his marriage in 1921 to Clara Sargent, a medical missionary from the United States. In 1925 he applied for appointment as a missionary under the auspices of the American Board of Commissioners for Foreign Missions. The application was not a straightforward one for the staid Boston-based Board of Commissioners. They were being invited to take on a candidate from a foreign country, an apparent backwoodsman, lacking any formal qualifications. He did, however, come with the enthusiastic endorsement of the board's team in the field. 'Don't let any high Brahman caste traditions in the Board stand in the way,' warned the secretary of the Shaowu Mission. 'He is a rare and growing man.'

Shepherd was given the appointment he sought. In 1926 he returned from the US, where he had been on furlough, to take up a position in Kienning (Jianning), in the Shaowu region of northwest Fukien (Fujian). It was a challenging assignment. While Fukien is a coastal province, it reaches a long way inland, and the Kienning mission station lay close to the border with troubled Kiangsi (Jiangxi) Province, which before long would become the seat of the rebel Communist regime.

Nor was Fukien itself in any way stable, as Chiang Kai-shek's Northern Expedition made its way upcountry, and local warlords weighed their options.

Against consular advice, Shepherd made his way from the coastal capital, Foochow (Fuzhou), to his inland post, although he took the precaution of sending his wife and their two small daughters to stay in Kuling (Guling), a hill resort inland from Kiukiang (Jiujiang) on the lower reaches of the Yangtze River. There the family found themselves in distinguished company, the missionary revealed to the *Otago Daily Times.*

> While at Kuling in December at the Fairy Glen Hotel, Chiang Kai-shek and his charming young wife came to live in the room adjoining that of Mrs Shepherd and her children . . . Mrs Chiang loaded the children with all manner of candies until their mother, who is a qualified doctor, began to be concerned about their health.

Shepherd himself did not meet Chiang until 1933, by which time the military strongman had acquired a quite different charming young wife.

(An entrepreneurial English missionary named E.S. Little had established Kuling as a temperate haven for missionaries and other expatriates at the end of the nineteenth century. His wife was a New Zealander. Little coined the name 'Kuling' as a bilingual pun intended to describe the resort's main attribute. By the time of the Shepherd family's visit, Kuling offered a variety of accommodation including two European-style hotels (the second, the Journey's End Inn, was noteworthy for providing in each room a copy of the Bible and an album of French pornography). As a businessman in later life he was the energetic promoter of a scheme to attract expatriates in China to a land development project in Kerikeri, where he retired to live.)

Chiang Kai-shek's purpose in travelling to Kuling was to convene a meeting with the political leaders of the central government, which had moved north to Wuhan in the wake of his military successes. The meeting presaged a split between the left and right wings of the coalition government that came to a head in the anti-Communist purges launched in Shanghai in April 1927. The uncertainties and violence associated with the northern progress of Chiang's troops had by then caused

Kuling: China's premier Health Resort, 1920.

George Shepherd with Soong Meiling (Mme Chiang Kai-shek) in *Time* magazine in 1939.

foreign consular authorities to take pre-emptive action to gather their citizens in the relative security of Shanghai's foreign settlement. The Shepherd family, reunited in Shanghai, there witnessed the Nationalist takeover and its aftermath.

Shepherd was no longer inclined to gainsay any consular advice, and more particularly the protection offered by the foreign troops deployed to Shanghai. Residents, he said, 'knew beyond all doubt that, had they not enjoyed such protection, the Communists who had entrenched themselves in and around the settlement would certainly have massacred two-thirds of the foreign population and looted every dwelling-place'. In the face of such perils, and with no immediate possibility of resuming missionary work, Shepherd took his family home to Dunedin to meet his parents.

The Shepherds returned to China, and to Kienning, at the end of 1927. Over the next five years they were four times driven out to the coast, in the end definitively, by the ebb and flow of military action, Communist incursions and the depredations of bandits. Often it was not easy to distinguish one from the other. 'We have been kept out of our field,' he wrote to his father in 1931, 'as the road between Foochow and Kienning was invested with more vigorous gangs of bandits then we ever had on the Min. Defeated troops had hived off inviting seven times more wicked spirits to unite with them in wholesale robbery and kidnapping.' The home the missionaries had built for themselves was in their absence occupied successively by a displaced magistrate, Nationalist troops, and Communist forces, who 'ruined our delightful little bungalow, that was home to us and the children, and when they were about to leave they buried three men in the centre of the garden'.

Despite being a victim of Communist depredations (as well as destroying his home and repurposing his garden, they made off with all the family's personal possessions and blew open the mission safe to destroy property deeds), George Shepherd was ambivalent about the effect of Communist governance on the areas that came under their control. On the one hand, he was shocked by the cruelty with which they imposed their rule. On the other, 'There is much that is good in their programme, and they certainly get rid of a lot of parasites and corrupt officials.'

Shepherd came to believe that evangelical Christianity alone did not offer a sufficient response to the challenge communism posed in rural areas. More and more, he immersed himself in programmes of rural reconstruction which drew both on the traditional role of the church and on more revolutionary responses to the social and economic problems of the countryside.

It was 1934 before successive Nationalist campaigns succeeded in dislodging Mao Tse-tung's Communist forces from the soviet they had established in the mountainous border areas of Kiangsi Province – the beginnings of the Long March. Even before then, however, the Nanking government had begun to give thought to how best to undertake reconstruction in previously Communist areas. The National Christian Council of China (NCC) was invited to make an input, and it in turn sought advice from Shepherd, who was considered to be better informed than anyone else in the missionary community about the conditions and the possibilities in the Kiangsi border areas.

He was keen to contribute, even though, as he warned, 'all the hsiens [districts] mentioned, and as many more, are as Red as the old barn door'. With a Chinese colleague, he made his way to Kiangsi's capital, Nanchang, to discuss possibilities for cooperation in a programme of rural reconstruction. This is where he met Chiang Kai-shek for the first time. In the course of three long meetings, Chiang set out his plans to enrol the assistance of the Christians whose ranks he had joined following his marriage to Soong Meiling: 'We must organise the local Christians as soon as the armies enter a district. The Christian farmers and workers will be our right hand men in establishing law and order.'

Shepherd quickly produced the blueprint for an experimental reconstruction programme, entitled 'Rural Reconstruction in the Communist Devastated Areas of Kiangsi and Fukien'. The Kiangsi Christian Rural Service Union was soon set up following the lines of the blueprint, with Shepherd as associate general secretary of the project. He re-established his family (there were by now four children) at Kuling, and, like Rewi Alley a few years later, set out on a frenetic round of travel in pursuit of funding, personnel and ideas. He fixed upon Lichuan hsien, just across the border from his old stamping ground in Shaowu, as the focal point for what became known as the Lichuan Experiment.

The Lichuan Experiment was not unique. By 1934 the parlous state of China's rural communities had prompted a wide range of approaches to agricultural reform and rural reconstruction. Among them was J. Lossing Buck's pioneering study of land utilisation, undertaken at Nanking University with input from a succession of New Zealand economists. What did set Lichuan apart was the urgency imparted by a need to win support back from the reform programmes set in place by the Communists. Chiang Kai-shek and Soong Meiling lent their support to the project, including through financial contributions, and endorsed Shepherd's role. Mrs Shepherd let it be known that (the new) Madame Chiang had invited her to her home to tell her 'how very pleased they were that George had been allocated for the work for they felt that with his experience, knowledge and love for the people added to his easy language facilities he was just the man for the project'.

At the end of an eventful first year, marked by the introduction of technically trained workers into formerly wholly political areas of decision-making, Shepherd found himself tripped up by his own lack of technical training. In the view of his mission's China secretary,

> For the present, George's assets are his intimate knowledge of the communist ridden areas, his abounding energy, his ability to work with others and get things done, and a certain amount of rural background in New Zealand with a large amount of practical common sense, added to the Christian spirit of devotion which makes all these things usable in the finest way.

Christian zeal, however, was not in itself sufficient. The mission board advocated another course of study in the United States, focusing this time on approaches to agricultural development.

January 1935 therefore saw Shepherd in the US to undertake a truncated course at the Cornell School of Agriculture. By October, in response to a personal plea from Mme Chiang, he was back in China. The opportunity to put his newfound book learning into effect was fleeting, as it became clear that Mme Chiang had other plans. In March the following year, at the invitation of the Generalissimo, Shepherd shifted to Nanking, and a new role as advisor to the New Life Movement.

The New Life Movement was a nationwide moral campaign launched in 1934, allegedly as a result of Chiang Kai-shek's seeing a schoolboy 'behaving in an unbecoming matter' in the street. 'If we are to restore the nation and gain revenge for humiliations,' he pronounced, 'then we must first talk about washing our faces in cold water.' The movement fitted in well with the Generalissimo's regard for military order and asceticism, but it was in fact largely the brainchild of his Wellesley-educated young wife. It owed something to parallel movements in the West such as the Oxford Group and its successor, Moral Rearmament, and something also to what were represented as the defining impulses of Confucianism. As Soong Meiling explained to visiting English poets W.H. Auden and Christopher Isherwood:

> The New Life Movement is based on the practice of four moral virtues: *Li* or Reason, *I* or Propriety of the Outward Man, *Lien* or Moral Judgement, and *Chih* or Conscience. It aims at instilling into the people ideals of civic responsibility and social service. Volunteers have been sent out to check administrative corruption, clean city streets, and generally raise the standard of public health. Hospitals and relief works have been established. Mah-jongg and opium smoking have been forbidden. Government officials are not allowed to visit brothels.

In the same way that rural reconstruction was intended to provide an alternative to the Communist land reform policies, so the New Life Movement was offered as an alternative to the Communist ideology that threatened to take a grip on China's proletariat. There was never a serious possibility that the puritan ethics it prescribed would find favour among the more moneyed classes. 'It is doubtful whether the personalities interested in the movement are sufficiently pure themselves to give the movement much prestige', US minister Nelson T. Johnson dryly advised Washington.

It is unclear how apparent this moral ambiguity was to Shepherd. Certainly he was torn whether or not to become involved. But in the end he saw the opportunity to provide a Christian perspective to plans to reshape Chinese society as a chance that could not be passed up: 'What would Borodin do with a chance like this?'*

The most senior of the Soong sisters, Soong Ailing, welcomed

* Mikhail Borodin was the Comintern agent seconded to Sun Yat-sen's government in 1923. His advice was central to party structures, and to the Communist policies pursued by the KMT's left wing. He returned to Moscow after Chiang Kai-shek's crackdown on leftists in 1927.

Shepherd aboard. Could you not as a first step, she requested, provide university students with a programme of work that they could carry down to the villages over the summer break? Her husband, H.H. Kung, would happily meet the cost. As an opening shot in his new role, accordingly, Shepherd sent students off with a *Summer Manual* for grassroots interventions:

I What you can do for the local barber shop.
II What you can do for the tea-houses.
III Some suggestions for the local inn.
IV Cooperation in the village community.
V Organise recreation and sports for young men and women.
VI Conduct discussion groups in the evening.
VII What you can teach the farmer about keeping his family healthy.
VIII About cooperatives.
IX How to improve the farmer's home.
X Some things to investigate.
XI List of subjects for evening talks in tea-houses.
XII Special supplement for work amongst women and girls.

The campaign with which Shepherd now associated himself was not universally acclaimed. Rewi Alley thought it was fascist . He was not alone in that view. In one critic's opinion, the only thing that distinguished it from the early days of Mussolini's regime was that 'the "castor-oil cure" has not yet been invoked'. Like Italian fascism, the New Life Movement placed a heavy emphasis on patriotism, and harked back to the nation's past glories. It emulated Italy's Blackshirts, and the Brownshirts of Nazi Germany, by creating a force of Blueshirts – young men who took to the streets to enforce the dictates of the movement. This led to the sort of excesses that first caught the attention of 'the poets', and prompted their raising the subject with Mme Chiang.

> Priggery and hypocrisy, it seemed, were flavoured unpleasantly with police bullying. A specimen frock, showing the correct length of sleeve for a chaste woman, had been exhibited in Peking. A young English traveller has been reprimanded in the streets of Sian for smoking a pipe out of doors. Some people had even had their teeth compulsorily

scrubbed. Mixed walking, it was rumoured, was forbidden in the cities of the interior.

That Mme Chiang set out to associate missionary interests with the 'curious moral crusade' of which she had taken charge (eventually she appointed herself director-general) owed much to the advice of the first Westerner to take up a position of trust within the Chiangs' kitchen cabinet, W.H. Donald. An Australian newspaperman, he had been in China in various guises since 1903. He distinguished himself by living there for 37 years without making any attempt to learn the Chinese language, a feat in which he took some pride.

When around this time Ilona Ralf Sues, a volunteer worker from Geneva, proposed to give Donald her address over the phone, he startled her by cutting in with 'Don't swear at me in Chinese', then calling for a 'boy' to take the address down. Sues soon discovered that the language gap ran in both directions. Her commission was to reform the foreign propaganda section of the Information Ministry. This, Nanking's main link with the outside world, was staffed by 60 men, most of whom spoke no foreign language whatever, but all of whom were intimately connected by birth or friendship to senior members of the KMT.

Donald, a strict teetotaller, also took pride in refusing to eat Chinese food. When he dined with the Generalissimo and his wife, as latterly he did most nights, two separate meals had to be prepared. He carried his own knife and fork. It was said that when he was constrained to attend official banquets, he took a loaf of bread with him. Blunt and outspoken, Donald nevertheless won the trust of Chiang Kai-shek, serving him as his advisor on foreign policy until 1942, when the two parted company over Chiang's wish to pursue ties with Nazi Germany.*

Donald advised Chiang to develop links with foreign missionaries, not because he thought they carried great weight within China – they did not – but because he perceived their experiences and reporting as being disproportionately influential in their home countries. In this he was quite right. Particularly in the US, missionary perceptions counted for a lot. They were given an extra fillip in that country by the advocacy

* After his resignation Donald refused as a matter of principle to go back to Australia, which he had last seen in 1903, because of what he considered its policy of appeasement towards Japan. He did spend some time in New Zealand.

of media giant Henry Luce.

Luce, the founder of *Time*, *Life*, *Fortune* and *Sports Illustrated* magazines, was born in China of missionary parents and received his early education at the China Inland Mission school in Chefoo (Yantai). He was passionate in his support for Christian activism, and for China's Nationalist government, and exercised direct editorial oversight over the reportage in his magazines to make sure it conformed with his views. (In Chungking in 1944, *Time* correspondent Theodore H. White posted a disconsolate notice on his door: 'Any similarity between this correspondent's dispatches and what appears in *Time* is purely coincidental.')

In Nanking, Shepherd was accommodated in a bungalow within what had previously been a school campus. The house opposite was occupied initially by W.H. Donald, and later by the Generalissimo and Mme Chiang, who shifted there for security after the onset of Japanese bombing. As well as the bungalow, the Chiangs gave Shepherd a small Ford car. They offered to pay his salary, but at this the mission board demurred. It preferred that his position should be at least to this extent at arm's length from the Chinese government, so that his advice could be seen to come from a missionary perspective, rather than that of an advocate for China's leader and his wife. It was a useful distinction, but one that would become blurred over time.

By the end of 1935 the New Life Movement was faltering – because of its perceived superficiality and because it appeared to be attacking the symptoms rather than the underlying causes of China's social discord. Shepherd's appointment was intended to give new impetus to the movement, by linking it more directly to general goals of national reconstruction. Initially the mandate was linked to Shepherd's work in rural reform and the Lichuan Experiment, but before long it came to have a broader focus. Shepherd set in train labour reforms along New Life lines, he arranged a training programme in rural reconstruction for hsien magistrates. He even, at some personal risk, made efforts to disrupt the supply of opium in Shanghai and Canton.

Donald's advice on the worth of cultivating foreign mission interests came to weigh heavily with Chiang Kai-shek as Japanese incursions became more blatant. His inclination to play a waiting game was predicated on eventual intervention by the Western powers. To that end, support from Christian interests could be instrumental in promoting his cause in the West, and might even help burnish his own somewhat dubious Christian credentials. The Chinese leader found a number of occasions to impress upon Shepherd the importance of securing church support for the extension of the New Life Movement. 'The Generalissimo is about as talkative as Calvin Coolidge . . . so when he speaks it usually means something. Once in Kiangsi, and then again last night, he drew me aside and earnestly requested me to link the Church with this work for the uplift of the people.'

From the time of Shepherd's arrival in Nanking, the Generalissimo and Mme Chiang were increasingly prone to draw him aside in order to seek his views on the situation in rural China, progressing the New Life Movement, and how best to present China to the outside world. W.H. Donald was the only other foreigner to have such unfettered access to the seat of power. While Donald's contact was more frequent on a day-to-day basis, Shepherd did have the advantage of being able to communicate directly with the non-English-speaking Chiang, while Donald needed an interpreter, most often Madame.

In his dealings with foreigners, the Generalissimo's views were on most important occasions conveyed through his wife, to the point where it was not always easy to tell whose views they really were. When Chiang attended the Cairo Conference in 1943 his wife attached herself to the discussions, to Churchill's considerable displeasure, in order to convey 'the full meaning of the thoughts the Generalissimo wishes to express'. Allegedly, when the Chinese leader faltered, Mme Chiang created a diversion by rearranging her feet to provide a glimpse of 'the most shapely of legs' through the long splits in her skirt. The British military advisor General Sir Alan Brooke, who reported this, claimed to have heard 'a suppressed neigh' from a group of the younger observers.

In one respect, Shepherd's remit exceeded that of Donald. In mid-1936 Chiang Kai-shek formally entrusted him with 'executive authority', the only foreign advisor ever to be accorded administrative power of this sort. In granting the mandate, the Generalissimo was explicit that 'this establishes no precedent for giving any other foreigner executive authority'.

By the end of 1936 Shepherd had been brought to the view that the only alternative to Chiang was 'chaos'. In this he was reinforced by events surrounding the 'Sian Incident' of December 1936, when Chiang was held captive by rebel troops to force him to combine with the Communists against the Japanese. Called to the side of Mme Chiang, in Nanjing, Shepherd became aware of threats not just from the left but also from the right, in the form of fascist sympathisers who favoured bombing Sian, and with it the Generalissimo, in order to facilitate a coup d'état.

When Madame Chiang, escorted by Donald, travelled to Xian, Shepherd remained in Nanjing. There he maintained the Generalissimo's contact with loyal elements in Nanking through an ongoing exchange of messages with Donald. When Chiang was finally released, both Shepherd and Donald joined him in eight days' 'sick leave' – self-imposed seclusion at Funghua, Chiang's ancestral retreat in eastern Chekiang (Zhejiang).

From the time of Sian, Shepherd came more and more to act as a counsellor to the Generalissimo and his wife. He also took on a role, presumably with the Chiangs' tacit approval, as a conduit to American officials in China. Chiang Kai-shek, he told Nelson T. Johnson, now US ambassador rather than minister (the legation had been upgraded to a full embassy), lived like an 'oriental despot', estranged from those about him, but he was nonetheless indispensable to what passed for national unity. The ambassador told Washington that Shepherd seemed to him both 'modest and honest' in his dealings with the Chinese leader. Clearly, however, by this time it was becoming increasingly difficult to differentiate between Shepherd's role as an advisor on social reform, and his personal advocacy on behalf of the Generalissimo and the policies of the KMT.

The ambiguity of Shepherd's position was not lessened when Mme Chiang asked him to travel to the US and the UK to present the New Life Movement, and the China situation more generally, directly to the people of those countries. By that time (the summer of 1937) China was on course for all-out war with Japan. There was a need for contributions to war relief, and equally, an end to the supply of raw materials and scrap metal that fuelled Japan's war effort.

The brief Soong Meiling gave Shepherd was very similar to that which her sister, Soong Chingling, was to entrust to James Bertram the following year: to underline the global nature of Japan's threat, and to solicit political and material support for China and its struggle. Only the preferred destination for funds raised was different: Meiling's New Life Movement and the KMT in the first instance; Chingling's China Defence League, with its links to the CCP, in the second.

By the time Shepherd returned to China in 1938, Nanking had fallen to the Japanese. He followed the Nationalist government first to Hankow and then to the wartime capital of Chungking, and resumed his work in support of the New Life Movement. By the end of the year, however, Mme Chiang, possibly by then disillusioned by the movement's failure to grip the nation, dispatched him back to the UK and the US to garner more support for China's war effort. Henry Luce's *Time* magazine reported his speaking tour, describing him as 'next to William Henry Donald . . . today the closest white collaborator of Mme. Chiang Kai-shek'.

Time quoted part of a radio address delivered to a New York audience. Criticising the material assistance still flowing from United States sources to Japan, Shepherd expressed fear that Japan might in the short term prevail in China. 'I find it difficult to decide whether I am needed more in America than in China.' As it turned out, Mme Chiang made the decision for him. Always jealous of approaches that appeared to trespass on her authority, she made it known that she was 'rather resentful of the reports reaching her from America that George was appearing as her "representative"'.

Shepherd had intended to return to China after placing his children in school in the US. It was only through a third party that he learned that his commission had lapsed and that the resentful Mme Chiang had recruited a Canadian missionary, James Endicott, to take over his New Life Movement responsibilities.* Settling in the United States, George Shepherd continued to speak out in support of the Nationalist cause throughout the war years, but he never returned to China.

It is an interesting question why George Shepherd, arguably the most influential of the New Zealanders in China over the Republican period, is so little remembered in his homeland. In part it is because the Americans made him so wholeheartedly their own. To *Time* magazine

* Endicott remained in the position for a relatively short period before resigning, first sharing with Madame his view that 'It's like fascism. There's no value in it. There's no individual thought'.

he was 'a Congregational missionary, Rev. George W Shepherd of Auburndale, Mass.' For *Newsweek*, he was 'the one trusted American' in Chiang Kai-shek's innermost circle. The celebrated travel writer John Gunther described him in *Inside Asia* as 'an American missionary' and good friend of Chiang Kai-shek. The fullest account of Shepherd's work, James Thompson's *While China Faced West*, takes as its subtitle *American Reformers in Nationalist China*, and scarcely mentions Shepherd's links with New Zealand.

In part, too, it is because he was on the wrong side of history. A record of support for Chiang Kai-shek and the Nationalist regime did not count for a lot in the years following Japan's defeat, and certainly not after the Communist takeover. Rewi Alley consigned him to the scrapheap of failed missionary endeavour without ever publicly acknowledging that he was a New Zealander at all. Alley's first book, *Yo Banfa!*, relates an encounter:

> In Chungking, I was invited to the room of an advisor to Madame Chiang Kai-shek, a Protestant missionary called Shepherd – 'Mu Ku-wen' as he was called by the gendarmes of the Gissimo. I had been pleading for the continuation of the United Front against Japan. 'Mu Ku-wen' after a solemn pause, in order to give his words more effect, proclaimed, 'We shall rely on the great middle-class of China. Only they can understand.' And he made it plain that the anti-Japanese war meant little compared with the holy task of crushing the Communists.*

And yet. It was to New Zealand, not to the US, that Shepherd had taken his family when conflict forced a withdrawal from Kiangsi in 1927. In Dunedin for more than two months, he re-established amicable links with his former Brethren associates. The Brethren HQ at York Place Hall provided the venue for a vigorous lecture programme: 'What's What in China Today?', 'Livewire Christians', 'China's Needs', 'Will

* *Yo Banfa!* was written at least in part to shore up Alley's own revolutionary credentials at a time when he faced an uncertain future in China, and the book dealt summarily with anyone likely to be thought unacceptable to the new regime. If there was genuine hostility, it was one-sided. Shepherd wrote to New Zealand at about the time of this encounter to describe the work of the cooperatives, and Alley himself, in positive terms: 'A New Zealander, Rewi Alley from Christchurch, is in charge of this work under the head of cooperatives, and he is doing a mighty good job. He has been in China for 15 years and speaks the language fluently.' *Otago Daily Times*, 17 February 1939.

Christian missions Survive?', 'Experiences of Travelling in China'. The lectures were buttressed by interviews published in Dunedin's *Evening Star* ('Thrills in China: Escaping the Reds'). From that time on, as long as he remained in China, Shepherd made it his business to send back to New Zealand occasional reports for publication, either directly to the newspapers, or to family and friends for onward transmission.

The Shepherds travelled once more to Dunedin, in 1929, when a furlough fell due. Shepherd was received as a favourite son. Once again he gave public lectures, and he was welcomed at the University Club as 'an old Dunedin boy'. (His presumed special knowledge saw him called upon to pass a vote of thanks to a speaker who had as his subject 'Ghenghis Khan – the Greatest Emperor'). According to the *Otago Daily Times*, Shepherd paid a final brief visit to Dunedin in 1938, a year before his mother's death.

It was not just the local newspapers that played up Shepherd's New Zealand connections. Rev. George McNeur, who travelled to China in 1902 to establish the Presbyterian Church's Kong Chuen Mission and remained there for almost 40 years, drew upon his example. During a visit home in 1934, lecturing to theological students on 'The Missionary in Changing China', he described the Lichuan Experiment. 'A programme of all-round rural reconstruction has been introduced, for the carrying-out of which the Government has enlisted the cooperation of the Church. The Rev. George Shepherd, of Dunedin, is one of the workers set apart to this special and difficult task.' Six years later, McNeur bracketed Shepherd with Rewi Alley:

> Two New Zealanders who are doing valuable work in China in co-operation with the Chinese leaders are the Rev. George Shepherd and Mr Rewi Alley. The Rev. George H. McNeur, senior Presbyterian missionary in China, who has just returned to Dunedin, told an *Otago Daily Times* reporter yesterday that Mr Shepherd, a Dunedin boy, who has had a highly interesting career, is advisor to Chiang Kai-shek and Madame Chiang Kai-shek in the New Life Movement, which has as its aim the uplifting of the nation morally and spiritually. Mr Alley, whose headquarters are in Hong Kong, but who spends much time in the interior, is assisting the Chinese in the establishment of co-operative enterprises, farming, education, etc. Both are held in high regard by the Chinese authorities.

Not all New Zealanders viewed their compatriot in quite so favourable a light. Agnes Moncrieff, the New Zealand YWCA foreign secretary, met him over breakfast at Bishop Root's house in Hankow soon after his return from the US in 1938. 'They have a New Zealander there, a Mr Shepherd from Dunedin,' she wrote home. 'He works in the New Life Movement which is the pet hobby of the Generalissimo and Madame Chiang. It has gone to his head rather and he is inclined to think he is the whole works.'

Closer acquaintance evidently did not reconcile Moncrieff to her fellow countryman. The two coincided again at the Anglican Guest House in Hong Kong early in 1939. 'The latest arrival is Mr Shepherd, a New Zealander who is a secretary in the Generalissimo and Madame's New Life Movement. I knew him up in Hankow and don't like him very much.' Shepherd's demeanour led the plainspoken Moncrieff to a very New Zealand judgement. 'He is', she confided to her mother, 'rather a skite.'

6. The Journalist

James Bertram and the Eighth Route Army

James Bertram arrived in China later than either Shepherd or Alley, and was there more fleetingly. That said, the fact that his autobiography, *Capes of China Slide Away*, devotes almost half of a 70-year memoir to the years he spent in China and Hong Kong is testament to how deeply he was affected by his time there.

Bertram was on hand to record and present to the world some of the most important passages in the evolution of revolutionary China. The first Western journalist save Agnes Smedley to reach Sian after the 1936 coup against President Chiang Kai-shek, he provided, in his book *Crisis in China*, an authoritative account of Chiang's arrest and its aftermath. Late the following year he took advantage of a rare opportunity to spend time with the Communist Eighth Route Army in Yenan, and to carry out a series of interviews with the Communists' most authoritative spokesman, Mao Tse-tung.

His experiences formed the basis of his second book, *North China Front*. The transcribed interviews later found a place in the four-volume *Selected Works of Mao Tse-tung*, and even (suitably abbreviated) in the Little Red Book (*Quotations from Chairman Mao Tse-tung*) during the Cultural Revolution. His reporting made him, in Peg Snow's estimate, 'the most famous Britisher of his years in China'.

If New Zealand was ever home to a generation of Gilded Youth, James Bertram was part of it. He had his secondary education at Waitaki Boys' High School in Oamaru, at the time a famously spartan establishment ruled over by the equally famously autocratic Frank Milner ('The Man'). Bertram's autobiographical account of his time there reads like the opening chapters of Kipling's *Stalky and Co.*, down to the 'possies' in the gorse, the literary cabals and the all-pervading imperialism.

The Man was knowledgeable about international affairs, and concerned that his charges should be so too. China was one of his favourite themes: 'If all the world's population filed past you one by one, do you know how many would be Chinese? *One fifth*! Think of that.

One, two, three, four, *Chinaman*! One, two, three, four, *Chinaman*!'

At Waitaki, Bertram formed two lasting friendships – with Charles Brasch, the poet and founder of the literary journal *Landfall*, and with Ian Milner. Milner, the rector's son, later wrote perceptively for the Institute of Pacific Relations about New Zealand's place in the Asian region, and later still was accused (on very doubtful grounds) of spying for the Russians.

From Waitaki, Bertram went on to Auckland University College. There he found ready acceptance as part of a group whose members shared his literary interests and high sensibility. As during his school days, there was a sense of exclusivity. In the view of Courtney Archer, a near-contemporary, 'They all felt that they were rather an embattled group, being battered by the Philistines.'

At the end of his time in Auckland, Bertram's academic achievements and sporting prowess (he was a member of an Auckland University rugby team that toured Fiji in 1930) earned him a Rhodes Scholarship to Oxford University. His sartorial flair may have helped tip the balance: Robert Lowry judged him on first acquaintance to be 'a most refined young fellow of the very perfectest thing in taste in every dashed thing under the sun'. Certainly a photograph of the 1932 Auckland Rhodes candidates shows him set apart from the others by his appearance in a rather startling double-breasted tweed suit. When he went to Wellington to be interviewed, he left his card at Government House.

Oxford was everything that Bertram could have hoped for. There he studied English under C.S. Lewis, dabbled in left-wing politics, and played football. At the end of four years, his term as a Rhodes Scholar at an end, the question arose, what next? After brief and unrewarding flirtations with journalism and teaching, he chose not to pursue either profession. (Not before he had established a place in the annals of the prestigious Saint Paul's Hammersmith, as the only master to have caned an entire class of unruly schoolboys – a nod perhaps to his Waitaki heritage.) The dilemma resolved itself when the Rhodes Trust called out of the blue to ask whether Bertram had any interest in travelling to China.

The opportunity arose out of the concern of the general secretary of the Rhodes Trust, Lord Lothian, that the South Pacific dominions, Australia and New Zealand, should be better informed and equipped to take a lead in dealing with the countries of Asia. Prompted by Edward G. Carter, secretary-general of the Institute of Pacific Relations in New York (which had provided a home for a number of New Zealand graduates), Lord Lothian proposed setting up a small number of travelling scholarships that would allow former Rhodes Scholars to study and travel in China and Japan. C.K. Allen, warden of Rhodes House, put forward Bertram's name, with the minor reservation that 'He has a slightly precious manner that is not to everyone's taste'. Precious or not, and apparently in the absence of a suitable Australian candidate, Bertram was offered £300 and travelling expenses to spend a year in China. He jumped at the chance.

For its foreign residents, Peking in 1936 embodied all that was best in Old China. The foreign colony, Bertram's memoir recalls nostalgically, 'were a fairly cultivated group, with a high proportion of aesthetes'. The city had never been a commercial centre like the brash treaty ports, Tientsin and Shanghai. It was no longer the seat of government, for Chiang Kai-shek had established his administration in Nanking. The fact of that shift, however, had not been enough to persuade most diplomatic envoys to renounce the comfort and charm of the northern capital. There they remained, making occasional forays south to consult with the government to which they were accredited. Chiang Kai-shek's regime had to build a state guest-house in Nanking especially to accommodate them on their visits.

The charm of Peking is captured in the titles of books that foreign sojourners devoted to life there at this time – Harold Acton's *Memoirs of an Aesthete*, Osbert Sitwell's *Escape with Me*, John Blofield's *The Years That Were Fat*. James Bertram recalled the experience most vividly through *Peking Picnic* and the other novels of Ann Bridge.

> You think that's impossible, but it's actually quite accurate. Paomachang, the racecourse and hunt, trying to ride horses round paddy fields . . . It was a good life, for foreigners anyway, weekends in the Western Hills – if we needed to go up to temples, just pack up the truck or something – we charged around. All that was very easy-going.

Between times, Bertram's first task was to learn Chinese. He began classes at a language school organised by a former US Marine lieutenant.

The textbook survives ('A Textbook for Beginners who intend to undertake the serious study of the Chinese language, and written to serve as a concise and sound basis for their future endeavours.'). Some translation exercises at least must have been helpful to him in his later travels: 'What is that man holding in his hand in this picture? He is holding a shotgun in his hand. That which he is carrying on him is a bullet container. That man is holding a pair of field glasses and a camera. Oh, so that is it. Excellent! Excellent!' When the time came Bertram in fact equipped himself not with a shotgun but with a small Browning automatic, which happily he was never called upon to use.

Before he left England, Bertram had made contact with three major newspapers: *The Times*, the *Manchester Guardian* and the *New Statesman*, to test the market for China-based journalism. All had confirmed that they were open to publishing occasional reporting and background articles on Chinese affairs. Unsurprisingly, therefore, he made it his business to establish links with the members of the foreign press corps early in his time in Peking. In particular, he soon built a close friendship with Edgar and Peg Snow.

Edgar Snow, by then already eight years in China, wrote primarily for the American magazine *Saturday Evening Post*. When he and Bertram first met he was on the eve of the journalistic scoop that was to change profoundly the outside world's perception of the political situation in China. Through the intervention of Soong Chingling (Mme Sun Yat-sen), Snow was able to break through the blockade surrounding the Communist-held areas in northwest China and engage first hand with Mao Tse-tung, Chou Enlai and other Communist leaders.

The book that resulted, *Red Star Over China*, shone a light on a little-known force within China. Even after nine years of civil war, Snow wrote, 'Red China was more *terra incognita* than Arabia Felix'. The book sold in very large numbers, and it informed international consideration of events in China from that time on.

Peg Snow was the sort of woman who invited adjectives. In James Bertram's public assessment, the former socialite was 'attractive and irrepressible', 'slim, casually elegant'. His less charitable private view, that 'she was a scatty, crazy woman', accorded more closely with that of Rewi Alley, and may owe something to the nature of their personal relationship. In her own memoir, *My China Years*, Helen Foster Snow devoted an entire chapter to 'James Bertram, Rhodes Scholar from New Zealand' – 'he and Ed and I formed a charmed circle'.

> Jim was very attractive – tall, muscular, athletic, and handsome, with curly hair and a sensitive Scottish–English face, quiet, well-bred, diffident, sweet, and shy, and though deeply emotional, totally self-controlled. His blue eyes were full of quest; he was reaching out for new experiences. He was my Sir Galahad – and I had to keep him from becoming my Sir Launcelot. I had to be 'cruel' to him, as he put it.

In his review of *My China Years* for Wellington's *Dominion*, James Bertram wryly acknowledged his occasional appearance 'as a well-intentioned moonstruck follower of the leading lady', while reaffirming his regard for her 'undaunted spirit, her crisp intelligence, and her unfailing gaiety and good humour'.

While Edgar Snow was in the Communist HQ at Pao An, gathering the material for *Red Star Over China*, Jim Bertram and Peg Snow holidayed together at Peitaiho (Beidaihe), north China's beach resort. It was a situation that could have given rise to misunderstanding: 'It's lucky you are a lady and Jim is a gentleman,' one of Peg's friends remarked supportively. Peg was unabashed – 'He was the son of a clergyman in Auckland, and ideal for the sort of relationship we had – the sort we had to have.' Nevertheless, when the possibility arose of their travelling together to Korea and Sian in the following year she thought it best to demur, not least because of concern about her husband's likely reaction.

Bertram had by now exchanged his quarters at the North China Language School for dormitory accommodation at Yenching University, the American-funded institution that later morphed into Beida. He found himself sharing a room with two apparently model students, both of whom would before long make distinctive contributions to the revolutionary movement in China. The first he knew as Wang Ju-mei; under his party name of Huang Hua he was to become an integral part of China's foreign policy establishment, and ultimately the country's foreign minister.* The second, Chang Chao-lin, was already playing

* As China's first permanent representative to the United Nations, Huang Hua signed the 1972 communiqué establishing formal diplomatic relations between China and New Zealand.

an active role in support of the Communists. In the months ahead, Bertram would meet him under different circumstances in Sian.

The 'Sian Incident' played out in December 1936, providing Bertram with his first opportunity for a journalistic breakthrough. It arose when Generalissimo Chiang Kai-shek travelled to Sian to oversee a renewed offensive against the Red Army. There he met with the commander of his northern armies, 'the Young Marshal', Chang Hsueh-liang (Zhang Xueliang). Chang, frustrated at the Generalissimo's determination to direct the KMT's military efforts against the Chinese Communists rather than the invading forces of Japan, kidnapped Chiang and held him hostage. Not until a three-cornered negotiation had secured acceptance that KMT and Communist forces should form a united front against the Japanese was China's Nationalist leader released to return to Nanking.

The outside world knew little of these events as they were unfolding. Foreign correspondents vied to reach Sian but were thwarted by the breakdown of all conventional travel links. Airlines declined to fly because they could have no certainty that their planes would not be commandeered on arrival. The train service was on hold because the branch line to Sian ran through districts affected by the civil war. Anyone who wanted to report first hand faced the prospect of a long overland hike under the harsh conditions of a north China winter.

Edgar Snow, a few weeks back from Pao An and engrossed in distilling the reporting from that trip, chose not to attempt the journey. He did, however, use his contacts to create the possibility of travel for Bertram. With only a few hours' notice James Bertram found himself, together with Mac Fisher of the United Press, at the West Peking railway station, keeping a rendezvous with a mysterious stranger who had links to northeast China, and allegedly to Chang Hsueh-liang himself. The plan, he learned, was to travel by train as far as possible, and then make their way by whatever means were available through Shansi and across the Yellow River.

The journalists' travelling companion was introduced as Mr Chou. To avert suspicion, he was to travel as Fisher's secretary. He wore a dark coat with a fur collar, a dark suit, and had donned, for the purposes of disguise, a pair of lavender-coloured spats. The three were nearly two days into their journey before Mr Chou thought it worth mentioning

James Bertram with Peg Snow
on the beach at Peidaiho in 1936.

that he was in fact a wanted man, with a substantial price on his head. One of a group of young radicals, he had used the Tungpei Military Academy in Sian as the forum for a scathing attack on Chiang Kai-shek. As a result, an order has been issued for his arrest. He had achieved notoriety under his real name – Miao Chien-ch'in, and the nickname associated with it. 'I am Miao Feng-shan, Miao the Madman!'

This disclosure put the journey west in a different light. Fisher thought it necessary to withdraw, rather than risk compromising his news agency through association with a fugitive – especially one who seemed disinclined to temper his revolutionary zeal. Bertram did not face the same dilemma, nor could he see any other way of reaching Sian. He opted to carry on, and 'Mr Chou' transferred to him his secretarial allegiance.

It took 11 days to reach Sian, travelling by train, by rickshaw, by donkey, on foot over the frozen Yellow River, and finally on a military truck provided by one of Miao's shadowy associates. By the time the party arrived at their destination, the immediate crisis was over. In return for a commitment to a united front against Japan, Chiang Kai-shek had been permitted three days earlier to return to Nanking, with Chang Hsueh-liang accompanying him.* Two foreign advisors to the Nationalist government had been instrumental in brokering the deal: the Australian W.H. Donald, who travelled to Sian with Mme Chiang, and former New Zealand missionary George Shepherd, who was left to hold the fort in Nanking.

Disappointed though he was to have missed the denoument, Bertram realised that the circumstances surrounding the crisis, and the new directions established by its resolution, remained largely unexplained to the outside world. He saw himself presented with a unique opportunity, the more so because he had been preceded to Sian by only one other foreign journalist. The morning after his arrival, he met her.

American journalist Agnes Smedley was already a legend within China's foreign press corps for her immediate, caustic and strongly left-wing reporting. She had travelled to China by way of Germany, and reported for the authoritative *Frankfurter Zeitung* until it was taken over by Nazi interests. She was an equal-opportunity activist: over the

* The outcome was less than ideal as far as Chang was concerned. The Generalissimo held him under house arrest, first in China and then in Taiwan, for the next 53 years.

course of her journalistic career she was accused by the British of being a German agent, by the Chinese Nationalists of acting for the Bolsheviks, by the Japanese of being an agent of the Chinese Communists, and by the Americans of spying for Russia. Her first-hand accounts of China's war, set down in two books, *China Fights Back* and *Battle Hymn of China*, were unrivalled then, and remain fundamentally important to this day.

As a Marxist, a feminist and a free spirit, Agnes Smedley had few friends within the staid society of treaty-port Shanghai. She was subject to public attack both for her politics and for her personal life. One Shanghai tabloid alleged she had entered the Communist areas to attend a Soviet congress, taking along a case of whisky to corrupt semi-indoctrinated students, and opened the congress by singing the 'Internationale' in the nude, except for a Red Army cap.

Smedley responded to such claims with derision:

> Nor could I be impressed by the attack upon my personal life. For years a British official lived with the mistress of an upper-class brothel to which only white men able to pay '$50 a shot' were admitted. This brothel mistress once had her picture taken with the Britisher. Incidentally, one such brothel mistress had a daughter studying in an exclusive finishing school in California.
>
> I also recalled that when Mrs Margaret Sanger once visited Shanghai, her crown of auburn hair had caused an elegantly dressed woman to approach her in a tea-room and ask her if she wished to earn a handsome sum of money, a fur coat, and other fine clothes. Margaret pretended interest. The elegant woman explained that the British fleet was coming in and Margaret was just the type for the Admiral.

Knowing something of this background, it was with a degree of trepidation that Bertram approached Agnes Smedley over breakfast at the Sian Guest House. Nor did he improve his position by promoting his link with *The Times*: 'The London *Times* is no friend of China.' More to his advantage was establishing his friendship with Chang Chao-lin, his former Yenching roommate, who had popped up in Sian as the editor of Chang Hsueh-liang's daily newspaper. This, together with his link to Sian's young revolutionaries through his travelling companion, Miao the Madman, served to give him some credibility.

Smedley had not, it turned out, broken through the blockade to reach Sian. Quite by chance, she had been staying at a hot springs resort at Lintung, near Sian, to recuperate from illness and to do some writing. She had shifted to the Sian Guest House when she was evicted from the resort to make way for Chiang Kai-shek's entourage. It was at Lintung that the Generalissimo had been taken into custody early one morning, in nightshirt and bare feet, and lacking his false teeth.*

The task was now to provide the outside world with accurate information about events in Sian, not least because of the wildly inaccurate rumours that were gaining currency. Bertram was able to file one report by wire, based on an interview with Sian's military commander, before full censorship was imposed from Nanking. After that, he offered his services to Smedley, whose solution to the embargo had been to commandeer time on a local radio station, Station XGOB, which operated beyond the reach of the Nationalist authorities.

The two settled into a double act, each day broadcasting news that was, as far as they could make it, objective and accurate. Fearing that listeners would dismiss items known to come from her as Marxist propaganda, Smedley did her best to disguise her voice, an effort largely thwarted by the passion of her delivery. Bertram, by contrast, did his best to imitate the urbane and neutral tones of a BBC announcer. The broadcasts were closely monitored by foreign embassies in China. They were largely accepted as being moderate and factual, although Bertram's diction fell under suspicion. A British Embassy file noted: 'This male announcer is clearly a Russian, since he follows the style of the English-language news bulletins from Moscow. These imitate the accent of the

* His false teeth were important to Chiang. When his wife joined him in Sian her first act was to draw him aside and discreetly pass over a spare pair. In Chungking, when their relationship had become less ardent, she reproached him that he only put his teeth in when he was going to visit his mistress. – John S. Service, *Lost Chance in China* (New York: Vintage, 1975), p. 95. (Service, who provided Washington with this lapidary piece of diplomatic reporting, was one of the US foreign service China hands later pilloried for predicting all too accurately the likely outcome of postwar events. His punishment was a posting to Wellington, where he befriended founding members of the New Zealand Foreign Service. He acknowledged ruefully in a letter to Michael Green that he had come in for 'some good-natured, friendly and sympathetic joshing – even as high as Peter Fraser. It had an added dimension because General Hurley, my nemesis in China, had served earlier as the first American minister to New Zealand – so they had experience of his enthusiasms and eccentricities'.)

BBC overseas service, but never get it quite right.'

What became known as the '55 Days Revolt' ended with the stationing of Nationalist troops in Sian in early February 1937. A condition approaching normalcy returned to the city. With the rail service reinstated, Bertram was able to make the return journey to Peking in considerably greater comfort than the outward leg.

Back in Peking, a first priority was to furnish an account of his activities to his Rhodes Trust sponsor, Lord Lothian. On the strength of that report, the trust was persuaded to fund him for a second year. Thus secured financially, he set about producing the considerably longer second version of his account that became *Crisis in China*. The book, swiftly accepted for publication by Macmillan and Co., threw a new light on what was happening in China and established Bertram's journalistic reputation.

On 7 August 1937 the Imperial Japanese Army entered and occupied Peking. This was the prompt for Edgar Snow and James Bertram to leave the city once more, Snow in search of his wife Peg, who had taken herself off to the northeast three months previously, Bertram in the hope that he might find a way to build on his earlier reporting by linking up with the Red Army. This time they travelled with a Chinese fugitive of much greater political significance than Miao the Madman. Teng Ying-ch'ao, Chou Enlai's wife, who had been receiving medical treatment in Peking, boarded the train with them as Snow's household amah, and parted from them without incident at Tientsin.

The two journalists made their way by sea and rail to Sian, where Edgar and Peg Snow were reunited. (Not without incident: Peg had departed for the coast just four hours before Edgar's arrival, and when a telegram of recall saw her summarily removed from her train, she not unnaturally concluded that her years of flouting government regulations had finally brought about her arrest.) Together, the Snows travelled to Shanghai, which had become the focus of international attention following the outbreak there of open warfare between Chinese and Japanese forces. Bertram remained in Sian, still seeking to link with the Red Army, now renamed the Eighth Route Army in deference to the new United Front.

It came as a surprise to Bertram (although perhaps it should not have) to discover that Sian was hosting another foreign guest of note. Agnes

Smedley had travelled down from spending time with the Communist forces in the northeast to seek medical treatment after her horse rolled on her. She moved about encased in a raincoat to conceal the fact that she wore a Red Army uniform. The two were invited to attend a mass meeting celebrating the first major victory of the Eighth Route Army, at Pingxingkuan in northeastern Shansi. Inevitably, they were called upon to add an international dimension to the celebrations. 'I tortured the audience with two songs,' Smedley reported. 'The New Zealander contributed an aboriginal Maori dance of his country.' Bertram's haka was, he admitted, a souvenir of football days, but 'was militant enough to be received with great enthusiasm'.

The newly renamed Communist forces had by now come to recognise that it would be worth taking steps to present themselves in a more favourable light to the outside world. Within a week of his arrival in Sian, Bertram found himself wedged among a pile of rice sacks on the back of a truck, jolting towards the northast and the Communist HQ, now relocated to Yenan. He was the first 'British' reporter to be so honoured.

The morning after his arrival in Yenan was by chance graduation day for students at the army's military academy. Bertram was strongly urged to attend the ceremony, on the grounds that it would be a unique opportunity to meet Mao Tse-tung before his normal rising time of early afternoon. As an additional incentive, he was invited to scrutinise a banner proclaiming (in English): 'Welcome to the Foreign Friends of China', illustrated by an alarming sketch of two foreign friends, one in a bowler hat smoking a cigar, the other with a check cap and a monocle. After this, the first encounter with Chairman Mao himself could only come as an anti-climax:

> Some remnants of the legend had left me unprepared for this first impression of the man himself. It was not easy to reconcile his smooth, unlined features, the still-youthful figure with a slight student's stoop, above all that boyish, mischievous, completely infectious good humour, with all one had heard of the 'iron bolshevik' and fighting leader of China's Red Armies.
>
> 'Sit down, won't you?' Mao said in his thick, rather pleasant Hunan dialect, 'and have a cigarette.'

An open-air banquet followed speeches delivered by Mao and others. At its conclusion Mao drew upon his limited stock of English to provide Bertram with an invoice.

> 'Promise to pay,' he enjoined me, 'five hundred dollars. *After* one hundred years.' I initialled the bill he presented, which Mao folded up and placed carefully in his pocket as he rose to go.
>
> 'If anyone ever claims this bill,' he warned me solemnly, 'there won't be enough money in the English Treasury to meet it – *at Chinese rates of interest*!'

The approved texts of Bertram's interviews with Chairman Mao are preserved in Volume II of the *Selected Works of Mao Tse-tung*: 'Interview with the British Journalist, James Bertram'. Although a date is assigned to the interview – 25 October 1937 – the discussions in fact extended over weeks, generally around Mao's preferred time of close to midnight. They took place in Mao's cave-dwelling, with Mao often lying stretched out on a deckchair, allegedly the only luxury he allowed himself. From time to time the Communist leader interrupted proceedings to attend to incoming radio messages.

The discussions were somewhat less than spontaneous exchanges. Necessarily, the two worked through an interpreter. The procedure, as earlier with Edgar Snow, was for the journalist to present beforehand a list of questions. Mao's responses were translated for the foreign reporter to take down in English. The English text was then rendered back into Chinese for Mao's consideration and approval. Bertram recalled:

> My questions were not distorted, but were re-arranged and organised, and so what came out in the final version was a kind of edited version . . . So that in the end I was satisfied that nothing was twisted too badly, but it was certainly rearranged. And the emphasis fell where Mao wanted it to fall.

Bertram could have had no fears that the explanations he received were less than authoritative, although any reporter might have wished them more conducive to a lively narrative. 'The journalist,' he noted in his introduction to *North China Front*, the book he built around the interviews, 'is usually more concerned to have the first word than the last.'

James Bertram spent almost a month in Yenan before setting off under escort to spend time with the Eighth Route Army on the front line in southern Shansi. It was necessary once more to cross the Yellow River, this time not frozen but in full flood. The crossing, on a boat towed two miles upstream and then released into the current, was terrifying for the passengers, and even more so for their animals. Bertram found himself nursing his pony's head under his greatcoat until the crossing was complete. '"Were you afraid?" my guard asked cheerfully, helping me out of the chaos. "*Very* afraid," I said emphatically.'

Bertram's time with the army brought him into contact with Chou Enlai in his role as political commissar, and with the senior military commanders Chu Teh and Peng Teh-huai. He fell in again with Agnes Smedley, who was once more travelling with the army. Their earlier encounters had let Bertram dare to hope that there existed a basis for friendship: 'We shared – and this was perhaps the one thing that made her tolerate me – an unbounded admiration for the common Chinese people.' Smedley's reaction to their renewed acquaintance was more nuanced:

> In late December two foreigners arrived. One of them was James Bertram, the young New Zealander whom I had met in Sian at the time Generalissimo Chiang had been captured. He carried a copy of Shakespeare's works, and the halo of Oxford culture hovered about his head. This loftiness irritated me.*

The foreigner with whom Bertram was travelling at this time was Evans Carlson, a Marine intelligence officer attached to the US Embassy in Nanjing. Carlson, who had served in China off and on since 1927, was impressed by the Communist use of guerrilla warfare, and by what he termed the 'ethical indoctrination' of their troops. He was less impressed with his own government's policies. He resigned his commission the following year, 1938, in order to be able to give open expression to his views, and in particular to protest the folly of the United States providing arms to Japan.

* Agnes Smedley was not universally condemnatory. Rewi Alley she thought 'one of the most truly civilised and tender-hearted of the men who walk this spinning ball of mud'. – Agnes Smedley, *Battle Hymn of China* (London: Victor Gollancz, 1944) p.149.

When the Pacific War that he had predicted became a reality, Carlson re-enlisted. He was assigned leadership of the Second Marine Raider Battalion, 'Carlson's Raiders', which fought with great distinction throughout the Pacific War. Carlson's Raiders adopted Eighth Route Army tactics and a slogan from the Indusco movement, 'Gung Ho!'.

Bertram spent the following two months on the battlefront, to the extent that such a thing existed. In open conflict the Eighth Route Army faced being heavily outgunned by the well-equipped Japanese forces. It therefore adopted hit-and-run guerrilla tactics, striking at patrols and supply lines, and keeping constantly on the move. Bertram recorded these practical applications of the theoretical principles he had heard expounded in Yenan, and later brought them together in *North China Front.*

Hankow, one of the 'three cities' of Wuhan, had with the fall of Nanking become the headquarters of China's war effort. It was to Hankow that Bertram made his way after almost six months in the northeast. There he stayed as the guest of Bishop Logan Roots, head of the American Episcopal Mission. Inevitably, he found Agnes Smedley already in residence, her energies now diverted to medical relief work. The bishop, by then more than 35 years in China, was famously even-handed in his dealings with all competing factions. Dubbed by Smedley 'Comrade Bishop', he convened a daily lunch which became known as the 'Moscow–Heaven Axis' for the variety of opinions around the table.

Bertram himself had already determined that he should apply himself to helping to organise medical support for those in the northeast. The arrival in Hankow of Canadian surgeon Norman Bethune (later to be invoked as an icon of international cooperation by Chairman Mao) offered a way forward. Bethune's decision to go to China had been prompted in part by reading Bertram's *Crisis in China* (published in the US as *First Act in China*). He was later to be associated with the New Zealand missionary nurse Kathleen Hall, who procured medical supplies for his field hospital at great personal risk.

Bertram helped scrape together funds and medical supplies sufficient to allow Bethune to continue his journey. (Another doctor with whom he had been travelling had drunk up all the group's cash reserves during the Hong Kong stopover, and had to be shipped back to the US.) The beginnings of a scheme to create an International Peace Hospital to serve the Eighth Route Army were cobbled together. Before Bethune departed to pursue this goal, Bertram endowed him with all that remained of his own travelling gear: 'blue uniform, bedding roll, fur cap, a pair of Bedford cord riding breeches and lace-up riding boots'. He was interested subsequently to track the progress of all these items through photographs of Bethune at various locations in north China.

By this time (early 1938) the often chaotic conditions within China had made Hong Kong a key coordinating point for relief efforts, especially those drawing upon funding by overseas Chinese. It offered, if not a guarantee, at least a hope of probity and effective administration. Meanwhile, the situation in Hankow was becoming increasingly tenuous, as Japanese forces made their way up the Yangtze Valley. Bertram made up his mind to head south to Hong Kong, and seek opportunities for relief work there.

Republican China: A Brief Account

The wider war

Up to the end of 1941 and Japan's bombing of Pearl Harbor, foreigners in China were regarded as neutrals. After 7 December 1941, however, the war in China took on a wider dimension, ranging Japan's forces not just against China, but also against the countries associated with the Allied cause.

In the parts of China that Japan controlled, Japan took over the concessions and settlements that had been administered by Allied nations. The British colony of Hong Kong came under attack, and fell to Japan on 25 December 1941. The status in China of the citizens of countries with which Japan was now at war changed to that of enemy aliens. Over time, some were repatriated or included in prisoner exchanges. Those who remained were confined in internment camps.

Even before Pearl Harbor brought Western nations into the China war, the policy of the Chinese government had become to 'sell space for time', maintaining a holding action in the expectation that Japan's ambitions would in the end be thwarted by the intervention of the major democratic powers. Only the Communist forces in the northeast mounted an active opposition, relying on hit-and-run guerrilla tactics to harry the Japanese forces and challenge their authority in the border areas.

China's eight-year war against Japan came to an unexpectedly sudden end with the United States bombing of Hiroshima and Nagasaki. On 14 August 1945 Japan announced an unconditional surrender. The Allied High Command allocated the China Zone to the supreme direction of the Chinese government. At Chiang Kai-shek's request, the US Air Force airlifted Kuomintang troops to the occupied areas so that they, rather than the Communists, could accept the Japanese surrender.

This extended to the parts of the north and the Yellow River Valley where CCP guerrilla forces had long controlled the countryside. The Communists retaliated by cutting railway communication between the north and the south. With Japan vanquished, the stage was set for a resumption of China's civil war.

7. The Journalists

James Bertram, Iris Wilkinson and the war against Japan

In Hong Kong, Bertram was soon drawn to the work of the China Defence League (CDL), an ad hoc group set up to channel foreign funding to humanitarian causes in China. (Another was the ICCIC, established to manage resources intended for Rewi Alley's Indusco project.)

According to the CDL charter, its purpose was 'to act as a liaison between the needs of the Chinese people and the supplies, whether of cash or materials, contributed to their relief by foreign affiliated organisations'. Expressed more plainly, it was set up to see that funds got to where they were needed, rather than being siphoned off along the way. It had as its chair Soong Chingling (Mme Sun), whose experience within her own family probably left her better informed than most about the avenues that existed for converting public funds to private purposes. Profoundly out of sympathy with KMT policies, she had left China after the fall of Nanking and was living in a small apartment on Conduit Road as Mrs S.C. Ling.

Soong Chingling's plan for James Bertram was that he should undertake an overseas lecture tour on behalf of the CDL, on the one hand fundraising, and on the other speaking against Western countries providing material support to the Japanese war effort through sales of scrap metal and oil. In the meantime he oversaw publicity in Hong Kong, and set out to raise the necessary funds for his trip by working as a tutor for expatriate students hoping to attend British universities.

In Hong Kong, Bertram was able to access for the first time a copy of his book on the Sian Incident, *Crisis in China*. He was called upon almost immediately to lend it to two literary lions, W.H. Auden and Christopher Isherwood, who had descended on the colony en route to China. They had been commissioned to write an account of China's war with Japan. Bertram drew on his Eighth Route Army contacts to try to gain them access to the guerrilla areas, 'but Fatty Liao [the army's liaison officer] wasn't over-impressed by their high camp manner and general air of frivolity, so the trip didn't eventuate'.

The two carried the same manner into the parts of China they were able to visit: Auden invariably clothed in a woollen cap, a huge overcoat and carpet slippers; Isherwood in what he considered the correct garb for a war correspondent – beret, turtleneck sweater and oversized riding boots.

In Shanghai, where 'the poets' stayed with the British ambassador, they prevailed upon Rewi Alley to guide them around the devastated industrial areas. Their travel diary formed the basis of a successful book, *Journey to a War*, although in truth the journey did not very often carry them close to where the real war was being fought. In the autobiography he published 39 years later, *Christopher and His Kind*, Isherwood confessed that a significant amount of their time had been taken up with visits to Shanghai's gay bath-houses.

A lesser literary figure, albeit one who showed greater seriousness of purpose, was Iris Wilkinson. Bertram had known her in New Zealand, where (writing as Robin Hyde) she had published a number of well-received novels. En route to Europe she had stopped off in China and been swept up by the struggle there. Her ambition to report on the war had been fraught. 'She had been in Shanghai,' Bertram noted, 'and had quarrelled furiously with Rewi Alley, which was a pity, because he could have done more for her in China than most people.'

In fact Alley had done a great deal for her during her time in Shanghai, making his car available, accompanying her around the city's troublespots and providing helpful introductions. He did, however, come to regard her as impetuous and overly swayed by sentiment. The final break came when Wilkinson entered into a furious argument with Peg Snow ('"The lady deserved it," she later asserted. "Leftist prig!"') over Rewi Alley's lunch table, which led to his walking out, '[s]ince when,' she wrote, 'I have neither seen nor heard from him'. Wilkinson was left to reflect with regret on 'how much I had hurt myself by hurting, without premeditation but irretrievably, someone I admired and owed gratitude'. Towards the end of his life, Alley still recalled her with displeasure, although willing to concede that he had found her book, *Dragon Rampant*, 'surprisingly lucid, since she was nutty'.

In early 1938 Iris Wilkinson was in Hong Kong, looking to re-enter China through Canton. She joined with Bertram in an excursion to

Macau, where they spent a day with William Empson, the English poet and literary critic. (Empson had been appointed to a post at Peking University but because of the Japanese occupation was unable to take it up.) At the gateway to China, Bertram saw Wilkinson as 'very much the innocent Kiwi abroad, an unfashionable figure in a flapping coat and battered tricorn hat, limping along crowded streets and facing the world with a gaze as direct and trusting as Candide's'.

Armed with various commissions from Soong Chingling, late in 1938 Bertram took ship on an elderly freighter, the *Talthybius*, bound for the Pacific Coast of the United States. In San Francisco he had a happy reunion with Ian Milner, who was doing postgraduate work at Berkeley. Milner's academic inquiries, presumably illuminated by his association with Bertram at this time, found an outlet the following year in an insightful monograph in the Institute of Pacific Relations Inquiry Series, *New Zealand's Interests and Policies in the Far East*.*

Bertram and Milner joined forces with a Chinese economist, Walter Chan, and embarked on a barnstorming tour of the US west coast. Wedged companionably side by side on the narrow single seat of Milner's battered brown Plymouth coupé, they travelled from city to city in the US and on into Canada, addressing service club breakfasts, public meetings and seminars, and, whenever the opportunity for an interview arose, taking their message to radio audiences.

The essence of that message never changed: if Japan were allowed to conquer China, its ambition would extend to other parts of Asia, and eventually beyond that region to the world. American audiences commonly responded with a mixture of bemusement and complacency. For them, China and Japan were a long way off. 'It's no special comfort,' wrote Bertram, 'in such matters, to be proved a true prophet; at the time we wore ourselves out trying to prove the obvious, though we happened to be right.' Only in Vancouver and Victoria in British Columbia was the reception different – there substantial Chinese populations rallied to the flag of Mme Sun Yat-sen, and the CDL gained useful recruits.

For all her charm, Mme Sun was a hard taskmaster. She commissioned

* Milner's focus was courageously at odds with that of his blimpish father, who had declared in the Cawthron Lecture for 1934: 'As a matter of cold fact you will always find the British navy at the world's centre of political gravity – and that today is certainly the Mediterranean.'

William Empson, James Bertram, Iris Wilkinson and their host, Mr Rainer, in Macao, 1938.

The fundraising team in Manila, late 1940. From left: James Bertram, Edgar Snow, Peg Snow, Rewi Alley, Evans Carlson.

Bertram not only to continue his publicity efforts in Britain, but also to meet with the Soviet ambassador in London and seek permission to transport medical supplies by train across Soviet territory, and thence by truck to the Eighth Route Army in north China. He entered into meaningful discussions with the ambassador of the Union of Soviet Socialist Republics – meaningful only in that they established clearly that fraternal communist relations did not extend to the USSR providing any actual support to the Chinese Communist Party, even to the extent of allowing goods passage across Soviet borders.

In London Bertram also dutifully sought out the publisher Victor Gollancz (whose Left Book Club, with its distinctive red covers, had first afforded a readership to Edgar Snow and Agnes Smedley). Under Gollancz's aegis he thanked and encouraged English supporters of the China Defence League.

He also set to work to assemble the notes and observations arising from his time with the Eighth Route Army into a form fit for publication, and he extended a helping hand to his New Zealand friend, Iris Wilkinson, who had by then arrived in England with her own notes and observations, and very little else.

After the two had parted in Hong Kong, Wilkinson had succeeded in re-entering China and made her way to Hankow. There she had established herself within the small circle of foreign correspondents and renewed her efforts to secure the accreditation that would allow her to travel to the front. She met and interviewed, among others, Agnes Smedley, whom she presented with a large bouquet of wisteria. This, she quickly came to realise, was an inappropriate offering for someone of Smedley's strong convictions: 'She kept looking at the flowers as if she expected them to turn into string sandals, munitions, or a small donation for the Orphans' University in the North-west.' It is not clear whether Smedley encouraged her in her ambition to enter the battle zone, although given the American's general view of short-term visitors, probably she did not.

In Hankow, Iris Wilkinson found accommodation at the Lutheran Mission, where she encountered a fellow New Zealander (and indeed a fellow alumna of Wellington Girls' College*), Agnes Moncrieff.

* The two did not coincide at Wellington Girls' College. Moncrieff was head girl for two years in succession, 1915 and 1916, while Wilkinson first entered the school in 1919. It

Moncrieff, a foreign secretary of the Chinese YWCA, had by then spent more than eight years in China. Wilkinson dismissed with scorn the possibility of a 'YWCA tour' of disputed areas. Moncrieff, who had by then twice been driven further inland to escape the Japanese advance, and in Hankow was devoting herself at considerable personal risk to providing medical supplies to areas of need in the interior, may well have felt that a YWCA tour was just what the younger woman needed. At any event, she was not slow with her advice:

> I was one of the people who tried to dissuade her from going up to the front lines but she was very stubborn and she was just determined to do it, and of course she got caught . . . I thought she was extremely foolhardy . . . But you couldn't move her, you just couldn't move her.

Moncrieff had offered her advice in good faith, out of concern that Iris Wilkinson would come to harm, as indeed she did. The same motivation could not necessarily be ascribed to the small clique of foreign journalists, all men, then gathered in Hankow. All were seeking an opportunity to travel on to the major rail junction of Suchow (Xuzhou), a likely target of the Japanese advance. Iris Wilkinson had encountered misogyny as a journalist in New Zealand. Now she met it again, as the foreign press group actively lobbied the Chinese authorities to see her excluded from any travelling party.

Among their number was Rex Warren, a New Zealander representing an Australian paper, whom Wilkinson had known when he was writing for the *Auckland Sun*. It was Warren who, as a fellow New Zealander, was deputed to convey to her the group's objections. 'At that time, women writers were not widely accepted . . . as they are today . . .', he asserted in an exculpatory letter decades later.

> In stating my objection to her, I was merely acting as a spokesman for the party, who were unanimous that she would be a heavy responsibility, and would retard our mobility and speed of movement. This arose from the fact that in those days, there was a strong sense of chivalry towards women, and that, as you must know, she had an artificial leg.

---

is nonetheless possible to conjecture that memory of Moncrieff's name on the honours board strengthened the innately rebellious Iris Wilkinson's determination to disregard any advice her more experienced compatriot might have to offer.

In fact Wilkinson did not have an artificial leg but she did walk with a limp, the consequence of an accident in her late teens.

The correspondents' strong sense of chivalry did not in the event survive the need to vacate Suchow rapidly in the face of a Japanese advance. Iris Wilkinson, who had after prolonged representations received permission to join them there, found herself on her own, and without a means of retreat, when Japanese forces striking up from Nanking severed the rail link back to Hankow. On 19 May the Japanese occupied Suchow.

Some weeks passed before the Chinese authorities or British consulate officials were able to establish Iris Wilkinson's situation. Agnes Moncrieff, writing to her Dunedin friend Eva Skinner, combined concern with commentary expressed in her usual forthright terms:

> Mr Farmer of the Chinese Government Publicity told me the other day that Miss Iris Wilkinson, the New Zealand journalist, is missing. They are very worried about her. He said they absolutely refused to give her a permit but she went on several 'tear bats' (his own phrase) and they had to give her one. Now they haven't heard of her for days and don't know whether she has got mixed up in the retreat from Hsuchow or not. I think she was crazy to go near the front lines at such a critical time, especially as she is lame. Even if she was not afraid for herself she should have considered the Chinese who accompanied her. They, if caught, would be killed for certain but she might have got away alright. I must try to see Mr Farmer tomorrow and see if they have had any news yet.

Wilkinson first tried to escape from war-ravaged Suchow by walking along the rail line back to Hankow. When she was turned back by Japanese troops stationed on the line she set off in the opposite direction, again on foot, along the line that led to Tsingtao (Qingdao). It was a difficult journey. While her status as a foreigner afforded her some protection – 'If you were a Chinese woman, we would shoot you', she had been bluntly warned – it did not shield her from some very rough handling. She was beaten, stripped and humiliated by Japanese soldiers set to guard the railway. In the end their officers solved the problem of her presence by placing her on a troop train to Tsingtao and the sanctuary of the British Consulate.

In England, Bertram found Wilkinson impoverished and in poor health. He helped arrange hospital treatment, and worked with her to progress publication of the book of her Chinese experiences, *Dragon Rampant*. At the same time he was finalising the text of his own new book, *North China Front*. By April 1939 both books were with the publisher, and Bertram was on his way back to China, where Mme Sun had a new task for him: taking a truck convoy into Free China (that part of China's interior not occupied by Japan) via Haiphong in Vietnam. Iris Wilkinson remained in England, obsessed with a desire for a return to China that her ill-health and lack of funds rendered impossible. 'James [Bertram] had tried to dissuade her,' according to Charles Brasch, then in London, 'but once a notion took hold of her she was headstrong.' On 23 August 1939, at the age of 33, Wilkinson took her own life by overdosing on Benzedrine.

Late in 1938 Japanese forces had entered and seized Canton, cutting off the direct rail link from Hong Kong into China. Back in Hong Kong, Bertram plunged into preparations for the dispatch of a CDL convoy by an alternative route, staging through Haiphong and French Indochina into the guerrilla areas of the northwest.

Bertram had as a helper Max Bickerton, later, with Indusco in Shanghai, the custodian of Rewi Alley's sheep. As has been seen, Bickerton had a chequered past.

Arriving in Japan from New Zealand in 1924, he had developed great facility in both spoken and written Japanese. He taught at a school for the sons of the aristocracy, he achieved success as a translator of Japanese literature, and he became an active supporter of the fledgling Japanese Communist Party. It was this last that attracted the attention of Japanese authorities. In 1934 he was arrested on suspicion of 'harbouring dangerous thoughts', interrogated, beaten, imprisoned, and after 24 days released on bail.

Bickerton opted to jump bail and leave Japan rather than encourage the authorities to explore further the nature of his thoughts. In this he was aided by William Empson, then like Bickerton teaching in Japan. By one account, Empson booked Bickerton's passage on a foreign freighter under an assumed name, and provided him with a disguise of different clothes, dark glasses and a false moustache. Despite these precautions, as the two approached the ship they were intercepted by an officer of Japan's secret police. The policeman presented Bickerton with a brown paper parcel, which turned out to contain all the clothes he had left behind, freshly laundered. But did not seek to detain him. If this is true, it adds credence to the idea that the authorities were less concerned with arraigning him in the Japanese courts than with getting him out of the country.

Now Bickerton had turned up in Hong Kong, keen to get into China, but for the time being working in support of Mme Sun's China Defence League. Bertram found him a breath of fresh air.

> Whenever Rewi Alley could manage one of his flying visits to the British colony, he and Max and I would gather at Jimmy's Kitchen, pick up a kit of beer and an outsize apple pie, and head for one of Hong Kong's less frequented beaches, where we swam, lay in the sun, and imagined we were back at Takapuna or Sumner, breathing a cleaner air.

The convoy that was eventually assembled in Haiphong was made up of 23 vehicles, carrying 15,000 gallons of petrol and 500 cases of medical supplies. It was spearheaded by a gigantic ambulance, custom built on a British bus chassis, a gift to Mme Sun from shipbuilder Sir John Thornycroft. Sadly, the ambulance did not prove equal to the challenge posed by China's roads, and when the convoy reached Nanning in southern China a local garage was employed to lop off the tail section. This detracted from its appearance but did allow it to negotiate sudden dips in the road. In the end it found its metier in Shansi as a mobile operating theatre.

Bertram was not on hand to see the convoy reach its destination. Before the trucks had reached Sian, news came through that Britain and France were at war with Germany. Not doubting that New Zealand would follow Britain's lead, Bertram saw no choice but to offer his services to the war effort in his own country. From Sian he caught an old Eurasia plane to Hong Kong, the first step in his return to New Zealand.

As it turned out, New Zealand was less well placed to take up his services than he was to offer them. Three echelons of the New Zealand Expeditionary Force were already in basic training, and there was no immediate intention to increase that number. Bertram sought unsuccessfully to get a job as an official war correspondent. When the government announced a move from voluntary service to conscription (a decision that would in time prompt a flow of pacifist volunteers to ambulance work in China), Bertram's sense of exceptionalism shaped his response: 'I was prepared to be a volunteer, but I was damned if I was going to be a conscript.' A telegraphed appeal from Soong Chingling tipped the balance: he decided to fight his war in China rather than Europe. He applied for and received a dispensation to return to the China Defence League and 'the organisation of medical relief'. August 1940 found Bertram in Manila, on his way back to Hong Kong.

Manila was another of Mme Sun's deft diversions, aimed at building support among the Philippines' substantial and wealthy Chinese population. Bertram found himself among friends: Edgar and Peg Snow had been based at a nearby resort, Baguio, for some months, and Rewi Alley arrived soon after to make his own pitch for support for Indusco. Bertram was treated to the sight of a sturdy New Zealander in khaki shorts 'addressing a mass meeting of local Chinese (most of whom spoke Fukien dialect at a couple of removes) in racy vernacular for over an hour'. Bertram himself was glad to team up for a presentation with his North China Front colleague Major Evans Carlson, no longer constrained by his US Embassy position from warning publicly about Japan's military ambitions. The three – Alley, Bertram and Carlson – travelled companionably together on to Hong Kong.

The Hong Kong that Bertram returned to remained oddly divorced from what was happening across the border. *New Yorker* correspondent Emily Hahn, who had relocated there, noted from the superior perspective of a US citizen:

> Nobody among those British ever gave China a thought. You could go through the day, from the 11 o'clock drink in the Grips through lunch at someone's house and tea somewhere else down to dinner, stately on the Peak with plenty of cut glass and damask linen and heavy silver, and nobody would talk of the war in China except as a far-off exotic manifestation of the natives.

Bertram was once again occupied in arranging the dispatch of relief supplies to wartime China, necessarily circumventing not only the Japanese but often also the KMT forces in order to provide medical aid to the New Fourth Army. Agnes Smedley, who had just spent an extended and physically debilitating time with the Communist forces, turned up to promote their interests, having been admitted to the colony only on condition that she not make speeches or engage in political activities.

Bertram found himself occupying a room at Bishopsgate, the official residence of Ronald, Bishop Hall, the Anglican bishop of Hong Kong. Bishop Hall, central to Hong Kong support for Soong Chingling's causes, had redesignated his residence the Church Guest House, and himself decamped to a bucolic retreat in the New Territories. He kept goats there; he had a brother who was a sheep farmer in New Zealand.

From time to time Rewi Alley arrived to stay at the Church Guest House, 'sunburnt and travel-stained, with half the correspondence and most of the working plans of Indusco in his bulging despatch case'. Alley's purpose was to seek accounting advice: the opening shots had already been fired in what was to be a long-running battle with H.H. Kung over the allocation of Indusco funding.

Early in 1941 the British ambassador wrote to Bertram (the message immediately distinctive for being written in Clark-Kerr's habitual quill pen) asking him to fill the position of press attaché at the embassy in Chungking while the incumbent recovered from typhus. With Soong Chingling's blessing (he could, she thought, help preserve the United Front against the policies of sister Meiling and her husband, the Generalissimo), Bertram relocated to the new wartime capital.

Chungking, perched precipitously above the Yangtze River some 1500 kilometres inland from Shanghai and the coast, had become the target of heavy Japanese bombing. (The effectiveness of the bombing was mitigated by the actions of the Chinese workers loading the bombs in Hankow, who provided Chungking with advance warning the planes were on their way.) It was not a situation that offered great scope for orthodox press liaison work; nor did the perceived British policy of appeasement towards Japan add to the credibility of its representatives in Free China.

Bertram accepted with some relief a commission to travel to Rangoon (Yangon) in Burma (Myanmar) to bring back two trucks loaded with 'necessary equipment for the Chungking press office'. In contrast to the medical supplies and fuel carried in the earlier convoy he had supervised, the 'necessary equipment' on this occasion turned out to include substantial quantities of Scotch whisky and London gin, destined for a large garden party on the embassy lawn intended to bolster British prestige, if not necessarily credibility. Not long afterwards the regular press attaché reported fit for duty – 'a moustachioed outdoor type who looked like a white hunter from a Rider Haggard novel, and really knew more about cloak and dagger operations then he did about newspaper work'. It was back to Hong Kong for his temporary replacement.

The CDL was by now finding it almost impossible to get relief shipments into China. It had shifted its focus to publicising the realities of the situation in Free China, and the perilous state of the United Front. Hong Kong too had changed, with an influx of refugees from the mainland, and an exodus of foreign dependants to Europe and the United States. Not all welcomed the compulsory repatriation – an American Navy captain unfeelingly described his wife's distress to Emily Hahn: 'Somebody showed her a dishpan and a washtub, and she's scared to death.'

Emily Hahn herself had no intention of being repatriated. She was caring for a new baby, the result of a liaison with the (married) head of British military intelligence, Major Charles Boxer. After the colony fell she avoided internment by declaring herself Chinese by right of her earlier secondary marriage to Sinmay Zau.

On 8 December 1941 Japanese forces attacked Hong Kong. Having assured himself of Mme Sun's safety (she found a seat on the last flight out to Chungking), James Bertram sought to mobilise local Chinese forces to assist in the island's defence. It quickly became clear that this was out of the question, even though his friend Fatty Liao had already marshalled guerrilla forces on the mainland. The work of organisation had been left too late, and the British feared the possible emergence of a Fifth Column. Bertram equipped himself with an introductory note to the Hong Kong Voluntary Defence Corps – a force up to that time more celebrated for the consumption of gin slings than for military prowess – and made his way to the corps headquarters where he joined up. The same night he found himself, still wearing corduroy trousers and a grey tweed overcoat he had bought for diplomatic duties in Chungking, patrolling the waterfront with a Bren gun.

Japan's military planners had counted on taking Hong Kong in four days. In the event, the island's defences held out for almost three weeks, with the contribution of the rag-tag-and-bobtail HK Volunteers by no means least. Bertram became part of Second Battery, HKVDC, Fort Stanley, tasked with defending the gun emplacements on Stanley Peninsula against land attack.

Much to his own satisfaction he was able to equip himself with a Lewis gun, a weapon by then virtually antique, but intimately familiar to a former member of the Waitaki Boys' High School Cadet Corps. When, after days of waiting, the Japanese attack came, he combined with a Norwegian spotter and a Polish loader to contribute to a gallant and effective defence of the isthmus of the peninsula. Sadly, events elsewhere overtook this action. With the city of Victoria in enemy hands, on Christmas Day 1941 Hong Kong surrendered.

The experience of defeat affected different people in different ways. According to the habitually censorious Emily Hahn, 'There was a rush on the part of the leftists . . . to save their skins.' She admitted only two exceptions, both of them New Zealanders. 'Except for Jim Bertram, who simply enlisted with the Volunteers and fought, and was captured, and in general behaved well, and Max Bickerton, who did his job too and made no attempt to get away, the leftists behaved in a way that made me slightly sick.'

From the time of Pearl Harbor, Max Bickerton's Japanese language skills had been set to use monitoring Japan's shortwave radio broadcasts. It was he who first broke to a disbelieving Hong Kong military establishment the news of the sinking of the *Prince of Wales* and the *Repulse*, and with that the last hope of holding out in Singapore. After the fall of Hong Kong he provided interpretation for Selwyn Clark, Hong Kong's director of medical services, who was permitted to remain free for a time in order to set in place measures for hygiene and epidemic prevention.

After the Japanese had established a civilian internment camp at Stanley, Bickerton was sent there to interpret for the 2300 internees. He continued in that role until the end of the war. Playing a liaison role that risked attracting criticism from those he represented, he built a reputation for competence, and for attention to the needs of internees. For John Sterricker, administrative secretary of the council set up within the camp, he was 'our admirable interpreter, Max Bickerton'.

When, after the war, awards were being handed out, a letter to Hong

Kong's *China Mail* from 'one of the POWs' expressed disappointment that Bickerton had not been included. According to the correspondent, he was the Japanese authorities' preferred interpreter, and hence was called upon all hours of the day and night. He translated Japanese newspapers for the internees. He accepted no favours from the Japanese for his work, and refused to use the black market. He appeared to own no shoes. 'I cannot help feeling that our safety was very much in his hands. He had to plead with the Japanese on our behalf time and again and risk being "slapped".'

After the Allied victory, Bickerton was repatriated to the UK. But postwar Britain held few charms and it was not long before he was back in China, enjoying a much livelier lifestyle in Shanghai. By 1949 Bickerton had made his way to Peking, where he renewed his friendship with William Empson, by then married to Hetta, who became Max's lifelong friend and supporter. Empson was teaching at Peking University, where Max also secured a position as a teacher of English.

Bickerton's anti-establishment streak did not serve him well with what remained of the British expatriate community. Among his many accomplishments was that of a skilled puppeteer, acquired while helping out at his grandfather's Christchurch pleasure garden. Hetta Empson drew upon this to combine revolutionary theatre with a Punch and Judy show for Christmas 1949. Sadly, it did not end well, Hetta wrote to a friend:

> Some of the little ones were carried away screaming, and sad Mrs Kendall looked at me regretfully with her great cow eyes and said gloomily, 'We thought it would be something jolly' . . . It was all a lot of crap because it was a lovely show. Max made the Doctor say to Punch, 'I can't waste my time on lower middle class cases like yours', so Punch poked him in his lower middle until he was dead.

A subsequent puppet show, which dealt disrespectfully with General MacArthur and the forces of mperialism, led to a fracas among members of the expatriate audience, with both Bickerton and William Empson giving as good as they got. Not long afterwards, Bickerton's teaching position lapsed, and with it his right to remain in post-revolutionary China. Regretfully, he sold his Phillips bicycle and set sail for Marseilles, and then to England, on the proceeds. He was never to return to China.

While Max Bickerton appears to have come through his wartime experience of internment without suffering huge trauma, the same was less true of James Bertram and others living under the much harsher conditions of imprisonment as a prisoner of war. Bertram was a captive of the Japanese for four years. 'Over those years many died,' he recalled in his memoir, 'and things happened to all of us that would return to haunt our dreams.' In later life, his wife Jean related, 'He would wake up screaming and fighting with his Japanese prison guards who were beating him.' He came to rely upon sleeping tablets to help him find sleep.

Bertram's combatant status meant that he joined his comrades of the Hong Kong Volunteers and members of the regular army units in a POW camp established at Shumshuipo [Shamsuipo], on the Kowloon Peninsula. The Shumshuipo camp, formerly a British military barracks, lay on reclaimed land between the Kowloon hills and the harbour. Before the Japanese installed electrified wires around the camp there were several successful escapes, which prompted severe reprisals, including food rationing as a form of collective punishment.* Malnutrition and diptheria both claimed many lives, at the same time as the prisoners were required to undertake heavy manual labour.

After two years at Shumshuipo, Bertram was transferred to Tokyo as one of a small group of 'Specials'. What was special, it turned out, was his experience as a journalist. A persuasive interrogator offered him preferential treatment in return for expressing 'humanitarian views' through the Japanese press and radio stations. When Bertram declined, he was consigned to the 'Undesirables' and set to work on the Tokyo docks. The work was gruelling and treatment of the prisoners often brutal. Still, Bertram had cause to reflect that the situation in which he found himself might have been worse, had the interrogating officer not recognised him as a fellow student from their time together at New College, Oxford.

* Even after the electrified fence was in place there was a spectacular solo effort by Lieutenant-Commander R.B. Goodwin of the RNZNVR, who negotiated the fence by stepping on the insulators, swam Laichikok Bay and trekked 10 days across country to link up with Fatty Liao's Communist guerrillas. The exploit is recounted in Goodwin's book, *Hong Kong* Escape (London: Arthur Barker, 1953).

At war's end James Bertram was repatriated to New Zealand, emaciated and suffering from beri-beri. His treatment at the hands of the Japanese had taken a mental as well as a physical toll. Those close to him found him changed: 'His whole being was somehow blunted,' in the eyes of friend and fellow Rhodes Scholar Geoffrey Cox.

Bertram considered and rejected the possibility of a return to China. Now in the throes of a revolution, China was 'no country for old men. I just can't take things at the old pace. I have a most cowardly desire to stay in one place.' Meeting him once more 14 years later, Helen Foster Snow found herself reflecting soberly that 'Jim paid a heavy price for his China experience . . . I often think back on the youth and health and high hopes and real talent destroyed before they could flower or reach their prime, especially among the British, in both the World Wars.'

8. The Organiser

Agnes Moncrieff travels for the YWCA

Agnes (Nessie) Moncrieff, who thought George Shepherd a skite, was herself anything but. Reports, public presentations and even her personal correspondence over 16 years in China are remarkable for their reticence about the part she herself played in the events she witnessed. Her reticence extended into later life: a young teaching colleague was astonished to learn by accident of Moncrieff's China years. 'We were talking about China and evidently she hadn't realised who I was, and she said, "Do you mean to say that you're the person we put our pennies in the tin for?" I thought it didn't sound very appreciative.'

'The tin' was provided at meetings of the Young Women's Christian Association (YWCA) to help fund the organisation's international work. It was under YWCA auspices that Moncrieff travelled to and worked in China, her interest sparked by a 1922 visit as New Zealand representative to a conference of the World Student Christian Federation (in New Zealand, the Student Christian Movement – SCM), held at Peking's Tsinghua University.

Fascinated by China, Moncrieff was anxious to return, but she had no interest in following the obvious path. 'I didn't want to go as a missionary. I knew I'd be absolutely no good in some out-of-the-way place, tucked away by myself.' The YWCA, with centres established in China's major cities and a focus on the well-being and career development of young women, was more in her line. When the opportunity arose to return to China as a YWCA foreign secretary in 1930 she seized the chance, despite being realistic about what she might achieve. 'When you think of the influence of a mission or anything else in China, it's just a drop in the ocean, isn't it.'

Agnes Moncrieff arrived in Peking in February 1930, equipped with a Victoria University Master's degree in Latin and French, some teaching experience, and the fruits of a full year's tailored programme designed to familiarise her with the operation of the YWCA. The training was aimed at equipping her to take on a mentoring role with young women of high school or university age. Accordingly, after a year's language study, she was pitchforked into oversight of a newly opened hostel accommodating 70 students. It was, by her later account, not an easy beginning. 'They were a wild crowd. They were away from home and away from authority, and for the first time in their lives the world was theirs. Somebody asked me was I making any progress and I said, well, I think they spit less within the building.'

The early 1930s saw a stepping up of Japan's drive to establish dominance in China. In September 1931 Japanese army officers in Manchuria launched a successful attack on Mukden [Shenyang], leading to Japanese control of all Manchuria (later renamed Manchukuo) before the year's end. This was followed by the occupation of Jehol Province and, in May 1933, a military threat to neighbouring Hebei, including aerial attacks on Peking itself. For the first time Agnes Moncrieff found herself exposed to Japanese bombing. There was little damage, she told the New Zealand newspapers, and 'the people were more frightened than hurt'. Sufficiently frightened, nonetheless, for China to sue for peace, and agree to humiliating terms in order to secure a Japanese withdrawal to positions north of the Great Wall.

For the first time, also, it fell to Agnes Moncrieff to deal with some of the consequences of Japanese aggression. Many of her hostel charges were directly affected.

> They were terribly upset because they were from Manchuria and they didn't know what was happening to their families . . . and the whole place broke up. It was very hard to staff because with girls of that kind anybody in charge is losing face all the time, and of course . . . China must not lose face.

The dislocations of intermittent warfare were to form a constant background to Moncrieff's activities in China from that time on.

In 1935 Moncrieff left China for leave in New Zealand and further training in the United States and Europe. She returned to China late in 1936 to take up a new position in Shanghai. She was now tasked not with the care of students but with involvement in the full range of YWCA activities in China's most westernised city. The YWCA itself had by this time moved away from Western control: oversight was entirely in the hands of a Chinese board of directors, 'the finest group of women you could possibly imagine', and the proportion of secretaries from outside China had fallen dramatically. While in 1920 there were 85 'foreign secretaries', mostly from the US, by 1934 only 14 of the total of more than 100 were from overseas.

The role of foreign secretaries was to support and advise, and inevitably they were called upon particularly when it came to addressing the difficulties of women from other countries living in China, most notably in Shanghai. Often the YWCA became a de facto employment agency, seeking to match needy foreigners with available opportunities. In a sketch of her day's work, Moncrieff touched on some of the difficulties:

> Two girls were waiting in the office to join the tennis club and enquire about swimming lessons. A newspaper called. What was the meeting on Thursday and what would the speaker say? The secretary invented a probable speech, and hoped there would not be a libel case over it.
>
> It was long past 12. She shot round the corner for lunch, discovered another social worker munching a sandwich and learnt to her horror that 50 resource-less girls had just arrived from the north. Couldn't there be some law to prevent such girls from landing in Shanghai? But what would happen if there was such a law? It wouldn't really solve the problem. They must live somewhere. . . .
>
> 'Princess Elsa Kederoff' said the card on her desk and there she stood, but surely not quite a princess. She must have work, but knew no English. 'Man want drink, I understand. I work bar, you find, yes?' 'Really,' thought the secretary, 'a princess, a bar and a YWCA. They simply don't go together.' It took her 15 minutes to find English simple enough to make the princess understand that no bar owners ever rang the YWCA to look for assistance.

White Russians were the first wave of destitute foreigners to arrive in Shanghai. The late 1930s saw the advent of penniless refugees from another source, and in greater numbers. Jews desperate to escape Hitler's Germany flocked to the only port in the world that would allow them visa-free entry. Shanghai's expatriate population in normal times hovered around 50,000; to this was now added some 20,000 Jewish refugees. The YWCA accepted this new call on its resources, as it did the need to help deal the problems created by many thousands of Chinese

Agnes Moncrieff (right) with American colleagues at the YWCA's Peking Residence, Hsai Po Ko Shih, 1933.

The impact of Japanese bombing – train carriages concertinaed near Canton. (Presbyterian Research Centre Archives)

cramming into the foreign settlements as the war moved closer.

Recalling the impact of the Japanese advance in later life, Agnes Moncrieff remarked upon her own good luck: 'I was very fortunate really. I was always just out of the way.' It depends how you measure good fortune. New Zealand's foreign secretary was, fortuitously, out of the way when hostilities broke out in Shanghai, but her life was not made noticeably easier as a result.

The resort town of Kuling included among its amenities a boarding school for the children of missionaries, the Kuling American School. During the summer vacation it offered holiday accommodation in the school hostel. Agnes Moncrieff and an American colleague took the opportunity to travel there for a break from Shanghai's summer heat in early August 1937. Scarcely had they arrived when an ill-judged pre-emptive attack by Chiang Kai-shek against Japanese warships anchored off the Hwangpu docks precipitated all-out (if undeclared) war in Shanghai's Chinese districts and the surrounding countryside. Return downriver from Kuling was impossible; the pair were instructed instead to travel on up the Yangtze to Hankow and see how they could make themselves useful.

Hankow in late 1937 became a focus for anti-Japanese resistance and war relief efforts. Faced with the likely imminent loss of Nanking, Generalissimo Chiang Kai-shek nominated Chungking, above the Yangtze gorges, as China's wartime capital. He himself, however, chose to locate himself for the time being in Hankow (or, more accurately, in another of the three towns, Wuchang, in the first instance). With the onset of Japanese bombing, arrangements were made for his security, although unfortunately such precautions did not extend more widely. As Moncrieff wrote later: 'The only people who had bomb shelters were the government party, and they had enormous concrete-lined places that had been built for Chiang Kai-shek and his immediate surroundings. But the rest of us were out and about. I always used to feel a little safer if I had my umbrella up.'

She herself found lodging at the Lutheran Mission, an institution that was over that year as much of a magnet for expatriates as Hankow itself was for all who had dealings with the Nationalist government.

> I had one absolutely fantastic year in Hankow, the year that the

> government was there, and everybody in the world who came to China went through Hankow. And they all stayed in the same place that I was staying in because the Lutheran Mission had an enormous six-floor boarding house cum offices cum everything else and everybody who went through Hankow in the way of foreigners – and some Chinese too – stayed in the Lutheran Mission place. And you really met the most amazing people.*

Among the amazing people Moncrieff met in Hankow were several fellow New Zealanders: Iris Wilkinson and George Shepherd, with whom she crossed swords; and James Bertram and Rewi Alley, with whom her relations were apparently more amicable. Alley she already knew from when he was a factory inspector in Shanghai; they met again years later in Chengdu, when he turned up to reclaim some personal effects which he had entrusted for safekeeping to her cousin, a missionary teacher at the West Union University. In Hankow, Moncrieff also struck up an acquaintance with Agnes Smedley, upon whom she thought the influence of Bishop Roots had had a mellowing affect.

On 13 December 1937 the Japanese army marched into Nanking, the beginning of the prolonged period of atrocities that came to be known as the Rape of Nanking. Accounts of events there did little to ease concern about what Japanese occupation might mean for other cities in the path of their advance. Moncrieff was concerned for the welfare of her Chinese colleagues, less so for herself as a foreign national. Apparently in response to representations from her mother, she wrote home:

> There is not the least likelihood of the New Zealand Association asking me to come home and if they did I would never hold up my head again. N.Z. would be forever disgraced. Western secretaries are badly needed especially in the places held or likely to be held by the Japanese. In spite of many unpleasant incidents foreign flags are still respected a little more than the Chinese flag and if the worst occurred I would probably go and live in the YWCA and wave a British flag over the institution.

* The Lutheran Mission was a separate institution from Bishop Roots' American Episcopal Mission, although guests from the former often joined meals at the bishop's table. James Bertram, George Shepherd and Agnes Smedley all at one time or another stayed at the American Episcopal Mission, Agnes Moncrieff and Iris Wilkinson at the Lutheran Mission.

As it turned out, Japan slowed its ground advance out of concern that its supply lines might become over-extended. Instead, it subjected Hankow to sustained attack from the air. When Chinese forces responded with anti-aircraft fire, Japan threatened to bomb residential areas of the city unless the anti-aircraft batteries ceased their operations. Whether as a consequence of Chinese intransigence or through simple ineptitude, the attacks did come to encompass civilian targets. 'The Japanese are such rotten marksmen,' Moncrieff wrote to New Zealand after one air raid. 'They are jolly good at hitting hospitals and refugee camps and residential districts and leaving the points of military importance alone . . . The worst damage was done in a congested Chinese area where about 200 people were killed and many more injured.'

In a humanitarian gesture towards their fellow countrymen, the Japanese military had closed the Japanese concession, and required all Japanese civilians to leave, before the bombing campaign began in earnest.

Amid such carnage Moncrieff set to work helping to provide medical relief through a body called the International Red Cross. It was linked to the Geneva-based organisation in name only – it was in fact an ad hoc body set up by a group of missionaries, diplomats and other concerned foreigners under the leadership of a long-term medical missionary, Dr James Maxwell. Its objective was to arrange the import through Hong Kong of desperately needed medical supplies, and to facilitate their distribution to civilian hospitals and to medical centres serving the Nationalist army.

Rather against Maxwell's better judgement, it extended its reach beyond the Nationalists, supplying the Communist areas as well.

> There was a Canadian doctor who was in touch with them and he used to come down and put in an order and old Dr Maxwell, he didn't like the stuff going up to Communists. He and Dr McClure used to have a real dingdong. But he did get materials through, and after all, they were serving injured men and sick people and they should have been served, whatever their politics.*

* Dr Bob McClure was a Canadian missionary doctor who later headed the convoy that facilitated Kathleen Hall's re-entry into China, and later still served as medical director of the Friends Ambulance Unit's China Convoy.

Agnes Moncrieff's stay in Hankow was enlivened by making the acquaintance of Soong Meiling, herself a YWCA supporter in Shanghai in the early 1920s. At their first encounter, Moncrieff thought the Mme Chiang 'very gracious and most distinguished looking', although she did comment quizzically on her 'wings'. 'She was chairman of the Aeronautical Commission and is still a member of it. So she wears the badge done up in platinum and diamonds.'

Later, Mme Chiang had occasion to call upon the assistance of Moncrieff (by now once more with the YWCA) and her American friend Pearl Pollock when she was invited to give a broadcast address to the National Convention of the American YWCA.

> The poor woman, you know, she wanted to get out of it. So she asked this American secretary I was with to write a speech for her. Well of course that was a stupid thing to do, because what the American secretary would say in a situation like that couldn't possibly be put into Madame Chiang's mouth . . . Madame Chiang found she had to write the speech herself.

The episode did have one positive consequence: the two young women were invited to lunch at Madame Chiang's home. And one unexpected one:

> We stepped out afterwards with her for some reason – I've forgotten where we were going – and my brother was in a small cinema show in Pahiatua and all of a sudden he saw me [in the film] walking down the pathway with Madame Chiang Kai-shek. And he got up and shouted, 'There's my sister!' They must have thought he was nuts.

Travel by this stage of the anti-Japanese war was not a straightforward affair. The title of Agnes Moncrieff's collected letters, *You Do Not Travel in China at the Full Moon*, derives from the fact that Japanese bombing was at its peak at that time. Even setting aside the activities of the Japanese, there were gradations of difficulty and comfort. Before Margaret Garland set out for China as a member of a 'peace delegation' in 1952, she sought travel advice from both Agnes Moncrieff and James Bertram. Recalled Moncrieff: 'I, of course, had travelled mostly third class with my own wash-basin and my food supply and, you know, real hard travel. And James Bertram had travelled first class. What the poor woman made of it, I don't know.' This seems a little hard on Bertram, whose journey to Sian, at least, had had its problematic moments. Certainly, however, Moncrieff found herself confronted with considerable hardship and risk in her travels within wartime China.

Wuchang, on the southern side of the Yangtze, was the northern terminus of the railway line that connected the Yangtze Valley with Canton. In July 1938 Canton was under intermittent attack but had not yet been occupied by Japan. The line accordingly offered a possible route out to Hong Kong, albeit one that carried with it a considerable risk of being bombed along the way. In the absence of any viable alternative, Agnes Moncrieff set out by train to attend a YWCA staff conference in Hong Kong.

> I went down on that railway to Canton and we went through stations that were still smoking and smelling of, you know, water on burning wood, and there were wrecks and we would get an alarm and the engine would be detached and shunted off into a cutting or something like that where it would be a little more protected. And we'd be left sitting in the open and just waiting for it to come. It was very exciting and it took about twice as long to get down to Hong Kong.

Precautions against air raids, the need to deal with the consequences of air raids, and the right of way accorded the many military trains stretched the journey to a six-day odyssey. Arrival at the Canton terminal did little to raise travellers' spirits: 'I never saw anything so gruesome in my life,' Moncrieff wrote to her friend Eva Skinner in Dunedin.

> I think it gave me the creeps more than anything else on the whole trip. We had passed the wrecks of locomotives and rolling stock and the repair sheds had been badly bombed, but of course all the tracks had been repaired so we came through alright. I was all for getting off the station as soon as possible. I couldn't bear the sight of it. While we were waiting for a taxi the telephone rang somewhere in the building and I thought how typical of China carrying on in the midst of ruins.

Moncrieff returned to Hankow via Haiphong, Hanoi, Kunming and Chengdu. Scarcely had she arrived back before the YWCA, alarmed at the pace of the Japanese advance, ordered her back out to Hong Kong, and from there to Shanghai. By this time the rail link to Canton and Hong Kong was scarcely functioning. Instead she secured a place on the back of a truck, travelling with a loaf of bread and a bunch of bananas, overnighting in flimsy Chinese inns, and retreating under the truck during the intermittent air raids.

'The amah who brought me water to wash in asked me if I was afraid. "Scared to death," I said. "I got under the bed," she said. "What did you do?" "I got under the truck," I said, and we both laughed.' She never heard whether the train she might have travelled on got through to Canton. If so, it was the last one. Canton, and the three cities of Wuhan, fell to the Japanese in rapid succession in the second half of October. Before the Japanese takeover of Canton she had found a berth on a P&O coastal steamer and was back in Shanghai.

As Japan extended its grip over coastal China and up the Yangtze Valley, the situation of foreign nationals became increasingly anomalous. Technically, the treaty ports' foreign concessions were not part of China but the territory of the external powers to which they had been ceded. Moreover, the citizens of some of those powers were owed the respect due to allies of Japan. ('The Good German of Nanking', John Rabe, who saved the lives of many Chinese during the Nanking Massacre, went about his work ostentatiously wearing a swastika armband.)

The situation of the YWCA, as a Chinese organisation staffed in part by foreigners, was doubly anomalous. Because of her British passport (New Zealand passports were not introduced until 1947) and conceivably also because of her physical presence (she was tall and strongly built), once back in Shanghai Agnes Moncrieff was assigned the role of coordinator for all 10 city associations still in operation. It fell to her to do what she could to ensure their continued effective operation in the confused situation that prevailed. This could include judicious invocation of the principle of extraterritoriality:

> I had been sent up to sit on the doorstep of YWCAs in North China because the Japanese were being a nuisance and they arrested one of our secretaries in Jinan. And I was very interested and went up to Chefoo to the YWCA there. You were allowed to fly your own flag if there was property belonging to the country even in a Chinese building, you see.

> And I got up there to find the American flag flying over the YWCA and I thought, well I'm quite sure there is no property, there's nothing belonging to America in there. But I found a dressing chest – you know, a chest of drawers – full of empty cardboard boxes. And that was the American property that justified the flag. I didn't bother to change it for the Union Jack or the New Zealand flag, I just left things as they were.

The abstruse principles of extraterritoriality did not prevent the Japanese from asserting their authority through petty acts of humiliation. From the time Manchukuo was established it was required that anyone passing a Japanese sentry should remove their hat as a sign of respect.* The same requirement, with the addition of a slight bow, was progressively imposed as the Japanese moved south. There were refinements: in Shanghai, Rewi Alley was debagged and 'caught a crack over the bottom' for protesting at the mistreatment of captured Chinese soldiers.

The question of the status of foreign concessions came into sharp focus in June 1939 when four Chinese accused by the Japanese of assassinating a collaborator took refuge in the British concession in Tientsin. Legally unable to enter, the Japanese instead blockaded it, and subjected those entering and leaving to humiliating strip searches. Fortunately, Agnes Moncrieff had departed Tientsin in the course of a northern tour two days before these measures came into effect.

Unfortunately she had left personal possessions and money in the concession, to be retrieved on her way back. In the end she chose to leave her effects there indefinitely rather than run the Japanese gauntlet. 'There is a headline in the paper this morning about another British woman being stripped,' she wrote to Eva. 'They usually leave your corselette, but as I don't wear one there would be an element of uncertainty in the incident.' The situation was ultimately resolved by the British handing the fugitives over to the Japanese, who executed them.

The 'Tientsin Incident' had ramifications for New Zealand when its honorary consul, Cecil Davis, set out to cross the concession border in

* This requirement so incensed Raymond Ludden, a member of the US Consulate staff in Mukden, and later one of America's China hands, that he did away with his hat in the midst of a frigid Manchurian winter, and never wore one again.

the (as it turned out, mistaken) belief that diplomatic immunity extended to immunity from being stripped naked in the street. The episode saw the Japanese ambassador in London called in for a stern talking-to. According to the British Secretary of State, Viscount Halifax, 'I told the ambassador that . . . behaviour such as that reported in the telegrams was unworthy of any civilised people, and I was certain that he would be just as shocked by it as I was myself.'

Moncrieff returned to New Zealand for her second furlough in mid-1940. The expectation was that she would divide her time between rest and recovery (she had contracted pleurisy shortly before leaving Shanghai) and what was called 'deputation work'. This involved undertaking a programme of interviews and public addresses to inform the New Zealand public of the situation in China and the work of the YWCA there – and to encourage people to put pennies in the tin. 'I addressed six Rotaries in seven weeks. And I was the first woman speaker that the Dunedin University Club ever had. And you know, I just talked my head off around the country.'

The Wellington *Evening Post*'s report of one such meeting in the capital records that the vote of thanks was proposed by Janet Fraser, wife of Prime Minister Peter Fraser, with Lotty Nash, wife of future Prime Minister Walter Nash, also present on the stage. Janet Fraser in particular, in Moncrieff's recollection, 'was extraordinarily interested in China. And she knew a lot about it. She used to turn up at all my meetings . . . And I said to her one day, "Well, Mrs Fraser, I think you could make my speech even better than I could."'

Mrs Fraser's strong interest may conceivably have helped shape the thinking of her husband, who was over this period subject to strong and ultimately successful representations by the retired Presbyterian missionary Rev. George McNeur, over the immigration status of Chinese stranded in New Zealand by the war. Certainly the case presented by New Zealand's YWCA secretary had some impact on public perceptions – when she presented herself at the Chinese Consulate in Wellington to secure a visa for her return to China, she was met with expressions of deep gratitude for all her 'propaganda work' on China's behalf.

A return to China in mid-1941 was in no way a straightforward affair. Sea travel had been disrupted by the war in Europe. To complicate matters further, conditions in Shanghai had deteriorated to a point where the

YWCA had relocated its headquarters to Chengdu, Szechuan's capital, as far inland as possible from the Japan-occupied coastal areas. Travel into Free China overland from the coast was not possible.

Alert to their international responsibilities, the Japanese made it known that they would refrain from bombing trains carrying foreign nationals – an undertaking that offered less than complete reassurance, as the machine-gunned British ambassador had already learned to his cost.

While Hong Kong remained in British hands the option did exist of finding a seat on one of the spasmodic flights from there into western China, but Agnes Moncrieff perceived one fundamental flaw: 'Planes were being shot down. And I wanted to get there.'

The only viable option, it seemed to her, was to enter from Rangoon in Burma. The Burma Road ran from Lashio for 1154 kilometres to Kunming, capital of China's Yunnan Province. It had been built, largely by coolie labour, between 1937 and 1939 to provide a supply route into China that avoided Japan's coastal blockade. Hacked through precipitous terrain in a series of torturous bends, and exposed to Japanese bombing attacks, it was a travel option to which the New Zealand YWCA's World Fellowship Committee was implacably opposed. Despite a series of a strongly worded resolutions to that effect, Agnes Moncrieff could see no other option. 'I therefore booked a berth on a Dutch steamer to Singapore [from Sydney] and after a very pleasant 19 days at sea landed in Singapore and caught a small and very dirty tramp to Rangoon.'

All up, her journey from Rangoon to Chengdu covered a distance of 3860 kilometres. She made it in the company of three missionaries who had managed to acquire and fit out an International 2-ton truck. She was lucky in her companions, who turned out to be resourceful in often trying situations. 'Both John and Joe knew a good deal about the inside of an engine and what they did not know to begin with they knew long before the end of the journey,' she recorded in the diary she kept of the journey.

To mechanical failings were added frequent punctures, stripped tyres, a constant struggle to locate petrol supplies, and not a few glancing collisions with other road users. Counting a two-week enforced stopover in Kunming, when one of the party contracted malaria, the trip took 38 days, finally reaching Chengdu on 22 November 1941.

The road route into Free China – 2,100 miles from Rangoon to Chungking.

An aerial view of 24 hairpin bends.

A fortnight later, Japan bombed Pearl Harbor and the shape of its war in China fundamentally changed as a consequence.

Before the end of the year Japan had occupied Hong Kong, cutting off the last link between the coast and Free China. In April 1942 it took control of Lashio, and with it access to the Burma Road. Except for the limited possibilities of supply over 'the Hump'— the air route over the Himalayas from Calcutta to Kunming – inland China was entirely cut off from the outside world. It was under these increasingly straitened circumstances that Agnes Moncrieff passed her final tour in China.

One heartening discovery Moncrieff made after arriving at her new base was that a number of the female factory workers who had joined in classes in Shanghai had turned up in Chengdu – a consequence of the efforts to move industrial production inland of which Rewi Alley's Indusco formed part. In Chengdu, to an even greater extent than in treaty-port Shanghai, much of the YWCA outreach necessarily fell on the shoulders of the association's Chinese recruits:

> We had to find other ways of working. We had cooperatives going up in the rural districts around Chengdu and things like, well, any family that had its menfolk press-ganged could apply for cheaper rice. They didn't have to pay. And there were inspectors out who were supposed to help them. What was happening was the inspectors were getting the cheaper rice and the people were being absolutely fleeced. So our girls just went out and informed the whole township or village or wherever they were, of what their rights were in that situation. And they could've been mugged at any point, you see. They were very courageous really. And it was no good the foreigners going out, our Chinese wasn't good enough, and we didn't have the local Szechuan dialect. So they did things like that that really met some of the problems that they were up against.

Moncrieff herself also found other ways of working. On the basis of some tentative efforts at accounting towards the end of her time in Shanghai, she found herself appointed business secretary and put in charge of YWCA finances for the whole of China. In a time of runaway inflation, dealing in six different currencies, and facing major logistical challenges in distributing funds to the places where they were needed, it was a formidable task. Often it called for unorthodox solutions, including wholesale excursions into the black market. 'I had a very elementary knowledge of bookkeeping and I always remember there was a very nice, youngish American accountant there as a missionary and he used to audit my books for me. And he said, "Well, you've got your own methods, but you get there."'

'Seven years is a long time for a war to last,' Moncrieff wrote disconsolately in March 1944. The end of the war in China did not come about as the result of a significant victory or a successful campaign; rather, it was the more or less incidental by-product of the US decision to bomb Hiroshima and Nagasaki.

Before that, there was not a lot to buoy the spirits of those, Chinese or expatriate, blockaded in Chengdu. Moncrieff noted that many of the young Chinese seemed to have given up hope. Nor was the foreign community exempt. Commenting on a novel built around the strains of internment, Moncrieff told New Zealand's YWCA that she thought being on the wrong side of a blockade produced similar results: 'One certainly sees a lot of lowering of moral standards and a kind of disintegration of personality that is one of the tragedies of war.'

A sense of isolation was accentuated by the absence of news and commentary from the outside world. If it arrived at all, it was generally long-delayed. On 4 March 1944 Moncrieff welcomed the arrival of a sheaf of mail from the World YWCA (in the US), all dated January and February 1942. Magazines were generally a year or two out of date when they reached Chengdu. An enterprising Chinese publishing firm in Chungking produced photographic copies of the *Reader's Digest*, some months after publication, and sold them at prices so inflated that groups of people would club together to buy and circulate a single copy.

Towards the end of Moncrieff's third term, and with the China war still at stalemate, the YWCA decided to discontinue its sponsorship of a secretary in China. The decision was based upon increased costs in China, a lack of funding in wartime New Zealand, and Moncrieff's own account of the severe limitations imposed by the military standoff in China. The decision pre-dated Japan's surrender in August 1945, but was not affected by it. On 6 September Agnes Moncrieff ended a 16-year association with China by flying the now well-established route from Kunming to Calcutta. Ironically, her travel onward from India was impeded not by wartime conditions, but by their ending. Because returning troops were accorded priority on what transport was available, it was three months before it was possible for her to secure a passage home.

The years of life under blockade conditions had taken a toll on her health. Her journey was interrupted by two months' hospitalisation in Australia, a consequence of nutritional deficiencies. She finally arrived back in New Zealand on 21 April 1946. For the next 18 months her health continued to be precarious.

'I was very ill when I got back from China,' she recalled late in her life. 'We'd been living under rather impoverished circumstances up in West China, and I always remember the doctor saying to me when he finally discharged me, "Fit for anything but return to China." And I never went back.'

9. The Economists

J.B. Condliffe, Bill Holland and Brian Low's research projects

The YWCA and its counterpart organisation, the YMCA, were both active in promoting Western values and Western ways of going about things in the early years of the Chinese Republic. One initiative in particular, the establishment of the Institute of Pacific Relations (IPR), brought China into a convocation with its Pacific neighbours, and incidentally provided a home for a generation of able young New Zealand economists.

The IPR was pioneered by a YMCA group in Hawaii in the early 1920s. It was based on the perception (worthy but, as it turned out, erroneous) that building greater knowledge and mutual understanding within the Asia–Pacific region would counter any tendency towards dispute and conflict. The concept before long outgrew its YMCA origins and passed to the oversight of a group of American business and academic leaders.

The IPR (in some countries, including New Zealand, a forerunner to Institutes of International Affairs), was generously funded by private contributions, primarily from the Rockefeller and Carnegie foundations. Its mandate was to commission and carry out research, and to convene a major international meeting every two years. Fourteen national councils were set up, including in China and Japan in the north, and Australia and New Zealand in the south. J.B. Condliffe, then professor of economics at Canterbury University College, set up the branch in New Zealand, and in 1925 he travelled to Honolulu to take part in the institute's first conference. The meeting he characterised as a blend of uplift (the YMCA had paid his fare) and serious discussion.

John Bell Condliffe was himself a graduate of Canterbury University College. He had taught at the university briefly before travelling to Europe with the New Zealand Expeditionary Force. Wounded at Ypres, after convalescing he was awarded a scholarship to Cambridge University. From Cambridge, he returned to take up the economics chair at Canterbury.

Late in 1926 Condliffe was offered the newly created position of research director in the international headquarters of the IPR, based in Honolulu. The job carried with it responsibility for helping the various national councils organise their research activities. Not without some misgivings, Condliffe accepted the position, the first step on an academic journey that led ultimately to professorships at the London School of Economics and then the University of California at Berkeley.*

From the beginning, J.B. Condliffe identified China as a primary target for research. Having installed himself in Honolulu, established liaison with his American sponsors and equipped himself with an offer of research funding from the Rockefeller Foundation, in late 1927 Condliffe travelled to China to assess the prospects. Arriving in Shanghai, he was met on the docks by Rewi Alley, himself not long in the country. At that time Alley was working for the Municipal Fire Brigade. There had been family connections in New Zealand and, more importantly, 'He [Alley] had played wing forward when I was scrum-half in the army team that won the Wellington competition in 1917.'

Condliffe spent his first seven days in China exploring industrial conditions in Shanghai, with Alley as his guide.†

> It was like seeing the pages of the early Factory Commission's reports come to life – or the sections of Karl Marx's *Capital* that drew so heavily on those reports. We saw firetraps and unsanitary crowding, opium dens, brothels, sweated workshops and slums of incredible degradation – the worst of them in the no-man's land between the foreign settlement and the Chinese city.

Condliffe's visit to Shanghai coincided with the period of widespread unrest inland following the Nationalist army's initial strike to the north. In particular, the excesses in Nanking, where a number of foreigners

* While he never returned to an academic position in New Zealand, J.B. Condliffe maintained close links. His book, *New Zealand in the Making*, became a standard text in New Zealand schools, and went through a number of revisions over the years. Prime Minister Robert Muldoon credited him with providing the theoretical backing for many of his economic policies, although it is not certain that Condliffe welcomed the accolade.

† Condliffe kept in touch with Alley following his visit to China, and later supported Alley's work with the Indusco movement. When he moved to Berkeley he became associated with Indusco's Hollywood branch, which included in its membership such luminaries as Lin Yutang and Charlie Chaplin.

were killed and their homes and property looted by forces of the invading army, had prompted many (including the George Shepherds, reunited after the family's stay in Kuling) to retreat to the safety of Shanghai's international settlement. Condliffe took the opportunity to seek the perspective of those who had relocated from the interior. Among them was an American missionary with a background in agricultural economics, J. Lossing Buck, and his wife, Pearl Buck.*

Buck was at that time teaching and carrying out research at Nanking University's Department of Agricultural Economics. Condliffe did not form a particularly high impression of his abilities: 'Buck was an agricultural economist of quite limited equipment and understanding, but he had been a student with Warren and Pearson at Cornell and knew how to make sample agricultural surveys.' Sample agricultural surveys were high on the new research director's list of priorities: the second conference of the IPR had flagged the desirability of building a database on land use in China.

Condliffe elected to travel to Nanking, in the company of Lossing Buck, to make his own assessment of Nanking University and its Department of Agricultural Economics. Although conditions in Nanking remained unsettled, some foreign staff, including the dean of agriculture, were camping at the university, protected by their Chinese colleagues. The upshot of his visit was a decision to put the bulk of the funding available from the Rockefeller Foundation into a major project to describe and quantify land utilisation in China, the project to be administered by Nanking University.

Condliffe continued upstream from Nanking to Wuhan, where his sense of security was probably not much enhanced when he set out to renew acquaintance with a Chinese delegate to the IPR's inaugural conference in Honolulu, L.N. Chang.

> He was Mayor of the ex-British Concession and sent out an armoured car with guards on the running boards. When I reached his office he told me that the local general was mopping up all foreigners and Chinese suspected of being communists. His phone rang constantly,

* China-born Pearl Buck came to outshine her husband. Her first novel, *The Good Earth*, won her a Pulitzer Prize, and in 1937 she was awarded the Nobel Prize in Literature. By then she had left Lossing Buck and married her publisher.

> mainly with appeals from anxious wives whose husbands had been picked up on suspicion.

Tientsin and Peking also formed part of this tour. In Tientsin, Condliffe made the balance of his Rockefeller funding available to Nankai University, to underwrite work being done by a team of young Chinese economists on matters such as price setting and industrialisation. The Peking visit was less productive: an unfortunate incident, in which his local IPR host almost brought about his visitor's asphyxiation by placing him in a bedroom with a coke heater and no ventilation, led to a loss of face so profound that there was afterwards little possibility of useful discussion.

When the IPR research director returned to Shanghai to report to David Yui, the Harvard-educated chairman of the institute's Chinese Council, he found him preoccupied with matters less immediate, but yet more weighty, than those that had confronted his colleagues in Hankow and Peking.

> He [David Yui] was an Anglican but not in holy orders. The Soong family belonged to the Methodist Episcopal Church. After much negotiation, Chiang Kai-shek, the rising star of the Nationalist revolution, was to be married to the youngest Soong daughter, Mei-ling. He came of rather humble parents but had been through the Whampoa Academy and had also had some education in Japan. He did not speak English, but Soong Mei-ling was a graduate of Wellesley. Her two elder sisters had married Sun Yat-sen and H.H. Kung. Her brother, T.V., was Minister of Finance.
>
> This was an even more important marriage and might be the beginning of a new dynasty. Madame Soong wished Chiang to accept baptism which he was not ready to do though he was ready to take the Christian vows of fidelity, had sent his [then] wife home to her family, and paid off his two concubines. The Methodist bishop refused to officiate, so David had been approached as Chairman of the Chinese Christian Council and a family friend. His bishop threatened to excommunicate him if he exercised the priestly function.

David Yui eventually arrived at a compromise whereby, before the civil ceremony, he would read over the happy couple the Anglican service, but omit the priest's blessing. Relieved at having thus resolved his problem, he accorded Condliffe an invitation to the civil ceremony, a lavish affair at the international settlement's Majestic Hotel. At this event, Condliffe noted, 'The most self-possessed person was the bride, whose curtseys to her husband and to the picture of her late brother-in-law, Sun Yat-sen, were not profound.'

Safely back in Honolulu, Condliffe set about building up the resources and the research capability of the central office of the IPR. The following year he invited one of his former students from Canterbury, W.L. (Bill) Holland, to join him as a secretary and research assistant. Holland accepted with alacrity, travelling on money borrowed from the choirmaster of his local church ('who charged me six percent so that I had an incentive to pay it back quickly'). He arrived in Hawaii on 28 December 1928, the day of his 21st birthday, to begin an association with the institute that would continue for 31 years.

Holland's first task on arrival was to help with preparations for the third IPR conference, to be held in Kyoto, Japan, in October 1929. The conference was larger than its predecessors, with delegations from all around the Pacific, as well as Britain and France (as colonial powers) and the League of Nations. A future prime minister, Walter Nash, and Willis Airey, later professor of history at Auckland University and Rewi Alley's first biographer, attended from New Zealand.

Although the meeting preceded by two years Japan's occupation of Manchuria, the issue was already very much on the agenda, the subject of vitriolic plenary debates between delegates from China and Japan (whose representative, Yosuke Matsuoko, became Japan's wartime foreign minister). It fell to Bill Holland to provide a record of these debates, which were conducted in excited and heavily accented English.

> Since a great deal of the discussion had to do with obscure railway lines (at least obscure to me) and railway stations in Manchuria, names that I had never heard of before, I thought I would go crazy trying to make any sense out of my notes of these debates. It gave me my first awareness of the depth of the bitterness between China and Japan over the Japanese policy in Manchuria.

The creeping expansion of Japan's railway empire had at least one positive outcome for Holland. Determined that the conference should show Japan in the best possible light, its sponsors (including, it was suspected, the Japanese government) had laid on an extravagant programme of entertainment. That included a pass for each delegate allowing two months' free travel anywhere on Japanese government railways. 'Anywhere' included travel throughout Korea, then a Japanese colony, and most of Manchuria (utilising the Japan-owned South Manchuria Railway). At the end of the conference, Holland travelled first class all the way to Mukden (Shenyang), then reached into his own pocket to continue to Peking and Tientsin.

After his initial foray into China, Holland was soon back, and for a longer period. The opportunity arose out of a piece of lateral thinking that led Condliffe to invite the distinguished economic historian R.H. Tawney, of the London School of Economics, to pay a visit to China, and to set out his impressions in a monograph for the IPR. In extending the invitation, Condliffe was not looking for someone who might provide a straightforward account of contemporary China's economic situation. He could do that himself, and he subsequently did so, in his book *China Today: Economic*, published in 1932.

Rather, in approaching Tawney, Condliffe sought to have China's situation viewed through a different lens. Tawney was a pre-eminent authority on Tudor economic history and the rise of capitalism. The brief he was given was 'to go and look at the economic and social problems of China through the eyes of a mediaeval historian; with the idea that in many respects China was just beginning to go through the kind of economic and social transformation that took place in England in the 17th and 18th centuries'.

It was, Holland commented, 'an inspired hunch'. Tawney amply fulfilled his brief: his text came to be regarded as a classic and was still in print 50 years later. First appearing in 1931 as an IPR monograph, *A Memorandum on Agriculture and Industry in China* was republished for a wider audience the following year by Allen & Unwin, titled *Land and Labour in China*. The book attracted critical acclaim: 'No one should miss this extraordinarily interesting and valuable book'; 'A rare combination of exact information and uncommon insight'.

Tawney was indebted to his Chinese colleagues for the information

– a debt he fully acknowledged in his preface – but the insight was his own, and drew upon his profound knowledge of European economic history. Translated and serialised in Chinese newspapers, *Land and Labour in China* was influential in bringing a domestic focus to bear on the challenges the country faced. To the outside world it offered a powerful corrective to then-prevailing Western orthodoxy. As Tawney wrote: 'The modern state in Europe was not made in a generation. The European who derides the failure of China to build in thirty years a level highway from the old world to the new must have read to little purpose the tragic history of his own continent.'

Having secured Tawney's participation, J.B. Condliffe thought it appropriate to offer him some support, and turned to Bill Holland. 'Condliffe asked me to go to China and simply be a general factotum, valet, bag-carrier, and research assistant to Tawney.' For more than three months Holland travelled with Tawney and his wife throughout northern China and as far south as Nanking, where they spent time with Lossing Buck at the large research establishment he had set up to further his own IPR project on land utilisation.

Tawney established the base for his study at Nankai University in Tientsin, where he was able to draw upon the knowledge and research inputs of the team earlier identified by Condliffe for IPR financial support. Franklin Ho and others at the Nankai Institute of Economics included Tawney and Holland in their field investigations into the beginnings of industrialisation in north China – investigations that included visiting in person emerging small industries, an eye-opening experience for the young New Zealander:

> In many respects, the conditions under which these industries operated, and particularly the labour conditions, were literally medieval. Workers lived and slept in the workshops. Children of course worked nine or ten hours a day and lived there. The old apprentice system such as you read about in 18th century England was in full flower. I've often said I learned more economic history in those three months with Tawney as my guide than I did in three years of college in New Zealand.

In the course of his travels with Tawney, Bill Holland also learned something of the great man's eccentricities. The professor was a disappointment to treaty port luminaries, who found him 'scruffy looking', and 'brilliant but stodgy and unpretentious'. His relationship with his wife Holland initially found somewhat alarming.

> [Tawney] occasionally would get impatient with some of his wife's more inane remarks and, on occasion when she would interrupt with one of these irrelevant comments . . . he would lose patience and say, 'My darling, will you for Christ's sake, shut up.' He would then be overcome with remorse and would lean over and pat her hand.

Happily, Holland observed, 'She was quite accustomed to this sort of thing and took it all in good part.'

Holland's most important role was as Tawney's amanuensis, turning his written notes into a typescript. Mrs Tawney was essential to this process, as only she could read her husband's handwriting. She would read the manuscript out at dictation speed, while Holland took it down on the typewriter. When the first edition of the resulting book appeared, Holland asked the author to sign a copy for him. 'He did so, writing, "From one author to the other". It was a gross piece of flattery of course, but I must say I relished it.'

After the Tawneys returned to England, Holland occupied himself once more with IPR research initiatives, looking towards the next conference, scheduled to take place in Hankow in September 1931. From July that year he was in Shanghai making final arrangements. Not, as it turned out, final enough. The conference was due to begin on 20 September, then on 18 September Japan launched its pre-emptive strike on Manchuria. Such was the violence of the reaction within China that the Japanese delegation refused to travel to Hankow, fearing for their lives. It seemed for a time that the conference would have to be cancelled, but at the last moment the Japanese consented to attend a meeting transferred to Shanghai's international settlement, which was, at least in theory, not part of China.

Inevitably the discussions were dominated by the situation in Manchuria, and bitter to the point where a Japanese walkout always seemed imminent. It was a harbinger of the shape of IPR conferences in the years to come.

Rather than returning directly to Honolulu, Holland travelled by rail to Peking, sharing the crowded line with truckloads of Chinese soldiers mobilised against the likelihood that Japan would seek to push south into China proper. While he wrote up the conference notes in Peking, well-meaning New Zealand friends arranged to bring him together with Doreen, his future wife, whom he had met previously both in New Zealand and in Honolulu. The two were married in Hong Kong before travelling to New Zealand for their honeymoon – interrupted by a lecture tour that saw Holland addressing the local branches of the IPR in Auckland, Wellington, Christchurch and Dunedin.

In 1932 John Condliffe resigned from the IPR to take up a position with the League of Nations secretariat. Holland was appointed research secretary in his place and held the position until the institute closed its doors in 1960, with only a short break for war service. During that break another New Zealander, Horace Belshaw, professor of economics at Auckland University, took over the role, allowing Condliffe to record with satisfaction that 'the succession came to be regarded almost as a New Zealand prerogative'.

It was a guiding principle of the IPR that it should commission research, rather than itself maintaining a large research staff. The need to identify and monitor suitable projects took Holland to China in 1935, and again in 1937. He could hardly have chosen a worse time for the second visit. He and Doreen arrived in Shanghai just days after the 7 July Marco Polo Bridge incident, the event that precipitated eight years of warfare between China and Japan. They found the city sandbagged against Japanese bombing.

The two took a small steamer north to the Manchurian ports of Dairen [Dalian] and Port Arthur [Lüshunkou], parts of China already securely in Japanese hands, then travelled by rail down to Peking. Once again the railway was crowded with troops, but this time they were Japanese: the Hollands' arrival coincided with the Japanese occupation. 'I remember seeing the Japanese army roll into Peking on thousands of American Dodge trucks. It first made vivid to me the whole issue of American participation in Japanese aggression as it seemed to the Chinese.' (As both Shepherd and Bertram urged in their separate visits to the United States, Japan was heavily dependent on America for the supplies of war materiel, including trucks, and petrol and aviation fuel, which allowed it to prosecute the war in China.)

*

In Peking the visitors stayed with Owen and Elinor Lattimore, already famous for their travels, separately and jointly, through the western borders of China. Owen Lattimore had taken on the job of editing the IPR quarterly journal, *Pacific Affairs*. He went on to become one of the United States' most renowned Asia scholars and, possibly for that reason, a primary target for the anti-communist witch-hunts of the McCarthy era. His long-time association with the IPR was one of the factors that led to the institute itself being brought within the ambit of the various Senate investigations seeking to find scapegoats for the failure of America's Asian policies.

The international secretariat of the IPR had in the mid-1930s shifted its base of operations from Honolulu to New York, where Holland found himself answering to an activist international secretary-general in the person of the American Edward G. Carter. (Carter it was who had persuaded Lord Lothian of the need to pay more attention to Asia, leading to the Rhodes grant that took James Bertram to China.)

As the conflict in China deepened, Carter came up with a new research project for the IPR. Why not, he suggested, produce a series of monographs dealing with the consequences of Japan's invasion of China, and the issues that would need to be dealt with in any peace conference aimed at ending the conflict? (The expectation at the time was that the war would not develop into a wider conflict, but would eventually be resolved through negotiation.) Among the papers thought likely to be useful was a study of the historical background to Japanese militarism.

Carter instructed Holland to put this proposition to the Japanese IPR council, 'but in such a way as not to alarm them and without giving them too many details'. Unsurprisingly, the Japanese council (a civilian body) was very alarmed, and the more details it was given the more alarmed it became. Ultimately, what came to be known as The Inquiry did go ahead, in the face of formal protests from Japan.

To mitigate Japan's concerns, it was agreed that contributions would be reviewed for neutrality and fairness by a panel of three expert advisors (one of whom, inevitably, was Condliffe), and that the study should be broadened to include papers considering the effect of the Sino–Japanese conflict on other Pacific countries. It was the New Zealand contribution to The Inquiry that Ian Milner was working on when he met James Bertram in San Francisco in 1939. His paper, *New Zealand's Interests and Policies in the Far East*, was published the same year as a study in the IPR Inquiry series.

Neutrality and fairness were not obviously to the forefront of Holland's mind when he travelled to New Zealand for a six-week break in March 1938. Scarcely had he disembarked from the SS *Monterey* than he launched into a vigorous attack on Japan's aggression in China, and indeed on the US for facilitating that aggression. 'Japan was greatly disillusioned by the Chinese resistance, and what was intended – a short, sharp invasion into a slice of the northern province of China – has, because of this resistance, involved the country in a nation-wide war,' he told the New Zealand newspapers. To make matters worse, the American oil companies were selling huge quantities of petrol and aviation fuel to Japan. 'People are saying that they are in favour of neutrality, but they say that this move of the oil companies is a travesty of the word . . . The U.S.A. by this action is actually assisting Japan to defeat China.'*

As in 1932, Holland travelled throughout the country, talking to regional IPR councils and other groups. Newspaper reporting reflects a heightened level of interest in events in Asia, including a new concern that Japan's expansion might in time pose a threat to Australia and New Zealand. Holland was proudly touted as 'a Timaru boy'.

The IPR's increasingly fraught efforts to accommodate Japan within its fabric came to an end with the outbreak of war in Europe. Under the Axis Treaty, Japan was firmly aligned with Germany and Italy. It ceased to participate in IPR activities, and Holland was able to give up his attempts at a near-impossible balancing act.

With the onset of the Pacific War the US government found itself confronted by a pressing need for information and expertise relating to Asia. While it looked to the IPR to help meet that need, even the IPR's expertise was not infallible: a weekend conference in December 1941 spent an entire morning hearing a range of experts explaining why Japan would not go to war, before Carter as chairman announced after the lunch break that the afternoon's agenda would have to be revised, as

* New Zealand was able to avoid any such accusation of partisanship because wharf workers refused to load consignments of scrap metal destined for Japan.

Japan had just bombed Pearl Harbor.

The IPR acquired a new market for its publications, often in very large numbers, at the same time as it lost staff members and researchers to various arms of the government.

For a time Holland continued his work as research secretary. Remarkably, even under wartime conditions he found it possible to visit Free China where, equally remarkably, some research work continued. It was an epic journey, undertaken in the company of Edward G. Carter. In July 1943 the two flew by US military transport via New Delhi to Chabua in Assam, a jumping-off point for the US air force flights over 'the Hump' into China.* There they prudently separated, rather than run the risk of going down together in a malfunctioning aircraft, or being shot down by the Japanese – both reasonably common occurrences at that time. As a consequence of the attrition rate, Holland noted, morale in the air force base was very low, 'and on top of that, the food was pretty dreadful'.

The travellers survived both the flights and the food. After some days in Kunming they flew on to Chungking where, to Holland's evident approval, arrangements have been made for them to put up in the hotel suite normally reserved for Minister of Finance H.H. Kung. Even that privileged position, however, could not protect them from Japanese air raids, which forced them to take shelter in a cave dug for the use of the hotel's guests. Not did they avoid further culinary misadventures, this time at the hands of the Communist liaison office: 'One day we were invited to lunch with them and were taken to a very out of the way and rather dirty house, and were given an even dirtier meal which a few hours later gave us frightful stomach upsets.' Holland nonetheless managed to fulfil his liaison brief in Kunming and Chungking, and in the course of an excursion to Kueilin [Guilin], where meetings with old Chinese friends gave him access to 'a great deal, part of it rather malicious gossip, about the course of politics and military developments in Chungking and South China at that time'.

About this time (or perhaps earlier, given the nature of his activities in Kueilin) Holland took on part-time employment with the Office of

* 'The Hump' was the name given by Allied pilots to the peaks at the eastern end of the Himalayas. After the closure of the Burma Road, an airlift over 'the Hump' ferried supplies from Burma and India to Kunming in Western China.

Strategic Services (OSS), the wartime forerunner to the CIA. His hope was that this would lead to an overseas deployment, preferably in China. When it became evident that this was not going to happen, he transferred his allegiance to another agency, the Office of War Information (OWI), later the US Information Service, which offered the possibility of a posting in Chungking. Pursuit of this possibility involved transferring more than one allegiance: in order to qualify for the job he needed to become an American citizen. By calling on old friendships, Holland found a fast track to naturalisation and a US passport, and in February 1945 he took up the position of acting director of the OWI office in Chungking, where he remained until the end of the war.*

In late 1945 he returned to the US to succeed Carter as secretary-general of the IPR. In 1947 he visited China once more, to assess the possibilities of rebuilding the China Council, but in visits to Nanking and Shanghai he found little encouragement. All attention was focused on the civil war, marked then by Communist gains in Manchuria and north China. The possibility of any substantial new research programme appeared remote.

Some research did continue: when Holland called on Chi Chao-ting, research director of China's Central Bank and a henchman of H.H. Kung, he saw the fruits of work undertaken under Chi's direction at the bank. It turned out later, to the surprise of Holland (and presumably Kung) that Chi had long been a covert supporter of the CCP. After the Communist takeover he moved smoothly into the position of president of the newly created People's Bank of China. By that time, most senior members of the China Council had decamped to Taiwan or the US so a reinvigorated council was no longer a possibility. The parent organisation was itself coming under attack in the US for its perceived role in the 'loss' of China.

The old-boy network that had brought Bill Holland to the IPR continued even after J.B. Condliffe had severed his formal links to the institution. When, in 1933, Lossing Buck appealed to Condliffe for someone to provide support in his mammoth inquiry into land use, Condliffe sought a recommendation from Albert Tocker, his successor

* Holland later had cause to regret his cavalier disavowal of his New Zealand heritage, when in the early 1950s the American authorities for a time declined to renew his US passport on the grounds that his name had come up in the senate hearings of the McCarthy era.

as economics professor at Canterbury University. Tocker suggested a recent graduate, H.B. (Brian) Low, who was quick to accept the offer of a position as Buck's personal assistant. By mid-1933 he was installed as part of the project team at the University of Nanking.

The study upon which Buck was embarked was like nothing that had previously been attempted in China. (Borodin, when advising the KMT, had recognised the absence of the most basic information, had set out to produce an analysis of land use in South China, but his work was less structured and on a much smaller scale, and when he left China in 1927 his study left with him.) The breadth of Buck's research effort is indicated by the subtitle assigned to *Land Utilisation in China*, the report ultimately published as part of the IPR's international research series. It was 'A study of 16,786 farms in 168 localities, and 38,256 farm families in 22 provinces in China, 1929–1933'. It was all-encompassing in its scope, providing intricate detail on climate, land, crops, livestock, fertility, farm business, farm labour, prices and taxation, marketing, population, nutrition and standards of living.

Buck's study was built on methodology developed at Cornell University, his alma mater and among the top agricultural universities in the US. While Buck exercised overall supervision, and academics from outside China provided some specialist input, most of the groundwork was done by Chinese graduates, including returned students from Cornell. Particularly was this so when it came to undertaking the fieldwork. The programme enrolled and trained Chinese graduates as regional investigators, with a mandate to seek out other locals to carry the survey into individual districts and villages. As Brian Low explained it:

> Supposing the chap who was doing it was my old friend Shao Dexing. Now Shao would go out to his area, to the area that he had probably lived in himself, and he would train a young bloke who had a reasonable education to be doing the actual collecting of information. And that chap would be a locally-known young man who would be trusted by the local authorities, and would talk to them in the local language. And also they would make sure that on all the important things we got the same information from two directions.

Unlike the programme of agricultural reform that George Shepherd was seeking to implement in Kiangsi at around the same time, Buck's work set out to be descriptive rather than prescriptive – 'The idea being that you couldn't do anything very useful for improving the whole living standards of rural people if you didn't know what the basic facts were.' Buck's mandate, as he saw it, was simply to set out the existing situation, as a precursor to possible future policy initiatives. Brian Low did not always agree with him:

> Lossing Buck was a bit annoying because he thought it was not his business to draw out too many conclusions. He would say, you know, this is the fact . . . I wrote two or three of the chapters and I made an attempt to get as much as I could of the sort of lively stuff into it, but most of it was edited out.

By the time Low had arrived in Nanking most of the groundwork for the survey had been completed. Ream upon ream of basic information had been flowing in to Nanking University to be subjected to statistical analysis. Bill Holland saw the process in action in 1930 when he visited Buck's research establishment in the company of the Tawneys.

> Since at that time there were few mechanical aids available for statistical analysis, even small hand calculators being very hard to get, the greater part of the computations on this huge survey involving thousands of farms scattered over wide areas of China had to be carried on by hundreds of abacus operators all clicking away madly in a huge room. It seemed an extraordinary throwback to mediaeval times but, in fact, the abacus people were extremely fast and expert.

Just how fast and expert they were became apparent when, 70 years later, the microdata on which the survey was based was rediscovered and subjected to computer analysis. The process confirmed the accuracy of the original calculations.*

* In the face of Japanese depredations at the time of the 1937 occupation of Nanking, a recalcitrant Nanking University librarian destroyed all the library's catalogues, and found new homes for a number of the library's collections. Duncan Campbell, to whom I am indebted for this information, tells me that when he was a student at Nanking University in the 1970s, the (by then former) staff member in question still returned from time to

Low contributed to what eventually became a hefty report running to three volumes by helping compile the text that supported the data, and by taking primary responsibility for the accompanying maps. While his work did not require extensive travel, he profited from Buck's determination not to allow any data to go forward if he had not himself seen the area from which it had been collected.

Thus, soon after his arrival, Buck took Low with him far into northwest China, travelling successively by boat, train and bus. When those options ran out in Sian, 'Lossing said, well, let's hire a Dodge 6 truck with a White Russian in it,' the two apparently commonly being made available as a package deal. Thus equipped, the pair continued into the grasslands beyond Sining (Xining) and up to Lake Koko Nor (Qinghai Hu), where Low triumphantly swam at an altitude of 10,500 feet (3200 metres). Other excursions followed, but none quite so glorious.

Although it was then China's capital, Nanking was a social backwater compared to Shanghai. Low did not regret this. 'To a small extent I found myself getting to know people down in Shanghai. And I just got caught up on the edge of that for a very short interval just to be aware that that wasn't my sort of life.' He made an exception for New Zealanders in Shanghai. Agnes Moncrieff he already knew from student conferences both had attended in New Zealand; Rewi Alley invited him to have dinner and meet his adopted children when he travelled to Shanghai on a shopping trip.

James Bertram he met in Nanking, under circumstances probably more typical of Bertram than of Low. In Bertram's recollection, 'I remember we were all practising archery in some villa in Nanking. The only time I've ever done this, with Chinese bows which are frightfully heavy going – really hard work.' The two were not kindred spirits:

> I [Low] was in Nanking, and Nanking was the place where you last heard what the Communists were doing . . . So I think Jim Bertram regarded me as being unspeakably conservative, because I just naturally belonged in an enclave where one didn't hear what was happening with the Communists, and got on with one's own work.

---

time to help locate particular volumes. Buck's data was probably put out of harm's way as part of this process.

Brian Low got on with his own work at Nanking University for three and a half years. He was accorded generous acknowledgement by Lossing Buck in the preface to the book that finally emerged, eight years after the study had been set in motion. 'Especially I am indebted to Mr H. Brian Low who has done most of the work in bringing the materials together in the Atlas and has assisted in many other ways in compiling the text . . .'

By that time (1937) Low was back in New Zealand, drawn home by the opportunity to set up a programme of agricultural economics at Massey University. He left with reluctance – 'It was very notable with foreigners, either they hated China or it really got under their skin . . . I was contemplating quite seriously . . . a life in China.' As it turned out, it was a timely exit. Before the end of the year the Japanese had sacked Nanking, and China was plunged into disruptive warfare that would continue, with intermittent pauses, until the Communist victory in 1949.

With the Communist victory, some aspects of the research encapsulated in *Land Utilisation in China* became irrelevant. 'All our information about ownership of land and those sorts of things was happily – or unhappily, whichever you like – superseded.' Nonetheless, in retrospect Low believed that much that remained had continued relevance – 'The basic relation between land and people and so on was pretty permanent.' When, in 2019, academics from Nanking and Cornell universities considered the rediscovered data, they reached the same conclusion: 'Even today, Buck's book stands out as a standard reference of conditions on the ground in China.'

Land Utilisation in China stands with Tawney's *Land and Labour in China* as the two IPR studies that made, and continue to make, a fundamental contribution to the understanding of the forces underlying China's economic development in the 1930s. Both were commissioned by J.B. Condliffe, and both profited from the inputs of the young New Zealanders he appointed to provide support. Through their efforts, they helped earn the IPR the reputation it came to enjoy as 'the era's foremost research institute on the problems of modern China'.

10. The Nurse

Kathleen Hall with the partisans

It was late in 1938 before the Japanese began a serious effort to impose control over the countryside of north China. Even after that time, control could never be absolute in a country as vast as China. The Japanese adopted a 'string of pearls' approach, installing garrisons in the main towns and setting up zones of control along the connecting railways and other major transport routes. The mountainous regions that had formerly provided natural boundaries between provinces now became the base areas for anti-Japanese forces. In Shansi, the country people before long acquired a new saying: 'Japanese, too many killed; Kuomindang, too many taxes'; Communists, too many meetings.'

At this time, before the onset of the wider Pacific war brought the privileged position of most foreign nationals to an end, the occupying troops' efforts to monitor and control people flows did not extend to those holding foreign passports. This was the situation when Kathleen Hall fell in with the young Englishman George Hogg, who was later to become Rewi Alley's helpmeet. Hogg had crossed through the Japanese lines into northwest China in the hope of making contact with one of the guerrilla groups, but had fallen ill with typhus fever. By great good fortune New Zealand nurse Kathleen Hall, returning to her mission hospital from a foray to Peking, found herself at the same inn. She installed Hogg in a cart and set off for her hospital, two days away.

> I remember her scampering like a rabbit over the fields all day to find the best roads, while I sat jealously in my blankets. Later, when the mountains became too steep for the carts, I remember an almost insurmountable problem of how to keep my balance on top of a donkey's packsaddle piled with bedding. Then a clean whitewashed gateway and someone saying 'Tao-la' – 'Arrived', and the next thing was three weeks later . . .

Kathleen Hall was, in the estimation of James Bertram, 'such a really original and determined person'. 'If she had been a man,' Rewi Alley said, 'she would have been famous long ago.' Born in Napier, Hall had already been in China for 16 years at the time of her encounter with George Hogg. She had trained as a nurse in Auckland before enrolling for missionary service with the Society for the Propagation of the Gospel (SPG), a mission group based in England, and supported in New Zealand by the Anglican Board of Missions. Its field of endeavour was north China. In all, nine New Zealanders served there under its auspices.

The High Anglican origins of the SPG carried over into the standards it set for its missionary recruits. Before she left New Zealand, Hall had been assessed against criteria set out in one of the society's pamphlets, *What Sort of Women do we Need?* Prominent among them was the appropriate social background: 'While women of all classes may be suitable on grounds of character, the special skills required mean in practice women from "higher" social classes.' Social classes were a little more difficult to differentiate in New Zealand than in England, but Kathleen apparently met the test (her father was a lawyer, at that time Auckland's Registrar of Lands and Deeds).

Kathleen herself did not claim membership of the 'higher' social classes, and certainly did not look for it among those she had travelled to China to work with. In fact it was with dismay that, after a period of language training, she found herself allocated nursing responsibilities in hospitals set up to meet the needs of the well-to-do, rather than the most needy among China's population.

Her first assignment was to the Peking Union Medical College, the same Rockefeller-funded institution that Dr Turbott attended to learn about X-rays. Like Turbott, she saw the PUMC as providing a high standard of medical care, at the expense of producing doctors truly willing to serve the people. This perception was brought home to her with real force in 1936 when, in the face of Japanese advances towards Anguo, the only Chinese doctor at St Barnabas decamped, leaving her in sole charge of a hospital full of injured soldiers.

The same sense that her efforts were not being directed where the need was greatest accompanied Kathleen Hall as she took up responsibilities in the provincial mission hospitals the SPG established in districts bordering Peking. She undertook nursing and teaching duties at Datong, at Hejian, and finally at Anguo in central Hopeh (Hebei). At Anguo, some 225 kilometres south of Peking, she was entrusted with the responsibility of setting up and then serving as matron of a new base hospital, St Barnabas.

Anguo and St Barnabas Hospital came to provide a base for Hall's activities over the remainder of her time in China, but they did not in themselves satisfy her continuing determination to address the needs of those disadvantaged – the 'simple, good, hard-working people, ignorant and poverty stricken'. Before she travelled to New Zealand on furlough in 1934 she sought and received permission to broaden the mission's outreach by establishing a foothold in the mountainous region inland from Anguo.

Kathleen Hall was not alone among those who travelled to China in wishing to adopt a more grassroots approach to medical care. Far to the south, at the Kong Chuen Mission, another New Zealand nurse had already taken steps in the same direction. Annie James was already a longstanding member of the hospital staff at the time of Turbott's tenure in the 1920s, and recalled by him somewhat dismissively as 'full up of her objective'.

By 1935 Annie James had taken leave of the main hospital on the broad plain north of Canton and assumed sole charge of a cottage hospital at Kaai Hau, a hill village 70 kilometres distant. On her way north after furlough in New Zealand, Kathleen Hall joined her there for some days, learning from her colleague's experience and gaining familiarity with the fundamentals of baby care according to Dr Truby King and current Karitane practice.

Once back in north China, Hall set about instituting the outreach programme she had proposed earlier. Like Annie James, she established herself in a village too far from the base hospital for the local people to draw on its services, but not so distant that a link could not be established in real emergency. The village she finally settled upon was Songjiazhuang, in northern Shansi. There, supported by Chinese nurses who had accompanied her from Anguo, she set out not just to provide basic medical services, but also to set in place public health programmes to reduce the incidence of preventable illnesses.

Some among the higher social classes might have been hard put to adapt to the conditions under which she came to live and work. Her clinic occupied three rooms – the clinic itself, the waiting area and her own living space. She relied on the goodwill of the local people: as she wrote home, 'A girl nurse and I are living in "borrowed" rooms in a "borrowed" yard. Except for my camp-bed and camp-chair, a kerosene-box bookcase which I made and a cupboard, all our furniture is borrowed.' Her equipment was rudimentary – lacking instrument trays, she resorted to sterilising instruments in the bamboo baskets used for cooking dumplings.

There was little contact with the outside world: 'The village . . . is at the most 35 miles from the railway, and yet it might be hundreds of miles away, there is so little contact with the outside.' Her best information about the course of the conflict in China came not from what she could glean locally, or even on visits to Peking, but from reports in the pages of the *Auckland Weekly News*, relayed to her from time to time several months after publication.

Because there was no local source of pharmaceuticals and other medical supplies, Hall took on the responsibility of making occasional journeys to Peking to stock up on necessary supplies for her clinic, and also for the main mission hospital at Anguo. (It was on the return leg of one such journey that she encountered George Hogg.) Her status as a foreign national allowed her to move with relative freedom through the Japanese lines, although where possible she would skirt the major population centres that after 1937 fell under Japanese control.

Songjiazhuang lies in the Taihang mountains, east of Peking. As the Japanese laid claim to the plains, the mountains came to provide a refuge and a base for guerrilla attacks by partisans and by soldiers linked to the Communist Eighth Route Army. The village of Songjiazhuang itself became a base for such attacks. Kathleen Hall recalled in later life how the Chinese forces launched night-time raids:

> They often took with them only a few precious rifles and their hand grenades made out of scrap-iron, but brought back captured Japanese rifles – sometimes a machine gun and other equipment – and more scrap metal to be made into hand grenades and perhaps into some surgical and hospital equipment too! Many a time, in the early hours of the morning, we heard the clatter of the scrap-iron being dragged up

> the rough, stony tracks into the hills – laboriously carried by the men, or on the backs of mules or donkeys – those sturdy little four-legged friends who did so much for us in those perilous times.
>
> How heartening, too, was the cheerful humour of the men and boys – whether hastening down to attack or raid, or wearily returning with the heavy loads; and at other times, on parade ground, or marching at their base in the hills, their stirring and happy songs, looking beyond the hard times and sorrows to the good era to come. But how often, too, would we wait anxiously to see if all our young men (and some not so young) had safely returned. Sometimes it would be to give assistance to the wounded on their way up to the base hospital in the mountains – and sometimes to mourn for those who would never run cheerily down again.

'The base hospital in the mountains' came to impose new demands on Kathleen Hall. Norman Bethune, the Canadian surgeon to whom James Bertram had bequeathed most of his travelling accoutrements, had made his way north to the Wutai mountains, where he had set up a small foreign medical team, the Canadian–American Mobile Medical Unit. (The American part of the title was a nod to his need for funding from US donors: 'That's just to let the Americans get their money's worth – all three of us are Canadian!')

In June 1938 the region's United Front government had named him director of the International Peace Hospital – in fact a conglomeration of clinics scattered through the Wutai mountains. To support these clinics he established a model hospital, which the Japanese before long located and destroyed. A replacement was created in a series of caves dug deep into the loess hillsides.

A complex and driven man, Bethune came to be seen as emblematic of the CCP's international engagement when, after his death, Mao Tse-tung made him the subject of a still widely quoted inspirational address, 'In Memory of Norman Bethune': 'What kind of spirit is this that makes a foreigner selflessly adopt the cause of the Chinese people's liberation as his own? It is the spirit of internationalism, the spirit of communism, from which every Chinese Communist must learn.'

Bethune's association with Kathleen Hall began early in 1938. He travelled to seek her out at her Songjiazhuang cottage hospital, initially perhaps in part out of curiosity and a wish for the companionship of

Kathleen Hall with staff at St Barnabas Hospital, Anguo.

Dr Norman Bethune operating in the open, near the scene of a partisan engagement.

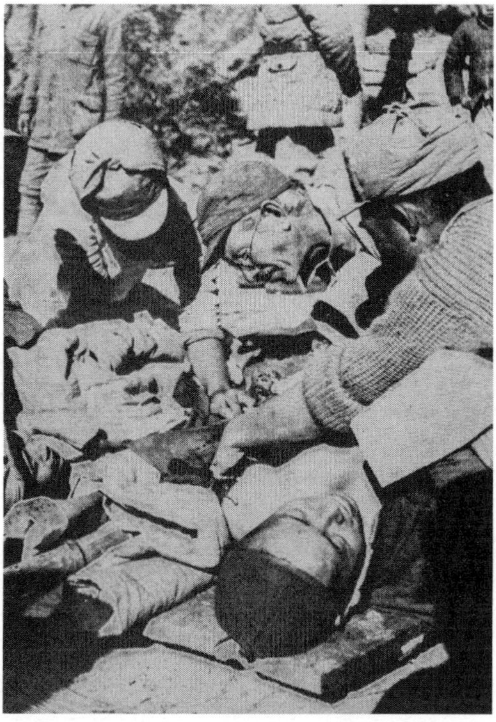

another foreigner (the other two Canadians had by that time left). Soon after that first meeting, however, he found an opportunity to discuss with her his hospital's critical shortage of drugs and other medical supplies. Would she be willing, he asked, to include in the consignments she was sourcing in Peking for St Barnabas and her own mission, medications and medical equipment for the centres set up to treat the soldiers of the Eighth Route Army?

It cannot have been an easy decision for the missionary nurse. The church of which her mission was part was ostensibly neutral in the conflict between China and Japan. Moreover, smuggling supplies to the Chinese forces would involve her in considerable personal risk. Nonetheless, Bethune, whose later writings make it clear that he was well aware of the danger he was placing her in, recorded in his diary in autumn 1938: 'I have met an angel . . . Kathleen H--, of the Anglican Church Mission here . . . She will go to Peking, buy up medical supplies, and bring them back to her mission for us. If she isn't an angel, what does the word mean?'

What precisely the word did mean has been debated over the years. Canadian writers, for whom the Bethune industry leaves for dead anything Rewi Alley ever inspired in New Zealand, have sought to suggest a romantic connection between the two. In an early Bethune biography, *The Scalpel and the Sword*, Kathleen Hall 'was tall, with an open strong face' (she was in fact little more than five feet in height), and the doctor neither confirms nor denies his interpreter's suggestion the two might be a good match: '"Tung, you wily dog," he exclaimed, "you've been dreaming up a romance for me!"' In the 1990 feature film *Bethune: The Making of a Hero*, 'Kathleen Hall' finds herself with Bethune in a rural hotel, where he plies her with wine and kisses her passionately on the way back to their rooms. To his disappointment she sends him packing, and he passes the evening contemplating her room wistfully from his window.

While there is nothing to support the biographers' wilder flights of fancy, Kathleen Hall spoke in admiring terms of the surgeon's commitment and his work. She valued the fact that he, like her, believed that medical services should be available on the basis of need rather than wealth. 'Here, in China, we were to see him with great devotion not only attending to sick and wounded with the armies, but also assisting in the carrying out of that idea of medical care for all the people, in the building of the first International Peace Hospital.'

She even managed to bring around Dr Bob McClure. While McClure supported providing medical supplies to the Communists as well as the KMT, he had reservations about Bethune personally (conceivably as a result of his having been called upon to retrieve the surgeon from a massive bender on his way to the front*). However, he came to concede: 'Contrary to what I have heard from a lot of other people, Miss Hall thinks rather well of Dr Bethune and evidently once he gets away from his alcoholic beverages he does a good job of work and is not a bit afraid of hardship.'

From late 1938 Kathleen Hall travelled regularly to Peking for medical supplies. She dressed each time in the most ostentatious clothes she owned, to underline her foreign status. Generally, the medical goods were directed to St Barnabas Hospital, and from there re-assigned to her own clinic and Bethune's International Peace Hospital. The usual method of transport was by mule cart, although sometimes it was possible to send the consignments by train as far as Dingxian, a town close to the border areas. Kathleen would travel there to see them repacked into carts or onto the backs of donkeys, and escort the convoy past the Japanese checkpoint at the city gate.

Over time the consignments came to include items for the partisans' use that, if intercepted, would certainly not meet the definition of medical supplies. Over time, too, Hall became involved in identifying and recruiting young people who wanted to escape Japan-held Peking and put their skills at the disposal of the resistance forces. To facilitate their travel to the liberated areas she established an underground of local inns whose owners she knew she could rely upon. Just how many times Kathleen Hall smuggled goods and personnel through the Japanese lines in this way is unclear. Her male nurse, Lu Zhongyu, later put the number at more than 30 but that seems high, given her commitments to her own clinic, and the time required for each journey.

Writing in 1958 for the twentieth anniversary of the China Welfare Institute (the successor organisation to Soong Chingling's China Defence

* The Chinese liquor Bethune had been drinking was more commonly used by local doctors as a hand rinse after scrubbing up. – Monroe Scott, *McClure: The China Years* (Toronto: Canec Publishing, 1977)

League), Kathleen Hall gave an account of one of her excursions as an 'innocent, good missionary':

> On this occasion, with the list for Dr Bethune as well as for our mission hospital, I managed to procure quite a large amount in Peking – labelling it all for our mission – and got it loaded on two mule carts. Some supplies were for the mission hospital at An Guo, some for our Cottage Hospital and Health Centre in the hill country in Ch'u Yang Hsien, and some for Dr Bethune and the army. On our route we usually passed around the outskirts of the city of Paoting, but this time our drivers on enquiring cautiously found that Japanese outposts blocked our way. I was horrified to learn that all traffic was compelled to pass through the city! My heart was hammering as our laden carts approached the northern gate and were stopped by the sentries. I can never forget the little Chinese policewoman (just a girl really), standing beside the Japanese officer and looking up to him with a smiling face, as she told him what a 'good woman' I was and that my carts contained only medical supplies for my mission hospital. No examination was made and the Japanese officer signalled us to pass on into the city.
>
> But the more dangerous place was when we wanted to pass out the other gate to the southwest. Here the Japanese officer had a Chinese 'puppet' policeman with him. The Japanese officer ordered the sentries to examine our packages and they began to unload them from the first cart. Again my heart thumped. Usually I was careful to bring only medical and educational items but this time I had also carefully packed among the medical supplies some radio equipment for our Chin-Cha-Chi Government! But again the Chinese policeman was evidently able to convince the Japanese officer that I was an innocent, good missionary, and after a few large hamper baskets had been taken off and just unfastened, the men were told to put them back and we were allowed to pass.

Smuggling goods for the partisans, actively recruiting to add to their ranks, and through her clinic providing them direct medical assistance, Hall's activities fell some way short of strict neutrality. They might have gone undetected by the Japanese for longer, however, had a local newspaper not published an admiring account of her contribution to the partisan cause. In July 1939 Kathleen Hall returned from a visit to Anguo to discover that Japanese troops had launched a sortie into the foothills that left Songjiazhuang in ruins, and the mission centre and cottage hospital razed to the ground. Added to that, when the New Zealand nurse travelled to Peking to report the destruction, she found that the Japanese authorities had complained to the British Embassy about her activities, and demanded that she be expelled from China. In compliance with Japanese wishes, the embassy had set in place arrangements for her to be repatriated.*

Knowing that she was now under close Japanese scrutiny, and risked endangering others, Kathleen Hall agreed to leave, but travelled only as far as Hong Kong before, like Alley and Bertram before her, seeking the good offices of Bishop Ronald Hall. Bishop Hall provided an introduction to Soong Chingling, at the forefront of the China Defence League's efforts to deliver medical supplies to the Chinese resistance forces. Through Mme Sun, Hall learned of a convoy of medical supplies and personnel planned to enter China via Haiphong (following the route adopted by James Bertram and the giant Leyland ambulance some months previously). She promptly severed her 18-year connection with the SPG and joined the Chinese Red Cross.

The Red Cross convoy was led by the hard-working Bob McClure, who had travelled to Hong Kong from Hankow to take delivery of two trucks designed to get around China's chronic petrol shortage by running on methane gas. (The gas was produced by burning charcoal in large burners mounted on the side of the engine.) From Hong Kong the two trucks were shipped to Haiphong, and from there they made their way via Hanoi and Nanning to Guiyang with a load that included spare tyres for the IRC, 48 French bicycles for IRC mobile public health units, a group of Scandinavian missionaries together with their three tons of supplies, and Kathleen Hall's consignment of medical equipment, financed by the China Defence League and intended for Norman Bethune's model hospital.

On 1 August 1938, before he had learned of Hall's expulsion from China, Bethune had reported to the region's military authorities on his

* Like all New Zealanders at the time, Kathleen Hall held a British passport and hence was subject to British direction. British policy towards Japan in 1939 was conciliatory, out of a fear of finding itself fighting a war on two fronts. The following year Britain acceded to a Japanese demand that the Burma Road be closed for three months to prevent supplies reaching the Chinese forces, adding to the importance of the supply route through French Indochina operated by the China Defence League.

plans to establish a medical school in the border region, in association with a revitalised model hospital. They included a role for the New Zealand nurse, if only she would devote herself to his cause.

> I am trying to persuade Miss Hall to join the Canadian–American Unit and give up her own missionary work. Around her I propose to gather a nucleus of trained graduate nurses from the P.U.M.C. (we have two now already) and with such a staff, set up a small model hospital to be used in connexion with the teaching of the Medical School. She is considering the matter. It would mean her leaving (resigning) from her mission.

By the time she set out from Hong Kong Kathleen Hall had indeed resigned from her mission, although whether she had any intention of pursuing Bethune's vision, one not easily attainable in the midst of an active battle zone, is hard to know. Certainly she left McClure with the impression that she was intent on something more than a simple delivery mission. 'There is a rather interesting lady going in with me, a Miss Hall,' he wrote to his wife in Canada. 'She has resigned from her mission and is going back for one year's work supported by a group of left-wingers in Hong Kong.'

In Guiyang, Kathleen Hall received the shattering news that Bethune had died. Operating without gloves, he had cut his finger and fallen victim to blood poisoning. Hall nevertheless remained determined to return to the border areas. 'I felt even more anxious, if possible, to get help to those men of the army and guerrillas, and the people in the north, who were so staunchly holding fast the bulwark there against the enemy.' She associated herself with a Chinese Red Cross medical unit that had been formed with the express purpose of reinforcing medical services available to the Eighth Route Army in northwest China. Led by a Chinese doctor of firm purpose, Jean Chiang, the group attended to pressing local needs for medical care while travelling steadily north – to Chungking, Sian and ultimately Loyang, in the valley of the Yellow River. There it stuck.

Whether the Red Cross unit was, as was alleged at the time, deliberately held up by the Nationalist administration in Loyang in order to prevent medical assistance reaching the Communist forces, or whether logistical support was simply not available, the unit found it impossible to make its way further north. At length, frustrated by the long stoppage in an area already adequately provided with medical services, Kathleen Hall sought and received permission to strike north ahead of the main group.

She travelled with one young medical worker for whom north Shansi was home, and took with her the medicines, serums, vaccines and other supplies intended for the Eighth Route Army. The pair dispensed such medical assistance as was possible to the isolated villages that survived on disputed ground that had been a war zone for almost three years.

> Now completely cut off by war, no means of buying food, no able-bodied people left to plant the ordinary poor crops, young men and boys had gone to fight, the old people and mothers and children remaining. Villages of death – in so many homes typhus fever and relapsing fever, dysentry and all the usual illnesses, and beriberi.

In the end Kathleen Hall fell victim to the same conditions that she had fought to counter among the people of the countryside. Severely malnourished, and worn out by the rigours of weeks and months of hard travelling, she fell ill with an extreme case of beriberi. It would not be possible for her to rejoin the anti-Japanese forces in north China. 'I had become too exhausted to continue. I could no longer be helpful but would only be a care to others.'

She did make contact once more with the Eighth Route Army, although not in the way she would have wished. In the village where her strength ran out, close to the rail line between Shijiazhuang and Taiyuan, she encountered a small detachment of soldiers who offered her support and assistance to return to Sian. No longer able to walk, the nurse whom George Hogg had first seen 'scampering like a rabbit over the fields all day', was carried by cart and by stretcher back to the Yellow River and from there placed on a train to Sian. In early 1941, when her health was sufficiently restored, Kathleen Hall returned as an invalid to the New Zealand she had left for China 19 years earlier.

The civil war

*With the defeat of Japan in 1945, the United States set out to identify a basis for effective power-sharing between the KMT and the Communist forces. Initially, Roosevelt's somewhat eccentric envoy, General Patrick Hurley, facilitated a meeting between Chiang and Mao that ultimately led nowhere.**

After Hurley came the highly respected General George Marshall, who did succeed in brokering a 'political consultative conference' in January 1946. The agreements that emerged from the conference, however, were never put into practice. A sense that he held the military ascendancy left the Generalissimo in no mood for compromise, while the Communist side saw no future role for a United States which, it justifiably perceived, was a less than honest broker. China returned to a state of civil war.

The Nationalist forces initially registered a series of victories, including taking Yenan, where the Communists had established their headquarters – an advance symbolically significant but strategically irrelevant. From the beginning of 1947, however, the tide began to turn. The forces of the CCP, now renamed the People's Liberation Army (PLA), step by step built up their position in Manchuria. Bolstered by massive defections from the Nationalist army, PLA forces established a presence in Shandong Province, placed Peking under siege and pushed south.

Encouraged by their early military successes, the Nationalists had taken steps to underwrite the legitimacy of their government. A new national assembly was elected in November 1947, which early the following year installed Chiang Kai-shek as president of the republic. In constitutional terms, it was a step towards the realisation of Sun Yat-sen's vision. By early 1949, however, Chiang's position was hardly tenable. His popular support had been eroded

* Hurley's only previous diplomatic posting had been as United States minister (heading a legation, not an embassy) in Wellington, New Zealand. There he demonstrated a propensity for Choctaw war whoops at public gatherings that he carried with him into China. He pronounced Mao Tse-tung 'Moose Dung' and called Chiang 'Mr Shek'.

not just by military failures, but also by the rampant corruption that characterised his government and a failing economy hit by skyrocketing inflation. On 21 January 1949 Chiang tendered his resignation as president, while continuing to exercise power behind the scenes.

April 1949 saw the Communists occupy Nanking, which the Nationalist government had re-established as its capital after Japan's defeat. The seat of government was relocated, first to Canton and then to Chungking. Shanghai fell to the Communist forces in May. After a final futile attempt to achieve a negotiated peace (on terms that amounted to KMT capitulation), the Communists resumed their rapid advance into China's southeastern provinces. Mid-October saw the fall of Canton, but even before that conquest the CCP declared victory. On 1 October 1949 Mao Tse-tung ascended the Tiananmen rostrum and proclaimed the advent of the People's Republic of China.

On 10 December Chiang Kai-shek flew from the Chinese mainland to the island province of Taiwan. Over the preceding year he had prepared a base there, and from that base he would continue for the next quarter-century to assert his right to rule China.

11. The Teacher

Marjorie Monaghan is interned in Shandong

At about the time Kathleen Hall was forced to concede that her health would not allow her to continue serving in China, another New Zealander arrived in Peking to begin work with the same mission, the Society for the Propagation of the Gospel (SPG). Westland-born Marjorie Monaghan (after marriage Marjorie Southward) travelled to China by a circuitous route. She first spent a year at a missionary college in Birmingham, having arrived from New Zealand just a fortnight before the outbreak of war. In 1940 she embarked for Montreal on board a ship called *Mid September* (the *Empress of Asia* in disguise), part of a complement that brought 12 young women together with 2000 naval officers and ratings travelling to pick up the first American lend–lease destroyers. Life could not have been more pleasant: 'I had a whale of a time – deck tennis all day and drinks at night.' From Montreal, a tightly choreographed route took her to Peking and language study.

Marjorie Monaghan had trained as a teacher, and the intention of the SPG had been that she should supervise the operation of a number of small country schools the society had established in north China. With Japan's occupation of the region, however, the schools had been forced to close. Worse was to follow, when the attack on Pearl Harbor rendered SPG staff, along with all other British and American citizens in China, enemy aliens. Those living in Peking were barred by the occupying Japanese from leaving the city, and required to wear a red armband emblazoned 'enemy' (a designation that did at least give them some standing along the Chinese.)

Life continued in this limbo until February 1943, when the Japanese instructed Monaghan and her colleagues, together with all other enemy aliens, to prepare to be transferred to a civilian internment centre in Shandong Province, where 'every comfort of western culture will be yours'. The transfer was put into effect a month later. It was a humiliating experience. As earlier in Singapore, and in Hong Kong and other parts of China, the Japanese engineered a situation that required those to be interned to parade past crowds of spectators, carrying what few possessions they could.

> I think our mana vanished forever the day we were marched to the station, pulling our own luggage, and the Chinese were in the streets watching us . . . any superiority the British may have felt before then was certainly taken away. I don't think the Chinese would ever feel the same about their masters, as they had been.

Monaghan and the other SPG missionaries were among 400-odd foreign nationals transported by train from Peking to the Shandong city of Weihsien (Wei Xian). There they were accommodated in what had been an American Presbyterian mission station – the birthplace, in happier times, of US media magnate Henry Luce. Similar groups from Tsingtao and Tientsin were already in residence. Later, after Italy capitulated, 400 Italians were added to the mix, 'and they had a lovely time, throwing teapots and knives at one another'. Including family members, at its peak the Weihsien camp accommodated some 2000 people.

In contrast to James Bertram's experiences as a POW, conditions in Weihsien, as in other civilian camps, were relatively benign. It was left for internees to establish their own administrative arrangements, working through a series of committees to sort out accommodation, catering, sanitation and all the other aspects of camp life. While it was considered a matter for regret that the Chinese servants on whom most foreigners had come to rely were denied entry, over time the internees learned to fill hitherto unaccustomed roles, although, to Marjorie Monahan's possibly biased eye, with discernible national differences: 'English people, in particular, were amazed at the things New Zealanders would do. Or contrived to do, out of virtually nothing . . . I presume having had pioneer forefathers, we've always been that much more resourceful.'

Weihsien camp brought together a disparate group of people – missionaries, businessmen, bankers, teachers, students, seamen, policemen, and a fair proportion of others whose previous occupations were less readily defined. Some adapted better than others. One contumacious (and, surprisingly, New Zealand-born) former member of HM Consular Service, E.C.T. Werner, found himself doomed to spend three years in close association with the Belgian dentist who he believed had murdered his 20-year-old daughter.* The missionary group included the 'flying Scotsman', Eric Liddell, who had played international rugby for Scotland, and who famously declined to race in the 100 metres at the 1924 Paris Olympics because the heats fell on a Sunday. He ran instead in the 400 metres and took the gold medal. (The film *Chariots of Fire* was based on his exploits.)

Liddell, who was born in China of a missionary family, returned to China to work as a missionary himself. A tower of strength in the early months of the camp's existence, he later participated less and less. Marjorie Monaghan was one of many concerned to see his energy wane.

> We all thought he'd thrown in the towel. Because from being a great inspiration to the young people, he suddenly got all slow and withdrawn and seemed very depressed, and was put into the hospital but they couldn't find out what was wrong with him. And I visited him, I remember, about the day before he died and said, 'Come on, Eric, I'll take you on for a dash up the corridor.' And he just looked at me and smiled, and said, 'Another day.' And of course he died very suddenly and they found he had a brain tumour . . . and we felt rather ashamed of ourselves for judging him in that way. But I suppose he understood.

The Weihsien camp was enclosed by barbed wire, with machine-gun emplacements commanding the walls. There was in any case little incentive to escape into an unknown and unwelcoming countryside. When in 1944 two men did break out, it prompted reprisals within the camp, but ultimately benefited their fellow internees a great deal. They linked up with Chinese guerrillas, and through them arranged for airdrops of much-needed drugs. These were transferred to the Swiss consul in Tsingtao, whom, as the representative of a neutral country, the Japanese had tasked with oversight of welfare in the camp.

The escapees had, before their departure, set in place a means of communicating in advance of the consul's visits:

* Werner, described as 'a by-word throughout China for maniacal quarrelsomeness', was one of only two members of Britain's Chinese Consular Service ever to be forced to retire other than on medical grounds. He subsequently took up residence in Peking, where he became a notable (although still quarrelsome) sinologue. – P.D. Coates, *The China Consuls* (Hong Kong: Oxford University Press, 1988), p. 440.

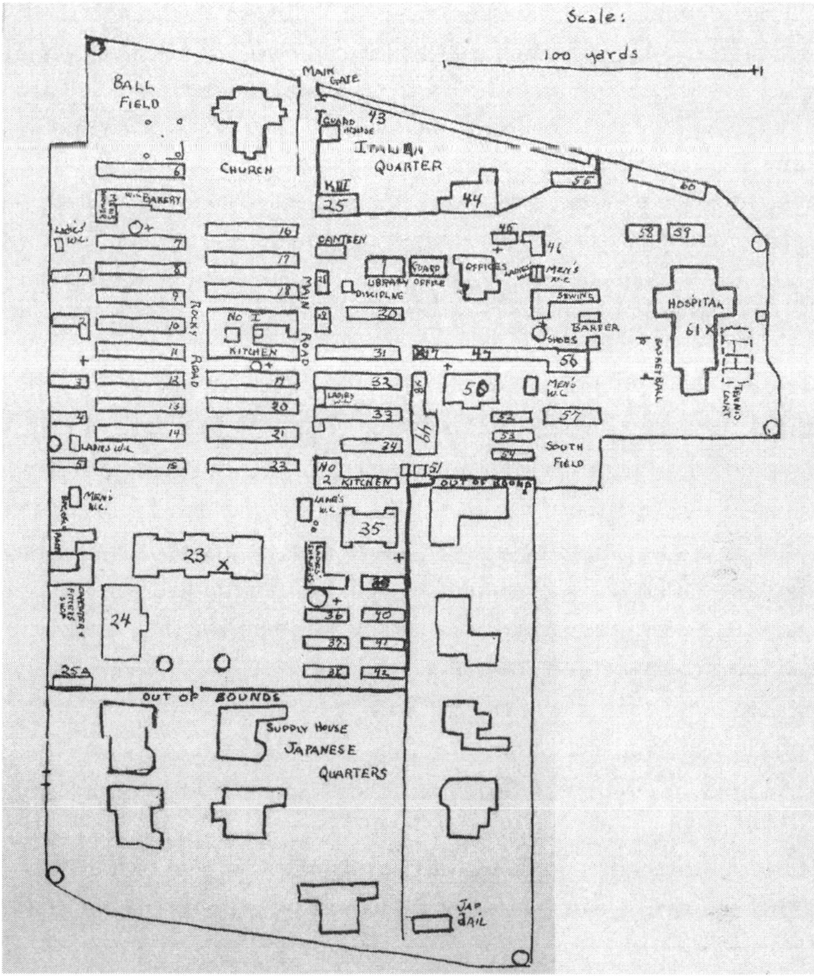

A plan of Weihsien Camp, Shantung Province, China.

Instructions in case there is a capitulation of the Japanese forces.

ATTENTION ALLIED PRISONERS

Allied Prisoners of War and Civilian Internees, these are your orders and/or instructions in case there is a capitulation of the Japanese forces:

1. You are to remain in your camp area until you receive further instructions from this headquarters.

2. Law and order will be maintained in the camp area.

3. In case of a Japanese surrender there will be allied occupational forces sent into your camp to care for your needs and eventual evacuation to your homes. You must help by remaining in the area in which we now know you are located.

4. Camp leaders are charged with these responsibilities.

5. The end is near. Do not be disheartened. We are thinking of you. Plans are under way to assist you at the earliest possible moment.

(Signed) A. C. WEDEMEYER
Lieutenant General, U. S. A.
Commanding

> Whenever he was going to come, they got a message in through the coolies. There was only one lot of Chinese allowed in, and that was to empty the cesspools . . . There were two Roman Catholic Belgian priests, who were very good men, we thought. They would always put themselves down for men's latrine duties . . . Whenever anything was going to come in extra, or anything like that, the coolies would have a message rolled up under their tongue or something, and they'd spit it into the cesspool, and so these priests had to have a reason for being there all the time, to retrieve these messages.

The Swiss consul, drafted into wartime service from his previous life as a small-time coastal trader, proved to be a courageous and resourceful man. Faced with the problem of introducing to the camp a large airdrop of sulpha drugs, manifestly not available locally, he had his secretary type up a list of the supplies he intended to take on his next camp visit, taking care of the list was double spaced. As required, he submitted the list to the Japanese consular police in Tsingtao for their approval, and secured their sign-off and official chop. He then used the same typewriter to fill the gaps in the list with the names of the new drugs. The officials in Weihsien were taken aback at the arrival of four large crates of medical supplies, but not inclined to query a document signed and sealed by their own consular authorities.

Marjorie Monaghan credited the consul with saving lives, including perhaps her own. 'I think a lot of us would have died without some of the new drugs that came in. I had dysentery very badly almost all the time we were there, and a lot of other people did too.' She did not survive entirely unscathed, as she noted unhappily more than 40 years later: 'My present condition is partly due to the camp, they say. I've got a malfunctioning liver, and I'm not allowed any alcohol, which I think is very poor, especially as I have to provide it for my friends and relatives.'

Repatriated to New Zealand at the war's end, by late 1946 Marjorie Monaghan was back in China. For the first time she was able to take up the teaching role she had trained for, joining the staff of a girls' school associated with the SPG in Peking. Over the turbulent years that saw the Nationalist administration swept away and the proclamation of the People's Republic of China, the school's programmes were remarkably little affected. Marjorie Monahan's time as a teacher there was uninterrupted until she chose to leave China in 1951.

Over this time she was fortunate to experience something of China beyond the confines of the mission compound. She found a place, effectively as an adopted daughter, in an old-style Chinese family home. The relationship began through a son who wanted to exchange English and Chinese conversation, and led to overnight stays, participation in Chinese New Year's festivities, and a wealth of instruction in the niceties of Chinese etiquette. 'The daughter of the house would say, "Don't hold your bowl like that! They'll wonder where you've been dragged up," and show me the correct way to do it . . . I gained a great deal from that introduction.' (The friendship survived the disruptions of the early years of the PRC, and was renewed by letter 30 years later.)

Under the Communist regime the possibility of offering religious instruction dwindled. It was not proscribed, but nor was it made easy:

> We had a chapel connected with the school, but the only teaching we could do would be out of school hours. And of course that made it extremely difficult because not only did the girls have to go to school all day, but then they had to open a night school and themselves teach the poor children in the area. So it meant they were frightfully tired. The only meetings we had were early, before school in the morning.

Under such circumstances, only those most committed could have been expected to apply themselves with enthusiasm. And, Monahan frankly admitted, their numbers were not high. 'Even in a school like that there were very few Christian girls, perhaps 20 or so . . . I myself only taught and prepared for baptismal confirmation about 12 girls, I suppose.'

Compensation of a sort was a requirement for the teachers themselves to receive political instruction. Twice a week Marjorie went with other staff members to be tutored on Maoist doctrine and how it could be applied to her work. In that time of Sino–Soviet friendship, the Soviet Union provided a shining example. They would be told: 'It isn't true to say that the Russians have taken over the mines in Manchuria, or something like that, because they're our friends. And even if they have taken them over, it's only because they're our friends.'

Monaghan was accorded a Workers' Party Ticket ('I was very cross when they made me surrender it as I left China'), and her photograph was included on a banner the school sent to Stalin as a birthday gift. In a letter to Australian missionary friends she reported that she had 'donned the Lenin uniform for teaching despite the Mission's disapproval' and had 'joined the Workers' Union'.

In at least one aspect of the new regime a New Zealand background helped to pave the way. Monaghan was accustomed to manual labour, which set her apart from her well-brought-up students.

> Each secondary school in Peking was given some land in which they were told to grow their own vegetables. We were given a section out at the Temple of Heaven . . . And the first time, the students looked at me in disbelief when I could pick up a spade and use it without being told how. There again, 'where have you been dragged up?' Because of course it was quite beyond the pale for any student to use their hands. And that, I thought, was a good thing about this new regime – that they were teaching them not to look down on labourers. And after every work day, they would read out the heroes of labour, those who had blisters on their hands through work. But I was never mentioned.

Not all the overseas teachers accommodates themselves so well to the new regime. One eccentric and autocratic English teacher had over the years made it her practice to cuff over the head any Chinese worshipper she thought was paying insufficient attention during cathedral services. When one of her pupils spat on the floor in class, she told him that such behaviour justified banning Chinese and dogs from public parks. This judgement was not well received – she was hauled before the People's Court and given two weeks to leave the country. The affair led to an epidemic of spitting among the young people (just as Agnes Moncrieff had experienced earlier) in unsuccessful attempts to provoke further intemperate reactions.

By this time, into the second year of Communist rule, Marjorie Monaghan was in any case beginning to have serious doubts about the worth of foreign missions' presence in China. It was, she thought, compromising the situation of the Chinese Christians rather than conferring any great benefit upon them. The perception was one she urged upon her bishop, but he was reluctant to accept that a cause he and other members of his family had pursued for many years had run its course. In the end it was the action of the New Zealand teacher, a junior member of the mission, that brought things to a head. 'It sounds rather conceited, but I think I precipitated our mission's withdrawal.'

Before Monaghan returned to China in 1946 she had promised her father that, having once been held prisoner, she would leave China if there was any prospect of a repetition. With the outbreak of the Korean war, some sort of internment of the nationals of countries ranged against Chinese forces began to appear a real possibility. Accordingly, she sought and received an exit permit from the Chinese authorities.

> Armed with this I went to the bishop and said, 'I'm very sorry, I'm afraid I'll have to resign because I promised my father I wouldn't run the risk of being a prisoner of war again.' And I'll always remember he said to me. 'You've got no right to promise your father that.' Which is a truly English sort of attitude.

The bishop delivered his uncompromising response in the morning, but by the afternoon, having reflected on the matter, 'He sent for me to go over to his house. And he said, "Oh my dear, I've been thinking it over. I think we'd all better go."'

12. The Pacifists

Lindsay Crozier, Courtney Archer and others with the China Convoy

The Friends Ambulance Unit (FAU) was a group set up during World War I by British members of the Society of Friends (the Quakers). It drew upon the resources of conscientious objectors to provide services compatible with their pacifist beliefs – driving ambulances, providing medical treatment and hospital care and undertaking relief activities. These services, available to both military and civilian populations, were intended as a demonstration of pacifism in action, even in the midst of conflict.

The unit was reactivated at the outset of World War II, albeit with a less direct link to the Society of Friends, some of whose members questioned whether any activities providing support in the war arena truly accorded with pacifist beliefs. China was a major focus for the efforts of the new FAU. The needs posed there led to an expanded range of activities, including large-scale transport operations, and famine and disaster relief. Reflecting that broader compass, the China operation was given the name the China Convoy. At its peak, in 1945–46, the China Convoy comprised about 140 members, mainly from the UK.

In New Zealand, conscientious objectors were often subjected to a harsh regime through the war years. Possibilities for involvement in relief work did not exist as they did in Britain. To counter this, the New Zealand Friends established a small committee under the leadership of Colin Morrison (the man who later headed Corso, and himself travelled to China postwar to assess possibilities for aid work there). The Quaker Relief and Reconstruction Committee identified some 90 candidates for voluntary work overseas.

From early on, the FAU was seen as a possible field of endeavour. In October 1944 the China Convoy indicated a willingness to accept a first tranche of six New Zealanders to undertake transport and medical work in China. A possible political hurdle was overcome with a promise of support from Prime Minister Peter Fraser (who consistently showed himself sympathetic towards the sort of China-related endeavours for which Agnes Moncrieff had found Mrs Fraser an enthusiastic champion). In early 1945 a British veteran of the China Convoy, Wilym Jenkins, arrived in New Zealand to undertake recruitment for the team.

In all, 12 New Zealanders travelled to China to serve with the FAU's China Convoy. Among the early recruits was Courtney Archer, who later gravitated from the FAU to Rewi Alley's school at Sandan, and worked with Alley to promote peace-related activities in the early 1950s. Archer was not an obvious recruit for an organisation with the motto 'Go Anywhere, Do Anything': When asked during his recruitment interview, 'Could you change the back axle of a truck halfway up a hill in the pouring rain?' he replied, 'My god, I wouldn't know where to start!' and was told, 'Okay, you can be a medical man.'

In accordance with this suggestion, Archer found an opportunity to train as a laboratory technician before leaving New Zealand.

> Only to arrive in China and they said, 'What training do you have?' and I said, 'A lab technician.' They said, 'God, we've got millions of lab technicians. You'd better end up as an anaesthetist.' So I had to go back to square one and train again and worked as an anaesthetist.

Archer's medical ambitions did not end there. When a cholera outbreak brought about an exodus of Chinese medical staff from the hospital where he was working as an anaesthetist, he found himself promoted to assistant surgeon. 'I got some experience amputating limbs and things like that, although I never got into it properly,' he recalled regretfully.

Courtney Archer was one of the first tranche of six recruits who left New Zealand to serve with the FAU in China. Even at that late stage of the Sino–Japanese war it was not possible to access from the coast the inland parts of China where the China Convoy had its operating bases. Their route lay from the south, via India and across Burma.

The New Zealand contingent were spared the lengthy and perilous land journey that Agnes Moncrieff had undertaken two years earlier along the Burma Road. Instead, like Bill Holland, they entered Free China as part of the US Army–Air Force airlift over 'the Hump', passing over the heights and valleys of the Eastern Himalayas and skirting Minya Konka, the little-known peak that James Edgar had sighted from the Szechuan side 40 years earlier. More rapid the journey certainly was, although arguably no less hazardous – over the three and a half years the airlift continued, 376 planes were lost to the uncharted terrain and Japanese fighter attacks. So frequent were the crashes that they gave rise to a new cottage industry in the mountainous areas of Burma, fashioning artefacts out of aluminium salvaged from the wrecks.

In recognition of the potential hazards of the flight, each passenger was equipped with a parachute and, assuming its successful deployment, a survival kit including such items as a compass, first-aid kit, matches, fishhooks and a note explaining who the survivor was in three different languages. There was a luggage allowance of 150 lb (70 kg) per passenger, together with what each stood up in, liberally interpreted. One member of the group, Lindsay Crozier, recalled their taking advantage of the latter provision to the fullest extent: 'When I weighed in . . . I was wearing the usual woollen underwear, a pyjama suit, a light suit, and on top a battledress outfit. I had three pairs of woollen socks and my climbing boots. I was so roly-poly I couldn't do up the fly of the trousers.' Thus equipped, the aspiring aviators 'waddled across the tarmac . . . like disabled ducks'. Five hours later they were in Kunming, the capital of China's elevated Yunnan Province.

Lindsay Crozier was, like Courtney Archer, a conscientious objector. Unlike Archer, he could boast some experience relevant to his future responsibilities, arising from his pre-war career as a photographer. In later years in China, film-making and photography came to occupy much of Crozier's time. Now, on first arrival, he was to help out in hospital work as a medical mechanic. X-ray equipment was relatively familiar; for the rest, it helped that he had a talent for improvisation – he was, as a Kong Chuen missionary later recorded with admiration, 'a very handy man – he could fix anything'.

It fell to the FAU to play a part in maintaining or re-establishing medical services that had fallen away over the years of conflict. Within a few days both Crozier and Archer found themselves in Kutsing (Qujing), a walled town some 150 kilometres to the east of Kunming, where the FAU had a major supply depot and a staff hostel. There Archer set about training as an anaesthetist at the Hui Tien (Hui Tian) hospital, which had been established in more peaceful times by the Church Missionary Society. Lindsay joined the group of 'med mecs' – medical mechanics

– who operated out of a workshop complex servicing both the hospital and the Convoy's mobile medical teams.

His background in photography saw Crozier take primary responsibility for maintaining the hospital's X-ray equipment, but inevitably the job expanded to improvising or remaking a whole range of hospital equipment that had been exposed to hard use and neglect over the war years. Imagination and invention were at a premium when the only materials at hand were cast-off truck parts, recycled fuel drums and similar leftovers from the conflict.

The med mecs, like the artisans of Burma, particularly prized the aluminium from downed aircraft. 'We had a slogan up on the workshop wall, 'BOMBERS INTO BEDPANS.' Not just the aluminium but

> the wiring, switches, motors and tubing were ideal for the multitude of improvisations we were asked to do in and around the hospital. Many a discharged soldier or badly wounded peasant hopped around on an artificial leg made from bits and pieces from one of these transports of death.

Others in the New Zealand contingent had signed up as driver–mechanics and became part of the FAU transport section. They too were based initially at Kutsing. Transport was integral to the FAU operation, carrying drugs and other medical supplies flown in over 'the Hump' to clinics and hospitals in China's interior. The driving was anything but easy, given the often horrendous state of the roads and the lack of maintenance facilities along the way. Every convoy included an extra truck at the rear laden with nothing but fuel and spare parts for the other vehicles.

The New Zealanders nonetheless sought any opportunity to be part of the often extended forays into the back country of China. Particularly prized was the chance to be part of the Hsuchow (now Jiuquan) run, undertaken to obtain precious drums of fuel from the Yumen oilfield. This long-range foray followed the route up the Kansu Corridor that Rewi Alley had earlier travelled with Joseph Needham. It even offered the opportunity to drop in on Alley at Sandan en route. Alan Jackson described the convoy in a letter home: 'The Gobi desert – the Great Wall – Rewi Alley and his Bailie schools – snow and dust storms – Central Asia – Mongolia – thousands of years old China – the romance is past

Flights over the Hump skirted Minya Konka, the lofty peak James Huston Edgar had viewed from the other side 40 years earlier.

Staff of the FAU garage at Kutsing, August 1945. (Crozier Family Collection)

In a Wuchang mission compound, Lindsay Crozier sets out to investigate a possible unexploded bomb. (Crozier Family Collection)

but the memories live forever . . .'

Within two months of the first tranche of New Zealanders arriving to join the FAU, Japan's long war in China came to an end. Over time, the nature of the challenges faced by the ambulance unit changed (so indeed did its designation – in April 1947 it was renamed the Friends Service Unit). Battlefield casualties were no longer the main concern; more and more the unit was called upon to address the plight of the refugees who were beginning to make their way back towards the coast in large numbers, and the associated threat of widespread outbreaks of disease. Another need was, as at Hui Tien, to bring back into commission hospitals and other medical facilities, often originally associated with missionary societies, that had been overtaken by the tide of war. In many cases little more than their shells remained.

Canadian missionary doctor Bob McClure had by this time become the FAU's medical director. Unsurprisingly, his mind turned back to his old stamping ground, Hankow, now a city in ruins. Wuhan, of which Hankow formed part, had been heavily bombed by the Japanese in 1938 to dislodge the Chinese forces, and even more heavily bombed by the Americans in 1945 to dislodge the Japanese. Lindsay Crozier found himself part of an FAU team dispatched to help rehabilitate Hankow's Union Hospital. The hospital, built by English missionaries, was then occupied by about 600 Japanese patients, cared for by 150 staff, part of the Japanese army medical unit. The staff included some 30 women – nurses and office workers.

At a time when remnants of the Japanese armed forces were by no means popular in China, Crozier insisted that those effectively in his charge be treated humanely and with dignity. On one occasion he went further: in the face of a perceived threat to the women in the group from night-time incursions by Chinese soldiers, he set about festooning the only gateway to their quarters with copper wire directed connected directly to the mains.

Happily, before this project was completed, a diplomatic solution was found, leaving a relieved Crozier to reflect that 'Perhaps this act of defiance was not the best demonstration of pacifist principles.' When Crozier later visited Japan he was accorded a 'party of gratitude' by repatriated internees – those who, in the words of the national daily, the *Yomiuri Shimbun*, 'had experienced unforgettable kindness at the hands of Mr Lindsay Crozier, a Britisher, in the Hankou hospital'.

Crozier established his credentials as a 'snowy-haired Kiwi angel' with at least one other group during his months in Hankow. The institution of a laboratory technicians' course at the Union Hospital brought him into contact with Catholic sisters whose hospital lay across the Yangtze, in Wuchang. When he learned that the hospital's main well could not be used because it had an unexploded bomb at the bottom, he expressed a possibly foolhardy willingness to go down the well and investigate the situation.

Climbing down two bamboo poles lashed together, he rummaged in the dark until he contacted what appeared to be a bomb's fin. 'A slight tug and the fin came away in my hand – the bomb had actually [previously] gone off and blown quite a large hole in the side of the well.' The nuns were both relieved and appreciative when Crozier reappeared from the depths of the well brandishing the remnants of the bomb.

In keeping with their pacifist beliefs, the FAU volunteers went unarmed. The FAU was seen as an impartial relief unit, and as a consequence was from time to time called upon to carry out tasks for which others' affiliations made them less well suited. This extended even to medical mechanics, Crozier recalled:

> Three of us were asked to go in away through the mountains from Hankow to bring out two UNRRA people who had helped behind the communist lines and couldn't get out. Leighton Stuart, who was then American Ambassador, approached the ambulance unit, to see if we would try and bring them out . . . We got to the Communist headquarters . . . and to make a long story short, we brought them out. We were actually held up, I think, five or six times in the one day by bandits. And I was always the Charlie who would get out and parley with them.

Crozier's personal qualities, and perhaps his country of origin, seem to have recommended him to more than just the bandits. At Yenan,

> We had an American and an English chappy and myself. And when we went into the Communist headquarters, we got talking to a lot of the students. And the Meiguoren – the American – he was buhao [not good]. And the Englishman was chabudwo [near enough]. And the

> Kiwi was dinghao [great]. You know, they didn't say this to me. They said it to the three of us – they were pretty frank.

It is unclear whether the students' warm endorsement of Crozier and his country of origin came before or after the locals had entertained the FAU visitors at a concert. Inevitably, the foreign delegation was called upon to provide an item.

> After some pressing and to save face for the foreigners I gave them a Maori Haka. You can imagine what a ridiculous sight I was. There was me with grubby clothes, three days growth, going through all the antics of a well-forgotten Scout haka. Believe it or not, it went down big and I had to repeat it.*

One member of the initial group to leave New Zealand did not share the pacifist views of the others. Graham Milne completed his medical training at the end of 1943. His intention had been to take up a position at Po Wai Hospital, the Presbyterian mission hospital at Kong Chuen, near Canton. With the Japanese occupation of south China that was no longer possible. Milne was in Trentham, destined for army service in Italy, when Wilym Jenkins approached him to put his medical knowledge to use with the FAU instead. 'And I said, "Well chum, I'm in the army, I'm not a pacifist." And he said, "No trouble, no trouble. We're a very tolerant mob."'

With the Italian campaign nearing its end, Milne's commanding officer was prepared to give him a temporary release from his military obligations, and sent him on his way with a copy of the army training manual for stretcher-bearers, the most relevant text he could find on his bookshelves. To this Milne added most of the elements of his existing uniform, which he shared with another FAU recruit, Owen Jackson, who was travelling as a motor mechanic.

> I designed – virtually – a uniform. I was very comfortable in battledress and it was a very useful thing to get around in, you know, all the

* The haka may claim to have been New Zealand's most distinctive contribution to Chinese popular culture in the Republican years. As well as Crozier's well-received performance, there was James Bertram's 'anti-Imperialist war dance' in Sian, and earlier the spontaneous performance that inspired terror in James Huston Edgar's band of would-be attackers.

> pockets. And I ended up getting Owen into a battledress and he was a true blue conscientious objector. But he didn't mind. We put a New Zealand flash on there – I took my pips off and got hold of some New Zealand Red Cross things. We put those on the top . . . and we ended up in a sort of paramilitary setup, between Red Cross and the army.

Graham Milne's service with the FAU was relatively brief. After a period at Qujing he travelled to Liuchow in Kwansi Province to join the team battling a cholera epidemic that had brought about deaths in the tens of thousands. Once the epidemic had been brought under control, Milne's team was redirected north to help with the rehabilitation effort in Hankow.

By that time news had reached him of the release of the Kong Chuen hospital staff following Japan's defeat. It was to that group that he felt his greater loyalty lay. The FAU, he believed, had agreed with New Zealand Presbyterian Church at the time of his recruitment that the FAU would release him when it became possible for the Kong Chuen hospital to reopen.

> At that point I got slightly unpopular at FAU because I adopted the usual Kiwi maxim of if something needs doing, go ahead and do it and ask questions afterwards . . . I didn't see any point in going north because I was eventually going to go east . . . So I managed to find an American pilot with a little spotter plane and when the rest of the team went north, I slung my bag in with this fellow to bring me down to Canton.

There Milne launched into the work required to bring the hospital at Kong Chuen back up to an operational standard.

One other member of the New Zealand FAU team eventually found his way to Kong Chuen. Lindsay Crozier's previous experience and skill as a photographer led to his being commissioned to produce a record on film of the China Convoy's activities. This became a valuable tool as fundraising grew more difficult in the years after the war. Other commissions followed. Basing himself in Shanghai, from mid-1947 Crozier travelled widely throughout China to produce publicity material for the FSU and a variety of other relief organisations. Shortly before he left China, a year later, he travelled to Kong Chuen to make a film for the Presbyterian Church of New Zealand on the work of the Po Wai Hospital.

The Kong Chuen Mission was by this time re-established on an operational basis. During Crozier's brief stay there as a filmmaker his range of other talents, already familiar to Graham Milne, were very much in evidence. No sooner had Crozier arrived back in New Zealand than the New Zealand Missions Committee was in touch to invite him to return to China as Kong Chuen's compound manager, 'with responsibility for hospital mechanics and oversight of many things practical on the compound'.

By February the following year he was on his way back to China, accompanied by Mary, his bride of just a few weeks, and 45 pieces of luggage, including two artificial legs for the hospital gateman, built to Graham Milne's specifications. Chancing upon these, shaken Hong Kong customs officials waved through the entire consignment without further inspection. The Croziers witnessed the Communist takeover of Southern China, remaining at Kong Chuen until the mission closed in 1951.

Courtney Archer, too, found himself changing fields of activity as the FAU adapted to a postwar role. The medical heroics of his early days gave way to administrative responsibilities. From mid-1946 he was assigned to Shanghai as the unit's medical purchasing officer, which involved close liaison with two parallel relief organisations, UNRRA and CNRRA. It was a difficult and often disheartening experience.

UNRRA did not have its genesis with the present-day United Nations, although latterly it was folded into that organisation. It was set up at a 44-nation conference hosted by the United States late in 1943, with the objective of providing relief for displaced persons and other victims of war. In China, the Republican government insisted that 'the dignity of the Chinese people' required the establishment of a counterpart organisation, CNRRA, to take charge of all relief supplies at the point of entry to China.

The result was what has been described as 'a giant blackmail scheme', which saw substantial quantities of relief supplies pilfered or diverted to the black market, little reaching those in most need, and virtually none being delivered to those parts of China under Communist administration. By mid-1946 the head of UNRRA, Fiorello LaGuardia, was writing despairingly to Generalissimo Chiang Kai-shek that '[UNRRA's] purpose is to help the rehabilitation of China and not the financial rehabilitation of warehouses', but his voice went unheard.

Far to the northwest, at Sandan, Rewi Alley was keen to recruit New Zealanders whose contracts with the FAU were nearing an end. Frustrated with his bureaucratic struggles in Shanghai, and keen to re-engage with the 'real' China, Courtney Archer decided to leave big-city life. In early 1947, after an exploratory expedition to Sandan undertaken on the FAU's behalf, he removed himself to Alley's Sandan Bailie School.

Archer's accountancy skills made him an important catch for the school. Officially working as a teacher of accountancy, he fulfilled a parallel role as an invigilator, as Alley had found it difficult to counter a tendency towards creative accounting on the part of students given financial responsibility. He also plunged back into the maelstrom of funding disputes, as he found himself caught up in Alley's continuing negotiations, by then with the international committee of the CIC.

The downside of focusing publicity efforts on an individual, the committee had come to discover, was that many donors in countries such as the US were earmarking their donations for the efforts of 'Blitzbuilder' Alley. So, more predictably, were the Rewi Alley societies in small-town New Zealand. The upshot was constant wrangling about how best to allocate funds. For the next six years, through the establishment of the People's Republic of China and beyond, Courtney Archer devoted himself to ensuring that there was ongoing financial support to allow Rewi Alley's 'adventure in creative education' to continue, and backstopping Alley's efforts to make it a success.

13. The Missionaries

Graham Milne, Alice Cook and Annie James see a mission's end

The Presbyterian missionary outreach programme to which Graham Milne attached himself after the end of hostilities had seen hard times in the preceding years. First, the Kong Chuen compound had suffered from the attacks of Chinese bandit gangs, one of which had resulted in the death of a New Zealand doctor, Owen Eaton, shot in the head. Then, after the Japanese occupation of Canton, it had been subjected to increasingly rigorous oversight by the occupying forces. Finally, after Pearl Harbor, the compound was commandeered by the Japanese, and the expatriate staff consigned to an internment camp in Canton. The end of the war presented the opportunity for a new start, building on the foundations of the long-established mission.

The New Zealand mission had in fact ceased to be distinguished as the Canton Villages Mission as long ago as the 1920s, when a series of interdenominational conferences set out to rationalise the efforts of Protestant missions. The result was the establishment of the Church of Christ in China, a broad-based coalition that included the mission at Kong Chuen. As part of the same effort, the CVM's founder, Rev. George McNeur, had earlier accepted a role in the training of Chinese preachers at Canton's Union Theological College.

Recognition of McNeur's achievements in China, both in setting up the Kong Chuen Mission and in supporting advances towards cooperation between differing evangelical groups, led to his nomination as Moderator of the 1926 General Assembly of the Presbyterian Church of New Zealand. Those who attended the assembly expecting to hear condemnation of China's unsettled state, and the anti-foreign riots that had driven most foreign missionaries from China at that time, may have been surprised to be told that '[China] cannot put her house in order while we persist in interfering with its arrangement'. At the heart of the problem, McNeur said, was the fact that 'There have been numberless instances where the insolently domineering attitude of fancied racial superiority has caused the sensitive and proud Chinese to abhor the foreigner.'*

On this and subsequent return visits to New Zealand McNeur added his voice to those of others such as George Shepherd and Bill Holland in promoting a view of China that was at odds with the more conservative accounts of treaty ports journalism. In a 1934 interview with the *Otago Daily Times* he scoffed at the idea that the central government had effective control of the country, criticised the role of Japan, and acknowledged an unlikely force for change:

> Communism was still very strong. It was driven underground in many parts, but it had a great many educated leaders. Some were educated abroad – in England, France, America, as well as Russia and Japan. Many very fine young men and women had given their lives for communism.

Prophetically, 'Mr McNeur said that he thought the conditions in China would settle down, but they would take a long time to do so.'

By the mid-1930s the mission compound at Kong Chuen had been built into a substantial undertaking. Occupying about 5 acres, it included four residential buildings for missionaries and medical staff, a 100-bed hospital, a girls' boarding school and a conference centre. Unlike, for instance, the compound that came to serve as Marjorie Monaghan's place of detention in Shandong, it was not secured against the outside world by any substantial wall, although its boundaries were delineated by a bamboo hedge. Walled in or no, it was unambiguously a foreign enclave, within which its New Zealand residents led lives quite divorced from those of the local community.

There were differing views on the matter of lifestyle. Alun Richards, a former New Zealand Student Christian Movement secretary who made his way from Shanghai to Canton with his wife Muriel and a tandem cycle in the late 1930s, thought the New Zealand group stuffy and insular. They were, he said, 'bilingual but monocultural'. (For their

* McNeur was not himself above passing judgement on particular groups of Chinese. Elsewhere he expressed the view that 'New Zealand has been unfortunate in the type of Chinese immigrant whose coming has moulded her earliest conception of China and its people – illiterate, conservative, Cantonese.' It was unclear which of these attributes he considered the most unfortunate.

part, the missionaries had some reservations about Alun Richards. Alice Cook, there at the time of his stay, remembered, 'He was rather unshaven and untidy and Paddy [Jansen] offered him his razor.')

McNeur, however, was unequivocal on the need for expatriate living conditions. 'Missionaries go out to China to work, not to die,' a semi-jubilee publication asserted flatly. 'The kind of house a missionary needs to live in if he is to preserve his health [is] a two-stor[ey] building with large, airy rooms and wide balconies . . .'

There was a good deal to justify such caution, particularly in relation to the living conditions of medical staff. 'We had awful bad luck, as far as doctors were concerned,' Alice Cook recalled of her time in China. 'Something was always happening to them, one way or another'. Dr Joseph Ings, of Forbury in Dunedin, who travelled in 1905 to set up the medical services, was in China less than a year before he succumbed to a virulent attack of dysentery. Dr H.B. Turbott, according to church records, had retired after a breakdown in health (although in truth, it appears his departure was prompted rather by a disinclination to remain idle in Hong Kong over a time of civil unrest.) Dr A.T. Howie, installed as medical superintendent in 1932, remained only four years before he was invalided back to New Zealand, where he died a short time later.

Howie was replaced by a recruit of great promise, Dr Owen Eaton, who had topped New Zealand's university scholarship list before training to be a medical missionary. Eaton held the post for less than two years before he was shot and killed when bandits raided the compound. Dr John Brown, recruited by Corso to reinforce the medical staff in the aftermath of the war, did not even survive to start work: he contracted Japanese-B encephalitis while passing through Hong Kong, and died soon after arriving in Kong Chuen.

That fatal disease was not the only threat is evidenced by the death of Owen Eaton. Robbers were considered an aspect of local life sufficiently constant to merit a separate section in a 25-year review of the CVM's activities:

> Most of them come from the villages and market towns in the district. Some have been professional robbers most of their lives; some have been driven it through sheer poverty; with many it has been the natural

> sequence to reckless gambling; while others take it on occasionally for the sake of wild excitement.

It was wild excitement of a kind that those resident in the mission compound could well have done without. Their obvious wealth, relative to conditions in the surrounding countryside, made missionaries engaged in outreach activities, and the compound itself, obvious targets for extortion and robbery. Paradoxically, it was only after the arrival of Japanese occupation forces that the sense of threat diminished.

Outreach was an integral part of the Kong Chuen Mission's work. It involved establishing regional hubs for worship and proselytising where the opportunity offered in the network of villages and small towns in the surrounding countryside. The Poon-yue area, which included Kong Chuen, had been allocated to the New Zealand Presbyterians because it took in the home villages of many Chinese who had travelled to New Zealand.

The connection seemed to have some validity, not least because right from the time of Rev. McNeur, missionaries had been entrusted with remittances to deliver to relatives in south China.* When Alice Cook arrived in 1935 she found a level of familiarity with her home country. 'They knew the name New Zealand. I don't know if they ever knew how many sheep we had, or anything, but I think they trusted us.'

From the mid-1930s, much of the responsibility for this aspect of the mission's work fell to Alice Cook. A proud Southlander ('I was actually born in Mosgiel, but I mean, I was only there for the event'), she came to the role well prepared: a history degree at the University of Otago followed by training at Deaconess College and two years' language study in China itself. Such extensive training was typical for those assigned to Kong Chuen: 'Everything had to be done decently, in order, in the Presbyterian Church.'

Possibly nothing could have fully prepared Alice Cook for the reality of south China under the threat of Japanese invasion.

* This could be a task of some delicacy, especially when it turned out that the intended recipients were no longer alive. Often the fact of their death had not been communicated to the donors in New Zealand, out of a wish to avoid causing distress – or perhaps ending the flow of remittances.

> I used to go out with a Chinese deaconess. We'd be biking around the villages, you know, and holding little meetings and that kind of thing. And we'd hear the sirens go. So you'd drop your bike and [lie] in the rice paddies until they passed over . . . Bombs were going all over the place. It [1936] wasn't a very good year, really, for getting around.

The New Zealand connection notwithstanding, for most purposes the Kong Chuen Mission was categorised as a British institution. As the Japanese bombing became more constant, a Union Jack was placed on the roof of the main building in the hope that this would prevent the mission becoming a target (although the constant failure of the Japanese bombers to hit their primary target, a railway bridge nearby, gave little confidence in the accuracy of their bombing).

The British consul in Canton, who was formally responsible for the New Zealanders' well-being, did his best to remove them from harm's way, according to Alice Cook.

> He said, when the bombing started, now you're all to leave except the doctors and nurses. Well, the rest of us said that we weren't going to do any such thing. But I did go into the hospital for two hours every morning for six weeks – this was me being a nurse. But he forgot about us and we just carried on.

The most concrete example of outreach was the establishment of a cottage hospital at Kaai Hau, a market town about 70 kilometres from Kong Chuen. Annie James, who set it up and ran it, was to become probably the best-known New Zealand missionary to serve in China, and ultimately a *cause célèbre*. In 1930, when the branch hospital was established, she had already been part of the Presbyterian Church's South China Mission for 18 years. For the next two decades, without the support of other expatriate workers, and largely cut off from the mission base at Kong Chuen, she dispensed maternity care, medical advice and Christian doctrine to the many thousands in the districts surrounding Kaai Hau.

As was the case with Rewi Alley and his support groups, Annie James became a focal point for fundraising in New Zealand. The Busy Bees, a children's missionary organisation associated with the Presbyterian Church, went beyond simple cash: aware of the distances James had to travel, the children presented her with a Ford V-8 car. The purchase was financed by the ingenious method of listing the car's constituent parts, then assigning each chapter ('Hive') of the Busy Bees responsibility for paying for one or more parts, so that Kelburn bought the horn, Otautau the accelerator, Wanganui the windscreen wipers, and so on. A minor hitch late in the process was the discovery that Annie James had never learned to drive. Over time, however, and with the assistance of mission colleagues, the deficit was overcome.

When Kathleen Hall visited Kaai Hau before establishing her own cottage hospital at Songjiazhuang, she found much to admire. 'I thoroughly enjoyed my time with Miss James, and not only got many helpful ideas from her, but received real inspiration. She is a wonderful woman.' James became an integral part of the community in which she had embedded herself. Especially was this so after her New Zealand colleagues were interned. When, towards the end of the war, she was called upon to interpret for the crew of a downed American bomber, it was the first time she had spoken English for nearly three years.

Japan's push south ushered in a long period of instability and hardship for Kaai Hau and the surrounding districts. Annie James, no less than her mission colleagues at Kong Chuen, was subject to strong representations from the British consul in Canton that she should remove herself from the danger zone. Her courteous response survives.

> Ping Tei Kong
> February 17, 1939.
> His Britannic Majesty's Consul-General,
> Shameen, Canton.
> Dear Sir,
> I wish to acknowledge your letter of the 1st inst., and to thank you for it. I note that you consider that it would be in the best interest of all concerned if I would vacate the Tsung Fa district.
>
> My circumstances at the present time, however, are so different from what they were in late December when the armed robbery occurred that I feel impelled to place these facts before you in preference to evacuating forthwith.
>
> The conditions making my safety more secure than formerly are briefly as follows:
>
> A robbery having already occurred, it is not likely to recur for many

months, for the robbers realise that there is nothing left to take.

Robberies are always more frequent towards the Chinese New Year, so from now on things are likely to be more peaceful.

I have moved from Lau Ha Wai to a district that has a much better reputation. I have done this in consultation with the Chinese Magistrate, who has taken a genuine interest in my welfare and has given special instructions to the village head and the village protection corps to guard my safety.

The temple we are living in here has the protection of several men who sleep in the building at night.

I realise that only in very exceptional circumstances should a British subject pursue a course of action that is contrary to the expressed wishes of his Consul-General, but I feel that these exceptional circumstances exist. Thus, whilst by remaining here I am disobeying the letter of your communication of February 1, I do not feel that I am disobeying the spirit of it; for I am sure that if you could see me in my present circumstances, and see at the same time the dire need for medical aid that exists in this district you yourself would no longer desire my evacuation.

I am, Sir,
Yours respectfully,
Annie James.

Having failed signally in his efforts to persuade her to quit China, the consul-general took another tack and recommended Annie James for an MBE instead. His recommendation was accepted, although she was not in fact invested with the honour until her return to New Zealand in 1952.

James had, by the time of the consul-general's letter urging her to evacuate, already been forced from Kaai Hau by Japanese bombing raids. The armed robbery to which she refers was the work of Chinese brigands. Over the remainder of the war years she would twice return to her base at Kaai Hau, and twice retreat in the face of renewed Japanese incursions.

While her mission colleagues were interned after Pearl Harbor, leaving her without external support, she herself was able to avoid the notice of the Japanese. 'I am afraid we are getting accustomed to running from the enemy,' she wrote to the mission director in New Zealand. 'Each time I run I feel a bit of a coward, but since we are at war with the Rising Sun, I find it best to keep out of their way. I do not want to land into a concentration camp "somewhere unknown".'

For those based at Kong Chuen, there was no possibility of avoiding internment. They had maintained a somewhat uneasy coexistence with the Japanese occupiers from the time Canton fell in October 1938. Since this involved constant interaction with the Japanese bureaucracy, there was no chance of their ducking under the radar when their status changed to that of enemy aliens. On 8 December 1941 the mission was served with a quaintly worded 'Verbal Note':

> As Japan and your country are, at this time, being involved in a state of war, His Imperial Japanese Majesty's Forces have decided to put all your properties, both private and public, under their control. Later, upon the arrival of the Japanese investigation party, led by the officer, definite settlement will be made between the master (manager) of this house (office) and that officer in charge of the party, so that, all the occupants, including employees, should remain in their own usual places.

Remarkably, receipt of this cyclostyled note was the first intimation those in the mission had that Britain was at war with Japan, something the Japanese had failed to mention while in the process of helping themselves to sundry objects within the compound in the preceding hours.

Even more remarkably, despite thus 'being involved in a state of war', the mission was able to carry on its work for almost another full year before the New Zealanders were moved to Canton and an internment camp, formerly the compound of the Oriental Missionary Society. The conditions under which they were held there were notably better than those experienced by Max Bickerton and others interned at Stanley camp in Hong Kong, and of a completely different order to the privations suffered by James Bertram as a military prisoner in Hong Kong and Tokyo.

Even after the New Zealand staff's internment the Kong Chuen compound served as a refugee centre, and the hospital was able to continue after a fashion through the efforts of the long-serving Chinese

A Shacklock range being carried into the kitchen at Kaai Hau hospital – a gift from the congregation of St Andrews Church, Dunedin. (Presbyterian Research Centre Archives).

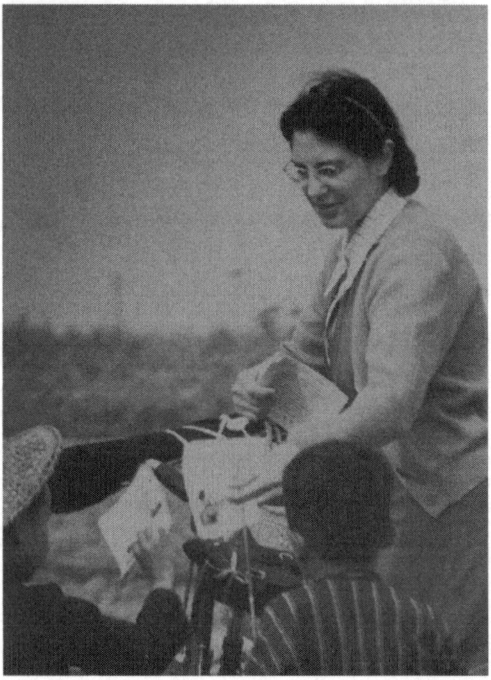

Alice Cook 'getting around' by bicycle on the mission's outreach work. (Presbyterian Research Centre Archives)

Annie James' prized Ford V8 forced into paddy fields to avoid a bomb crater, 1938. (Presbyterian Research Centre Archives)

Annie James at Kaai Hau in 1948. (Presbyterian Research Centre Archives)

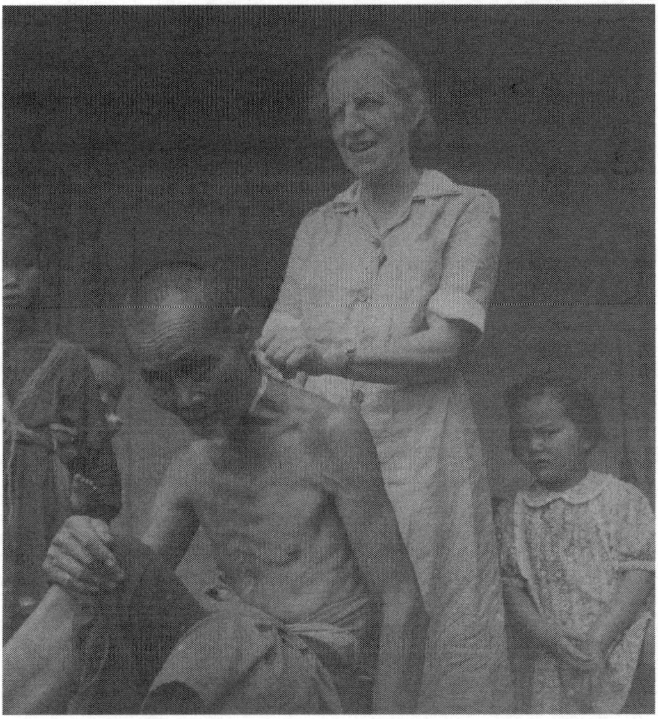

nursing and support staff, under the direction of the one remaining doctor, George Grätzner. (Grätzner, an Austrian refugee, was not considered an alien.) Only in the last year of the war, when there seemed a real prospect of out-and-out conflict in south China, did the Japanese take over the hospital premises in order to create a 1000-bed base hospital for their troops.

The occupying force showed surprising generosity in retaining basic hospital furniture but allowing all other equipment and personal effects to be removed prior to their takeover. The compound staff took full advantage of the opportunity, moving everything that could be removed into safe storage, and replacing it with meticulous care after Japan's defeat. When Graham Milne arrived he found that '[e]ven the wastepaper basket with the same stuff in it came back and was in exactly the same place'.

That it was possible to salvage so much in terms of medical equipment and personal possessions was a great help to Dr Milne as he set about making the hospital fully operational once more. While New Zealand staff members who had been held in captivity were repatriated for a period of recuperation, others, including Alice Cook, who had been out of China on furlough at the time of Pearl Harbor, were able to return and pick up other aspects of the mission's work. Rev. Paddy Jansen, who provided the New Zealand authorities with a clear and generally favourable account of conditions under internment, had returned and was playing a leading role in the mission by early 1947.

South China was now nominally under the control of the Nationalist government once more. In practice it was in a state of considerable lawlessness, to the point where in Canton the Japanese were prevailed upon to continue their armed policing of the streets until such time as the KMT could set a credible alternative force in place. The mission at Kong Chuen found itself once again facing the threat posed by bandit gangs, many of them now including former soldiers of the KMT.

Milne had his first experience of their activities when three men entered his bedroom one night.

> I woke up and there was some shadowy character there with a torch in my eyes and waving a very large revolver at me and another bloke alongside him. And I remember my first impression was, well by God,

> I'm nervous, but they look far more nervous than I am. They didn't seem to have done this very often and I was more frightened they'd pull the thing out of sheer fright than anything.

Possibly as a consequence of their nervousness, the would-be robbers fled when a nightwatchman raised the alarm, but the incident led the local police chief to recommend hiring four armed guards to patrol the mission at night. 'And he said, you ought to have a rifle too. I took the view that if we were prepared to employ people to shoot at someone who might bandit us, then I should be prepared to be armed too, just as a gesture of solidarity, if you like.'

Milne, who had already disavowed any pacifist instincts when invited to join the FAU, saw no problem in equipping himself with a rifle, which he placed out of sight and largely out of mind. 'And when Paddy Jansen and co. arrived back the armed guard situation went on. But I sort of forgot to tell anybody that I had one too.'

The fact that he did became apparent when another group of bandits broke in one night armed with hand grenades. Having secured his family, Milne recalled later,

> I thought – ha – I've got a rifle . . . We had a standard signal – three shots meant trouble, you know. And I grabbed this thing and went out on the balcony and went *boom boom boom*! Lovely noise. We learned later its effect downstairs was [that] these three guys were absolutely horrified and they took off. They didn't stick around. But the implications of it were far more serious than I realised.

The 'serious implications' arose from Milne's failure to appreciate the strength of pacifist feeling among some of the mission staff. Even though his shots had been fired in the air, the revelation that weapons were being held on the compound at all was enough to cause real concern. Frances Ogilvie, a longstanding and highly valued member of staff, felt strongly enough to offer her resignation. 'So I was put on the mat for that. And we agreed to disagree. But we finally agreed that I'd give up my rifle . . .'

By the end of 1948 the mission found itself faced with a concern more fundamental than the possibility of bandit incursions. China was once more enmeshed in civil war between the Nationalists and Communists. It was increasingly evident that the CCP forces had the upper hand, and their southward thrust would before long bring them to Guangdong Province and the mission field of Kong Chuen. The possibility of renewed conflict and the advent of an avowedly atheistic and apparently anti-foreign regime pointed towards an uncertain future.

Graham Milne was by then a married man, with three small children. As the Communist forces drew nearer he took the precaution of sending his family out to Hong Kong. He himself remained with the mission, while keeping a weather eye on the Communist advance. In October 1949, when CCP agents began to appear nearby towns and villages, he decided it was time to leave.

> One of the reasons I wanted to get out was that we knew they had a blacklist of Westerners who had been a bit in the forefront of succouring the Chinese, if you can put it that way. I had been pretty much involved not only in medical work but in relief work . . . famines and that sort of stuff. I worked in pretty closely with the local police chiefs in organising orphanages and food lines and so on, and we already knew that two American doctors who'd been in a similar position up in central China had stayed on under the mistaken impression that the Geneva Convention applied to doctors. They were promptly grabbed, and one of them died in prison as a result of the treatment he got. I had a sneaking suspicion that Mao's boys might have me on their list, and I didn't see any point in hanging around to find out, frankly.

His caution was justified. Nancy Jansen recounts that when her husband Paddy was questioned by the Communist authorities, a primary objective was to secure an admission that Milne had had access to UNRRA funds and had misused them. Given the level of corruption that had accompanied the allocation of UNRRA funds and goods under the Nationalist government, it was a not unreasonable line of inquiry.

Milne's departure from the mission and from China was more precipitate than he had envisaged. Plans for a farewell afternoon tea and a dignified departure were negated by a breakfast-time intimation that troops had entered the next village. He had time only for a precipitous drive to the airport, where he was able to book a seat on the 2 o'clock flight to Hong Kong.

> I went and had lunch with some American friends of mine at the big American hospital [in Canton]. And I said to Paul, 'What's your pick, what's going on?' He said, 'I don't like it'. I said, 'Well, I've got an airways ticket this afternoon.' He said, 'I don't think that'll be much bloody use. They took the airport about an hour ago.'

Remarkably, Milne was able to secure a refund on his plane ticket. He suspected the airline resold the non-existent seat to someone else. Instead he set his sights on the night ferry, due to depart at half past eight.

> Darkness fell about half past six and Paul said, 'Let's go.' His driver took us. And Canton had just gone like that. It was completely empty. There were no lights. There wasn't a soul on the street. Daylight had been reasonably busy and suddenly there wasn't a thing. It was the most eerie sensation, to go through a Chinese city and nothing was happening. Everybody was under shutters, you know.
>
> Paul just said to his driver, 'Keep going.' We whipped around one corner on some main road and there was a rattle of orders and rifle bolts clicking. They came out of the dark and we skidded to a halt. Half a dozen gentlemen in black silk appeared at the car window wanting to know where we were going and who we were. This was undoubtedly the underground who'd taken over, just on dark, and were working in – you know, very sensibly – working in with the local police force to make the takeover as easy as possible. Anyway, they said, 'Okay, get on your way.' They obviously didn't want to keep any foreigners.
>
> We went down to the wharf there at the Pearl River. There was one boat there and there was absolutely screaming pandemonium. All sorts of foreigners had turned up, from up country. A most extraordinary lot . . . And the Chinese – Hong Kong Chinese types, Chinese who feared Communism – were scrambling six deep over each other, trying to get over the wharf gates, and off the wharf sheds . . .
>
> I said, 'So long mate, I'll see if I can get on this thing.' I literally had to fight my way on with my bags. And I was barely on and they cast off, with people still trying to jump to get on the ship. Absolute panic situation. Chinese panic, which was interesting. Most of the foreigners got on. So then we set off. It was a very full ship, and darkened, and we got fired on about an hour downstream. Somebody had got news of us. One or two of the guards on our side started popping back and

that created a lot more pandemonium. We arrived in Hong Kong next morning.

The scenes surrounding Graeme Milne's departure on what was, as it turned out, the last ferry to make the Pearl River run under the old regime, were among the more eventful in the takeover of Guangdong Province and its capital. By and large, the Communists won by default. Neglect, misgovernment and corruption had left the Nationalists with little support in the south. Inflation was rampant – Lindsay Crozier reported having seen a peddlecab driver cleaning the chain of his cycle with a $1000 note.

In the view of Nancy Jansen, who remained with her husband Paddy at Kong Chuen, the Communist revolution was anything but. 'It was absolutely not a revolution. A revolution is when people rise up, they cannot stand the conditions. The Communists took over because no one would raise a finger to support [the KMT]. They were such a lousy government.'

Nor did the remaining foreigners initially come in for special attention. In Crozier's recollection, 'We were not molested at all. I would say we were more ignored than anything.' When the mission compound once more became the target of robbers, the nightwatchman was able to call upon a nearby PLA unit, who swiftly put them to flight (ironically, by firing shots in the air, the expedient that had earlier landed Graham Milne in hot water).

The order imposed by a disciplined political force was welcome, even though it came with some drawbacks, according to Nancy Jansen:

> They were very neat, they were very natty, they were very thorough. They never taxed half as heavily as the nationalists did, but they collected everything they taxed. And they were as shrewd as could be . . . They waited till they were ready and then they just took each little piece as they could.

With the passage of time the attentions of the new authorities came increasingly to limit the activities of the Kong Chuen Mission, and in particular its interaction with the local church. For Alice Cook it was a time of frustration, leading to an inevitable conclusion:

> Could you do Christian work under a Communist regime? We had to find out. Well, you couldn't. You needed a permit to go out your back door, really. It was a period of anti – anti-American, anti-British, anti-religion, anti-Western. These campaigns were going all the time . . . It meant the Chinese couldn't be seen with us, couldn't work with us. Well, we were no use there [if we could not] work with the people. So the church folk themselves said – the Senate said – I think you'll have to go. They were quite pleasant about it, but we did have to go – there was no doubt about it.

The situation was complicated further by the commitment of UN forces to Korea in October 1950, bringing Chinese and New Zealand troops into conflict. Like Marjorie Monaghan in Peking, members of the mission had to consider the possibility that they might be interned as enemy aliens. To Lindsay and Mary Crozier, with a baby (as it turned out, twins) on the way, it seemed prudent to move out to Hong Kong and wait.

On 29 December 1950 the mission council in New Zealand passed a resolution to the effect that '[i]t would best serve the ends of the indigenous church for foreign missionaries to withdraw from Guangdong . . . While it is not the wish of any of us to lay down our work we are unanimously agreed that the development of events requires this of us.'

With the council's decision the way ahead was clear, and preparations were made for an orderly withdrawal. Securing exit permits was time consuming and vexatious but ultimately relatively straightforward. Personal belongings being removed were subject to inspection. Books containing illustrations thought to reflect favourably on the Nationalists, or to show China in a bad light, had the photographs removed. (When Ann Lilburne, an evangelist of long standing, was asked why all the photographs in her album were of poor people, she replied, 'Because they're my friends.') A formal requirement that those departing be subject to criticism in accordance with communist doctrine was satisfied by ritual denunciations – Sister Eileen Reid, who had already left China, had sometimes spoken sharply to nurses in her team; Paddy Jansen once 'nearly kicked' the gardener.

By April 1951 the last of the mission staff had made their way out of China to Hong Kong. It was 50 years since Rev. George McNeur had arrived in China to establish a distinctively New Zealand missionary outreach.

There was one exception: Annie James remained. Having successfully avoided internment throughout the period of the Japanese occupation, she had travelled to New Zealand for a brief period of recuperation before returning to assist in the rehabilitation of her mission base at Kaai Hau. With her she brought 53 packing cases of goods and equipment donated by well-wishers in New Zealand. Drawing on these resources, Annie James' cottage hospital, the Hospital of Universal Love returned to serving the local community.

Under Communist rule from 1949, James found herself in a different situation to that faced by her colleagues at Kong Chuen. Geographically, she was isolated, the only foreigner in a district remote from the major administrative centre of Canton. In the atmosphere of accusation and counter-accusation that the new order brought with it, she was an easy target without the relative security of compound living, and found herself exposed to petty harassment. After a year of seeking to accommodate herself to the new regime she reluctantly came to the same conclusion as her colleagues at Kong Chuen – that her presence was a liability to her co-workers – and applied for an exit permit.

That in itself was not a straightforward process. Some within the local medical community had seen the Hospital of Universal Love as operating against their interests and took the opportunity to make their grievances known. On 26 February 1951 Annie James was summoned to the local authorities – not, as she had hoped, to receive her exit permit, but to answer accusations of manslaughter relating to the death of a baby in her care.

When those accusations were dismissed, others took their place. Careful record-keeping did not work in the hospital's favour because detractors could demonstrate that some 40 patients, mostly babies, had died in James' care over her time in the district. That was hardly extraordinary – patients only presented at hospital when all other avenues had been exhausted, and in any case, as Alice Cook tartly observed, 'People die in hospital, and that's that.'

Invited to admit to wrongdoing, Annie James refused, and found herself consigned to prison. Her place of custody was a small enclosure beneath the stairs of the police station. It had little natural light and no sanitation, and she was kept awake by the constant tread of those using the stairs overhead. More frightening were the sounds of groups of prisoners being led to execution following conviction on charges of crimes against society that paralleled those she herself faced.

At intervals over the following months, Annie James was taken from her cell to face further hearings. Her steadfast declarations of innocence became an embarrassment to the local authorities, not least because her case was beginning to attract international attention. Simple acceptance that she had been at fault, she was told, would see her released and repatriated forthwith.

Physically at a low ebb, and anxious about the fate of those who depended on her, she eventually provided the signature required – meaningless in her view, because extracted under duress. On 11 May 1951 she left Kaai Hau – permitted to acknowledge the calls of well-wishers, but forbidden to respond. Two days later she was at the Sailors and Soldiers Home in Hong Kong, still in the clothes she had worn throughout her captivity. When she was recognised and greeted with a kind word, she put her face in her hands and wept. Seventy years old, she had spent more than half her life in China.

Annie James' expulsion marked the end of the distinctly New Zealand school of missionary endeavour that had been set in train in south China 50 years previously, as the People's Republic of China set itself on a course of independence and self-reliance. More than that, it underlined the parameters within which China would from then on pursue its contacts with the outside world. Those changes applied not just to Western attempts at proselytisation, but to the broad range of foreign involvement in China.

Those foreigners who were permitted to stay, as Rewi Alley was, were likely to find themselves assigned new and different duties. Those who sought to return to China, such as Kathleen Hall, often discovered that not even sterling service in the past was enough to secure a visa. China had not ceased to face interesting times, but was positioning itself to face them on its own terms.

After China

H.B. Turbott rose to become New Zealand's Director-General of Health, and was for many years the 'Radio Doctor', broadcasting each week on health-related matters.

Rewi Alley remained in China until his death in 1987, writing and speaking extensively in support of New China.

Barbara Spencer became active in the NZ/China Friendship Society. A return visit to China in 1977 gave rise to a second book, *Thirty Years On*.

Bob Spencer became a surgeon in Whangarei; after his retirement he was instrumental in founding the North Haven Hospice to serve the wider Whangarei area.

George Shepherd became a Congregational minister in the United States, where he remained for the rest of his life.

James Bertram became a university teacher, retiring as professor of English at Victoria University of Wellington.

Max Bickerton spent the rest of his life in England, where he taught, and remained involved in oriental studies.

Agnes Moncrieff became a teacher with the New Zealand Correspondence School in Wellington.

J.B. Condliffe continued as a professor of economics at the University of California at Berkeley, while maintaining close links with New Zealand.

Bill Holland presided over the dissolution of the IPR in the early 1960s, then took up a post at the University of British Columbia, taking the IPR records with him.

Brian Low became head of the Department of Agricultural Economics at Massey Agricultural College, and later taught at Victoria University of Wellington.

Kathleen Hall helped establish a branch of the Mission to Lepers in Hong Kong, and later worked among Māori communities on New Zealand's East Coast.

Marjorie Monaghan (Marjorie Southward after her marriage) married the general secretary of the Anglican Board of Missions, Rev. John

Southward, and supported him in his later roles as the Anglican archdeacon in North Otago and in Central Otago.

Courtney Archer returned to New Zealand in 1953, assuming a role in the family flour-milling business in Rangiora.

Lindsay Crozier became a photographer and publicist for the Presbyterian Church of New Zealand, and later a field officer with Presbyterian Social Services.

Graham Milne provided medical services in the South Pacific before taking up general practice in New Zealand.

Alice Cook became dean of studies and later principal of the Hong Kong Theological Institute at Hok Fuk Tong. She retired to Invercargill in 1971.

Nancy Jansen worked with her husband Paddy in Hong Kong and the New Hebrides (Vanuatu). She later served as a teacher in Tonga.

Paddy Jansen became involved in evangelical training in Hong Kong, and later headed the Tangoa Teachers' Training Institute in the New Hebrides (Vanuatu).

Annie James worked at a home for refugee children in Hong Kong before retiring and returning to New Zealand in 1961.

Sources

Introduction

'At that time' – J.B. Condliffe, autobiography, typescript, ATL qMS-0511-0513.

'I knew I'd be' – interview with Agnes Moncrieff, 8 December 1985.

I don't know if' – interview with Alice Cook, 16 December 1985.

'a representative colonial type' – interview with James Bertram, 19 October 1985.

'a very handy man' – Cook interview.

'This kind of add-mix' – interview with Courtney Archer, October 1985.

'My god, I wouldn't know' – ibid.

'they were very competent men' – interview with H.B. Turbott, 16 November 1985.

'The finest group of people' – Moncrieff interview.

'a bit bossier' – Cook interview.

'Many very fine' – *Otago Daily Times*, 5 February 1934.

'extraordinarily interested' – Moncrieff interview.

'When you think of' – ibid.

'What would Borodin do' – Shepherd to W.C. Fairfield, China secretary of the ABCFM, Boston 7 March 1936, Shaowu Letters 1935–39, item 43, quoted in Thomson, p. 178.

Salvation could not be imported' – R.H. Tawney, *Land and Labour in China* (London: Allen & Unwin, 1964 [1932]), p. 186.

1. The Explorer: James Huston Edgar

'The Highest Town on Earth, and the Dirtiest' – chapter title in J.H. Edgar, *The Land of Mystery: Tibet*.

'a magnificent Lamasery' – J.H. Edgar, *The Marches of the Mantze*, p. 28.

'Bible distribution' – *China's Millions*, September 1922, p. 134.

'Your reports' – interview with Ron Malcolm, 19 June 1986.

'The new members were stupid' – Edgar to Anna Malcolm, 25 June 1922.
'He was basically' – Malcolm interview.
'The ravine' – Edgar, 'From Trapper to Missionary in China', unpublished ms.
'The cold blustery spring night' – Edgar to Anna Malcolm, 7 July 1935.
'A mass of sawtooth peaks' – Naval Intelligence Division, *China Proper*, Geographical Handbook Series, 1944, vol. 1, p. 83.
'suicidal lateral canyons' – Edgar, 'From Trapper to Missionary'.
'Owing to an idea' – Edgar, 'The Ganka, a Peak in Eastern Tibet', *Journal of the West China Border Society*, vol. III, pp. 157–61.
'the vast mountain systems' – Joseph F. Rock, 'The Glories of the Minya Konka', *National Geographic*, October 1930, p. 385. The American Joseph Rock started life as Josef Stein, an Austrian plant collector. His expeditions, often sponsored by the National Geographic Society, were on a grand scale, the caravan generally including a full dinner service, a portable bath, a gramophone, and two teams of Szechuanese porters to carry Rock himself from place to place.
'From Tapanui to Thibet' – *Otago Daily Times*, 7 May 1910.
'My thanks are due' – *China's Millions*, May 1916, p. 61.
'typical of the best class' – Frederick M. Bailey, *China – Tibet – Assam: A Journey, 1911*, p. 64.
'to another friend'— Ernest Henry Wilson, preface to *A Naturalist in Western China, with Vasculum, Camera and Gun*, p. viii. It was a peculiarity of Wilson's explorations that he always travelled with a whole-plate camera, whose size and cumbersome tripod added considerably to the difficulties of transport in broken country. His choice was vindicated, however, when he suffered a badly broken leg in a rock slide, and the legs of the tripod were called into use as splints to allow the expedition to continue.
'Here he was' – Malcolm interview.
'Whenever he came to stay' – ibid.
'Were I asked' – *Otago Daily Times*, 26 March 1908.
'the most critical incident' – Edgar Snow, *Red Star Over China*, p. 194.
'If I have to die' – Edgar to Will and Anna Malcolm, 3 January 1926.
'like the good old Duke of York' – China's Millions, May 1936, p. 75.
'Every day I am on the street' – ibid.

2. The Medical Man: H.B. Turbott

'You thought you were' – interview with H.B. Turbott, 16 November 1985.

'He was a sour customer' – ibid.

'While we were operating' – The Long Locum, Spectrum radio documentary #462.

'Canton city' – ibid.

'It was purely hospital work' – Turbott interview.

'The only other volunteer' – ibid.

'100 [students] a year' – ibid.

'Go to the laboratory' – ibid.

'We were hurried out' – *The Long Locum.*

'Hong Kong was under martial law.' – ibid.

'My time in China' – Turbott interview.

3. The Humanitarian: Rewi Alley

'to have a bit' – Rewi Alley to author, October 1973.

'a great internationalist fighter' – *Rewi Alley on Gung Ho*, introduction by Yang Bo.

'The scenery was great' – Alley to author, October 1973.

'He was a strangely out-of-place figure' – Edgar Snow, *Scorched Earth*, Book 1, 1941, p. 92.

'What the old Shanghai' – Rewi Alley, *Yo Banfa!*, 1953, p. 61.

'A woman who beat' – ibid., p. 64.

'The irrepressible gaiety' – ibid., p. 64.

'He had sandy hair' Helen Foster Snow, *My China Years*, 1984, p. 300.

'that I would be able' – ibid.

'She was a scatty, crazy woman' – interview with James Bertram, 19 October 1985.

'Right after Shanghai war' – Edgar Snow, 'The Dragon Licks His Wounds', *Saturday Evening Post*, 13 April 1940, p. 155.

'The old Chinese guild' – Edgar Snow, 'China's Blitzbuilder, Rewi Alley', *Saturday Evening Post*, 8 February 1941, p. 35.

'a good Scotchman' – Agnes Smedley, *Battle Hymn of China*, 1944, p. 149.

'"Suppose I did agree"' – Edgar Snow, *Journey to the Beginning*, 1959, p. 201.
'Old China Hands' Snow, *Scorched Earth*, Book 2, 1941, p. 191.
'Rewi Alley was already known' – Jacques Marcuse, *The Peking Papers*, 1968, pp. 118–19.
'In two years Indusco' Snow, *Scorched Earth*, Book 2, p. 192.
'A much later Chinese assessment' – brochure, Rewi Alley Memorial Cooperative Foundation.
'The indispensable man' – Helen Foster Snow, *My China Years*, p. 304.
'The most extraordinary man' etc – Snow, 'China's Blitzbuilder', pp. 12 ff.
'That man Rewi Alley is here' – Rewi Alley, *Fruition: The Story of George Alwen Hogg*, 1967, p. 46.
'Rewi Alley had been' – George Hogg, *I See a New China*, 1944, p.196.
'I did not even know' – Rewi Alley, *An Autobiography*, 1987, pp. 130–01.
'The brakes were put on' – Alley, *Yo Banfa!*, p. 177.
'it was not simply' – Pauline Keating, 'Cooperative Visions versus Wartime Realities . . .', NZ *Journal of East Asian Studies*, June 1997.
'As salary and allowances' – Alley, *Yo Banfa!*, p. 39.
'George had become convinced' – ibid.
'Some speak of it' – Hogg, *I See a New China*, p. 167.
'a large, amply-robed Buddha' – ibid., p. 170.
'He isn't exactly a pessimist' – Alley, *Fruition*, p. 79.

4. The Humanitarian – Sandan: Rewi Alley

'As things afterwards turned out' – Joseph Needham, letter, in Joseph & Dorothy Needham (eds), *Science Outpost: Papers of the Sino–British Science Co-operation Office 1942–1946* (London: Pilot Press, 1948), p. 127.
'I never met a better friend' – ibid., p. 128.
'When after five decades' – Joseph Needham, foreword in Rewi Alley, *Yo Banfa!*, 1952.
'made all six cyls. fire' – Needham, *Science Outpost*, p. 141.
'Wrote telegram to Embassy' – ibid., p. 147.
'practically the whole population' etc – ibid., p. 159.
'It was a place' – Alley, *Yo Banfa!*, p. 42.

'According to Rewi' – Needham, p. 163.
'When you are marching' – Rewi Alley, *Fruition: The Story of George Alwen Hogg*, 1967, p. 82.
'an adventure in creative education' – Rewi Alley, *Shandan: An Adventure in Creative Education* Christchurch: Caxton Press, 1959).
'To see how best Corso' – Colin Morrison, 'Report from China, 1947', typescript, p. 1.
'A man doing his job' – ibid., p. 37.
'I feel it only right to record' – ibid., p. 55.
'a whole group' – interview with Courtney Archer, October 1985.
'The sheep were exemplary' – Max Bickerton, *NZ Listener*, 20 June 1947.
'The native sheep' – Morrison, p. 53.
'It would do the average' – Rewi Alley, 'Lyttelton . . . to . . . Lhasa', *NZ Listener*, 16 February 1945.
'Bring your prince' – Barbara Spencer, *Desert Hospital in China*, 1954, pp. 58–59.
'We began a frantic search' – ibid.
'Small packages of a few potatoes' – ibid., p. 147.
'The work at the Shandan school' – *Training Rural Leaders*, UN FAO study, 1949, p. 135.

5. The Reformer: George Shepherd

'I commenced my first term' – George Shepherd, candidate's paper, American Board of Commissioners for Foreign Missions (ABCFM).
'Let me say right here' – ibid.
'I visited Shanghai' – ibid.
'Don't let any high Brahman' – ibid.
'While at Kuling in December' – *Evening Star*, 22 June 1927.
'knew beyond all doubt' – letter, ibid.
'We have been kept out of our field' – *Otago Daily Times*, 24 September 1931.
'ruined our delightful little bungalow' – *Otago Daily Times*, 3 November 1931.
'There is much that is good' – Shepherd to W.C. Fairfield, China secretary of the ABCFM, Boston, 29 October 1932, Shaowu Letters 1930–34, item 146, quoted in James C. Thomson Jr, *While China*

Faced West: American Reformers in Nationalist China 1928–1937, Cambridge, Mass.: Harvard University Press, 1969), p. 80.

'All the hsiens mentioned' – Shepherd to Fairfield, 19 September 1933, ibid., item 241, quoted in Thomson, p. 85.

'We must organise' – Shepherd to Fairfield, 5 November 1933, ibid., item 250, quoted in Thomson, p. 87.

'how very pleased' – Clara Sargent Shepherd, letter of 16 March 1934, ibid., item 32, quoted in Thomson, p. 261.

'For the present' – Fairfield to Shepherd, 22 May 1934, ibid., item 300, quoted in Thomson, p. 103.

'behaving in an unbecoming manner' – Hannah Pakula, *The Last Empress: Madame Chiang Kai-shek and the Birth of Modern China* (London: Phoenix, 2010), p. 232.

'The New Life Movement is based' – W.H. Auden & Christopher Isherwood, *Journey to a War* (New York: Random House, 1939), p. 57.

'It is doubtful whether the personalities' – Laura Tyson Li, *Madame Chiang Kai-shek: China's Eternal First Lady* (New York: Atlantic Monthly Press, 2006, p. 109.

'What would Borodin do' – Shepherd to Fairfield, 7 March 1936, ACBFM, Shaowu Letters 1935–39, item 43, quoted in Thomson, p. 178.

'What you can do' – *North China Daily News*, 24 March 1936.

'the "castor-oil cure"' – Thomson, p. 174.

'Priggery and hypocrisy' – Auden & Isherwood, p. 56.

'curious moral crusade' – ibid.

'Any similarity between this correspondent's dispatches' – E.J. Kahn, *The China Hands: America's Fereign Service Officers and What Befell Them* (New York: Penguin, 1976), p. 18.

'The Generalissimo is about as talkative' – Shepherd to Fairfield, 16 March 1936, item 45, quoted in Thomson, p. 181.

'the full meaning of the thoughts' – Field Marshall Lord Alanbrooke, *The Alanbrooke War Diaries 1939–1945* (London: Weidenfeld & Nicholson, 2001), p. 478.

'This establishes no precedent' – G.W. Shepherd, 7 December 1959, cited in Thomson, p. 182.

'modest and honest' – Memorandum on 'Conversation with G.W.

Shepherd, Nanking, May 1937', Johnson Papers, Library of Congress, quoted in Thomson, p. 195.

'next to William Henry Donald' – *Time*, 17 April 1939.

'rather resentful' – Fairfield to Shepherd and Mrs Shepherd, 28 May 1941, ABCFM, Shaowu Letters, 1940–52, item 300, quoted in Thomson, p. 194.

'It's like fascism' – Emily Hahn, *China to Me* (New York: Garden City Publishing, 1946), p. 127.

'In Chungking, I was invited' – Rewi Alley, *Yo Banfa!* (Shanghai: China Monthly Review, 1952), p. 18.

'A programme of all-round' – George Hunter McNeur, *The Missionary in Changing China* (Dunedin: Foreign Missions Cttee, 1935), p. 136.

'Two New Zealanders' – *Otago Daily Times*, 4 April 1940.

'They have a New Zealander there' – Agnes Moncrieff, letter to mother from Hankow, 19 June 1938, in Barbara Francis (ed.), *You Do Not Travel in China at the Full Moon: Agnes Moncrieff's Letters from China 1930–1945* (Wellington: Victoria University Press, 2017), p. 140.

'The latest arrival' – Moncrieff, letter to mother, from Hong Kong, 23 January 1939, ibid., p. 180.

6. The Journalist: James Bertram

'the most famous Britisher' – Helen Foster Snow, *My China Years* (London: Harrap, 1984), p. 177.

'If all the world's population' – James Bertram, in Ann Trotter (ed.), *New Zealand and China: The Papers of the 21st Foreign Policy School, 1986*, p. 5.

'They all felt' – interview with Courtney Archer, October 1985.

'a most refined young fellow' – James McNeish, *Dance of the Peacocks* (Auckland: Random House, 2003), p. 39.

'He has a slightly precious manner' – ibid., p. 80.

'were a fairly cultivated group' – James Bertram, *Capes of China Slide Away: A Memoir of Peace and War 1910–1980* (Auckland: Auckland University Press, 1993), p. 93.

'You think that's impossible' – interview with James Bertram, 19 October 1985.

'What is that man holding' – J.M. McHugh, *Introductory Mandarin*

Lessons (Shanghai: Kelly & Walsh, 1931), p. 201.

'Red China was more *terra incognita*' – Edgar Snow, *Journey to the Beginning* (London: Gollancz, 1959), p. 152.

'Attractive and irrepressible' – Bertram, *Capes of China*, pp. 94–95.

'She was a scatty, crazy woman' – Bertram interview.

'he and Ed and I' – Helen Foster Snow, p. 176.

'Jim was very attractive' – ibid.

'as a well-intentioned, moonstruck follower' – *Dominion*, Wellington, 15 March 1986.

'It's lucky you are a lady' – Helen Foster Snow, *My China Years*, p. 176.

'I am Miao Feng-shan' – Bertram, *Capes of China*, p. 103.

One Shanghai tabloid alleged – Paul Frillman & Graham Peck, *China: The Remembered Life* (Boston: Houghton Mifflin, 1968), p. 22.

'Nor could I be impressed' – Agnes Smedley, *Battle Hymn of China* (London: Gollancz, 1944), p. 72.

'The London *Times*' – James Bertram, *Crisis in China* (London: Macmillan, 1937), p. 176.

'Some good-natured, friendly and sympathetic joshing' – John S. Service to Michael Green, 8 December 1986. Service elsewhere expanded on this unlooked-for legacy in a footnote to a discussion of the eccentric American envoy's determination to 'sustain' Chiang Kai-shek at all costs. 'For a brief period in 1942, Hurley had served as the first American diplomatic representative in New Zealand. When I served in that country in 1946–1948, the memories of his stay were still vivid. One of the most common related to a national election. The incumbent Prime Minister, seeking re-election, was Peter Fraser. He and Hurley soon – and quite properly – became good friends. Fraser recognised Hurley's penchant for oratory and began to make it a habit to invite Hurley to accompany him to meetings during the campaign. The American Minister would at some point be introduced as an honoured guest and asked to make a few remarks. These would invariably start out as a rip-snorting, flag-waving talk about the war . . . but end up as a strong endorsement of his 'old friend, staunch ally, and great leader of the country', Prime Minister Fraser. The reactions to this story of the American Republican boosting the socialist New Zealander varied, of course, according to the party affiliation of the teller, though all could agree that Hurley was a most unusual diplomat.' – John S. Service, *The Amerasia Papers*, research monograph (Berkeley: University of California, 1971), p. 80.

'This male announcer' – Bertram, *Capes of China*, p. 112.

'I tortured the audience' – Agnes Smedley, *China Fights Back* London: Gollancz, 1938), p. 48.

'Was militant enough' – James Bertram, *North China Front* (London: Macmillan, 1939), p. 124.

'Some remnants of the legend' – ibid., p. 150.

'Promise to pay' – ibid., p. 156.

'My questions were not distorted' – Bertram interview.

'The journalist is usually more concerned' – Bertram, *North China Front*, p. vii.

'Were you afraid?' – ibid., p. 223.

'We shared' – Bertram, *Crisis in China*, p. 246.

'In late December two foreigners' – Smedley, *Battle Hymn of China*, p. 141.

'blue uniform, bedding roll' – Bertram, *Capes of China*, p. 142.

7. The Journalists: James Bertram, Iris Wilkinson

'To act as a liaison' – James Bertram, *The Shadow of a War: A New Zealander in the Far East 1939–1946* (London: Gollancz, 1947), p. 17.

'but Fatty Liao wasn't over-impressed' – James Bertram, *Capes of China Slide Away: A Memoir of Peace and War 1910–1980* (Auckland: Auckland University Press, 1993), p. 148.

'She had been in Shanghai' – ibid.

'"The lady deserved it"' – Derek Challis & Gloria Rawlinson, *The Book of Iris: A Life of Robin Hyde* (Auckland: Auckland University Press, 2002), p. 535.

'surprisingly lucid' – Lindsay Watt, quoted in Elspeth Sandys, *A Communist in the Family: Searching for Rewi Alley* (Dunedin, Otago University Press, 2019), p. 349.

'very much the innocent Kiwi abroad' – Bertram, *Capes of China*, p. 179.

'It's no special comfort' – Bertram, *Capes of China*, p. 151.

'She kept looking at the flowers' – Robin Hyde, *Dragon Rampant*

(London: Hurst & Blackett, 1939), p. 176.

'I was one of the people' – interview with Agnes Moncrieff, 8 December 1985.

'At that time, women writers' – Rex Warren quoted in Challis & Rawlinson, p. 571.

'Mr Farmer of the Chinese Government Publicity' – Agnes Moncrieff to Eva Skinner, 22 May 1938, cited in Barbara Francis (ed.), *You Do Not Travel in China at the Full Moon: Agnes Moncrieff's Letters from China 1930–1945* (Wellington: Victoria University Press, 2017), p. 133.

'If you were a Chinese woman' – quoted in Gillian Boddy & Jacqueline Matthews (eds), *Disputed Ground: Robin Hyde, Journalist* (Wellington: Victoria University Press, 1991), p. 381.

'James [Bertram] had tried to dissuade her' – Charles Brasch, *Indirections: A Memoir 1909–1947* (Wellington: Oxford University Press, 1980), p. 340.

By one account – Fujio Kano & Maurice Ward, 'Socialism is a Mission: Max Bickerton's Involvement with the Japanese Communist Party and Translation of Japanese Proletarian Literature in the 1930s', *NZ Journal of Asian Studies*, vol. 16, no. 2 (December 2014), pp. 104–06.

'Whenever Rewi Alley could manage' – Bertram, *Capes of China*, p. 156.

'I was prepared to be a volunteer' – ibid., p. 166.

'addressing a mass meeting' – Bertram, *The Shadow of a War*, p. 73.

'Nobody among those British' – Emily Hahn, *China to Me* (New York: Garden City Publishing, 1946), p. 216.

on condition that she not make speeches – J.R. & S.R. McKinnon, *Agnes Smedley: The Life and Times of an American Radical* (Berkeley: University of California Press, 1988), pp. 225 ff.

'sunburnt and travel-stained' – Bertram, *The Shadow of a War*, p. 79.

'necessary equipment' – ibid., p. 92.

'a moustachioed outdoor type' – Bertram, *Capes of China*, p. 181.

'Somebody showed her a dishpan' – Hahn, *China to Me*, p. 247.

'There was a rush' – ibid., p. 295.

'our admirable interpreter' – John Stericker, *A Tear for the Dragon* (London: Arthur Barker, 1958), p. 209.

'I cannot help feeling' – Gwolo: Old Hong Kong: https://gwulo.com/node/11872

'Some of the little ones' – quoted in Sandra Simpson, 'William Maxwell Bickerton: A NZ Footnote to the History of Haiku in English': https://poetrysociety.org.nz/affiliates/haiku-nz/haiku-poems-articles/archived-articles/william-maxwell-bickerton-a-nz-footnote-to-the-history-of-haiku-in-english. There is an account of the subsequent fracas, together with photographs of some of the puppets, in Rachel May & John Minford (eds), *A Birthday Book for Brother Stone* (Hong Kong: Chinese University Press, 2003).

'Over those years many died' – Bertram, *Capes of China*, p. 205.

'He would wake up screaming' – James McNeish, *Dance of the Peacocks* (Auckland: Random House, 2003), p. 404.

'His whole being' – McNeish, p. 287.

'Jim paid a heavy price' – Helen Foster Snow, *My China Years* (London: Harrap, 1984), p. 176.

8. The Organiser: Agnes Moncrieff

'We were talking about China' – interview with Agnes Moncrieff, 8 December 1985. Other quotations in this chapter are from the same source, unless otherwise indicated.

'the people were more frightened' – *Evening Post*, 30 August 1934.

'Two girls were waiting in the office' – Barbara Francis (ed.), *You Do Not Travel in China at the Full Moon: Agnes Moncrieff's Letters from China 1930–1945* (Wellington: Victoria University Press, 2017), p. 60.

'There is not the least likelihood' – Agnes Moncrieff, letter to mother, 13 February 1938, in Francis, p. 103.

The Japanese are such rotten marksmen' – Moncrieff to mother, 6 October 1938, in Francis, p. 157.

'very gracious and most distinguished looking' – Moncrieff to mother, 10 April 1938, in Francis, p. 120.

'I never saw anything so gruesome in my life' – Moncrieff to Eva Skinner, 24 July 1948, in Francis, p. 145.

'The amah who brought me water' – Moncrieff, shared letter to New Zealand, October 1938, in Francis, p. 160.

'caught a crack' – Rewi Alley, *Rewi Alley: An Autobiography* (Beijing: New World Press, 1987), p. 74.

'I told the ambassador that' – Confidential Despatch F6096/1/10 of 19

June 1939, Viscount Halifax to Sir R. Craigie (Tokyo).
'I therefore booked a berth' – Moncrieff, travel diary, January 1942, in Francis, p. 223.
'Both John and Joe' – ibid., p. 225.
'One certainly sees a lot' – Moncrieff, 'Life in Chengdu', *The YWCA Review*, July 1945, in Francis, p. 254.

9. The Economists: J.B. Condliffe, Bill Holland and Brian Low

'He [Alley] had played wing-forward' – J.B. Condliffe, autobiography, typescript, ATL qMS-0511-0513.
'It was like seeing the pages' – Condliffe, autobiography.
'Buck was an agricultural economist' – ibid.
'He was Mayor of the ex-British Concession' – ibid.
'He [David Yui] was an Anglican' – ibid.
'The most self-possessed person' – ibid.
'who charged me six percent' – William L. Holland, 'The IPR: A Historical Sketch', typescript, p. 2.
'Since a great deal' – ibid., p. 3.
'to go and look' – ibid., p. 12.
'The modern state in Europe' – R.H. Tawney, *Land and Labour in China* (London: Allen & Unwin, 1964 [1932]), p. 167.
'Condliffe asked me to go' – Holland, 'The IPR: A Historical Sketch', p. 12.
'In many respects' – ibid. p. 13.
'scruffy-looking' – Wilfred V. Pennell, *A Lifetime with the Chinese* (Hong Kong: South China Morning Post, 1974), p. 175.
'occasionally would get impatient' – Holland, 'IP Activities, 1930-1933', typescript, p. 3.
'He did so' – ibid.
'the succession came to be regarded' – Condliffe, autobiography.
'I remember seeing the Japanese army' – Holland, 'The IPR: A Historical Sketch', typescript, p. 23.
'but in such a way' – Holland, 'IPR Activities 1934–1939', typescript, p. 11.
'Japan was greatly disillusioned' – *Evening Star*, 18 March 1938, p. 8.

'People are saying' – *Auckland Star*, 18 March 1938, p. 8.
'and on top of that' – Holland, 'India–China Trip 1943', typescript, p. 2.
'One day we were invited' – ibid., p. 6.
'a great deal' – Holland, 'IPR Memoirs 1939–1946', typescript, p. 8.
'Supposing the chap who was doing it' – interview with Brian Low, 18 November 1985.
'The idea being' – ibid.
'Lossing Buck was a bit annoying' – ibid.
'Since at that time' – Holland, 'IPR Activities, 1930–1933', typescript, p. 5.
'Lossing said, well, let's hire' – Low interview.
'To a small extent' – ibid.
'I remember we were all practising' – interview with James Bertram, 19 October 1985.
'I [Low] was in Nanking' – Low interview.
'Especially I am indebted' – John Lossing Buck, *Land Utilization in China* (Taipei: Southern Materials Center Inc (reprint), 1986), p. xiv.
'It was very notable' – Low interview.
'All our information' – ibid.
'The basic relation between land and people' – ibid.
'Even today, Buck's book stands out' – Hao Hu et al, *Chinese Agriculture in the 1930s* (Palgrave Macmillan, 2019), p. 14.
'The era's foremost research institute' – James C. Thomson Jr, *While China Faced West: American Reformers in Nationalist China 1928–1937* (Cambridge, Mass.: Harvard University Press, 1969), p. 279.

10. The Nurse: Kathleen Hall

'I remember her scampering' – George Hogg, *I See a New China* (Boston: Little, Brown, 1944), p. 11.
'such a really original and determined person' – interview with James Bertram, 19 October 1985.
'If she had been a man' – Rewi Alley to Tom Newnham, cited in Tom Newnham, *He Mingqing: The Life of Kathleen Hall* (Beijing: New World Press, 1992), p. 171.
'While women of all classes' – Rae McGregor, *Shrewd Sanctity: The Story*

of Kathleen Hall, Missionary Nurse in China, 1896–1970 (Auckland: Polygraphia, 2006), p. 23.

'simple, good, hard-working people' – Kathleen Hall, 'Recollections of the Days of Bitter Struggle', in *The Twenty Years of the China Welfare Institute* (Shanghai, 1958), p. 90.

'A girl nurse and I' – Hall, quoted in McGregor, *Shrewd Sanctity*, p. 63.

'The village . . . is at the most' – Hall, quoted in ibid., p. 62.

'They often took with them' – Hall, 'Recollections', p. 93.

'That's just to let the Americans' – Roderick Stewart, *The Mind of Norman Bethune* Ontario: Fitzhenry & Whiteside, 1977), p. 91.

'What kind of spirit is this' – *Selected Works of Mao Tse-tung*, vol. 2, p. 337.

'I have met an angel' – Bethune, quoted in Sydney Gordon & Ted Allan, *The Scalpel, the Sword: The Story of Doctor Norman Bethune* (London: Robert Hale, 1954), p. 223.

'was tall, with an open strong face' – ibid., p. 221.

'"Tung, you wily dog"' – Bethune, quoted in ibid., p. 225.

'Here in China' – Hall, 'Recollections', p. 96.

'Contrary to what I have heard' – McClure, quoted in Monroe Scott, *McClure: The China Years* (Toronto: Canec Publishing, 1977), p. 273.

'On this occasion' – Hall, 'Recollections', p. 100.

'I am trying to persuade Miss Hall' – Bethune, quoted in Stewart, *The Mind of Norman Bethune*, p. 121.

'There is a rather interesting lady' – McClure, quoted in Scott, *McClure*, p. 273.

'I felt even more anxious' – Hall, 'Recollections', p. 106.

'Now completely cut off by war' – ibid., p. 109.

'I had become too exhausted to continue' – ibid., p. 110.

11. The Teacher: Marjorie Monaghan

'I had a whale of a time' – interview with Marjorie Southward (née Monaghan),17 February 1986. The Monaghan quotations that follow are from the same source.

'Every comfort of Western culture' – Langdon Gilkey, *Shantung Compound* (London: Anthony Blond, 1966), p. 1.

'I think our mana vanished forever' – Southward interview; see also

Gilkey, pp. 3–4.

'donned the Lenin uniform' – Jean Yule, *About Face in China* (Melbourne: Joint Board of Christian Education, 1995), p. 203.

12. The Pacifists: Lindsay Crozier, Courtney Archer

'The person who came out' – interview with Courtney Archer, October 1985. The Archer quotations that follow are from the same source.

'When I weighed in' – interview with Lindsay Crozier, 6 January 1987.

'a very handy man' – interview with Alice Cook, 16 December 1985.

'We had a slogan up' – Lindsay Crozier; 'Pieces of String', typescript, p. 14.

'The Gobi desert' – Owen Jackson to Ellen Jackson, 5 June 1945, quoted in Catriona Cameron, *Go Anywhere, Do Anything* (Wellington: Beechtree Press, 1996), p. 73.

'Perhaps this act of defiance' – Crozier, 'Pieces of String', p. 40.

'snowy-haired Kiwi angel' – ibid.

'A slight tug and the fin' – ibid.

'Three of us were asked' – Crozier interview.

'We had an American' – Crozier interview.

'After some pressing' – Crozier, *Pieces of String*, p. 44.

'And I said' – interview with Graham Milne, 12 January 1986. The Milne quotations that follow are from the same source.

'A giant blackmail scheme' – Hannah Pakula, *The Last Empress: Madame Chiang Kai-shek and the Birth of Modern China* (London: Phoenix, 2010), p. 481.

'[UNRRA's] purpose is to help' – *Time*, 22 July 1946.

13. The Missionaries: Graham Milne, Alice Cook and Annie James

'

[China] cannot put her house in order' – G.H. McNeur, *New Zealand and China* (Dunedin: W.H. Adams, 1926), pp. 3–4.

'New Zealand has been unfortunate' – G.H. McNeur, *The Missionary in Changing China* (Dunedin: Foreign Missions Cttee, 1935), p. 9.

'Communism was still very strong' – *Otago Daily Times*, 5 February 1934.

'bilingual but monocultural' – Rhys Richards (son), pers. comm. to author.

'He was rather unshaven' – interview with Alice Cook, 16 December 1985. The Cook quotations that follow are from the same source.

'Missionaries go out to China' – Rev. William Mawson (ed.), *The Story of the Canton Villages Mission of the Presbyterian Church of New Zealand*, Dunedin: Foreign Missions Cttee, 1926), pp. 15–16.

'Most of them come from' – ibid., p. 22.

'I thoroughly enjoyed my time' – Kathleen Hall to 'Civis', 9 April 1935.

'His Britannic Majesty's Consul-General' – D.N. MacDiarmid, *Tse Koo: A Heroine of China* (Dunedin: Missions Cttee of the Presbyterian Church of NZ, 1945), p. 14.

'I am afraid we are getting accustomed' – ibid., p. 27.

'As Japan and your country' – E.G. Jansen, *Jade Engraved* (Christchurch: Presbyterian Bookroom, 1948), p. 152.

'Even the wastepaper basket' – interview with Graham Milne, 12 January 1986. The Milne quotations that follow are from the same source.

'It was absolutely not a revolution' – interview with Nancy Jansen, 10 November 1985.

'We were not molested' – interview with Lindsay Crozier, 6 January 1987.

'They were very neat' – Nancy Jansen interview.

'It would best serve' – J.S. Murray, *A Century of Growth: Presbyterian Overseas Mission Work 1869–1969* (Christchurch: Presbyterian Bookroom, n.d.), p. 66.

'Because they're my friends' – Nancy Jansen interview.

Abbreviations

ABCFM – American Board of Commissioners for Foreign Missions
ATL – Alexander Turnbull Library, Wellington
CAT – Civil Air Transport
CCP – Chinese Communist Party
CDL – China Defence League
CIC – Chinese Industrial Cooperatives
CIM – China Inland Mission
CMS – Church Missionary Society
CNRRA – China National Relief and Rehabilitation Administration
Corso – Council of Organisations for Relief Service Overseas
CVM – Canton Villages Mission
FAU – Friends Ambulance Unit
FSU – Friends Service Unit
HKVDC – Hong Kong Volunteer Defence Corps
ICCIC – International Committee for the Promotion of Chinese Industrial Cooperatives
Indusco – Industrial Cooperatives
IPR – Institute of Pacific Relations
IRC – International Red Cross
KMT – Kuomintang (Nationalist Party)
NCC – National Christian Council (of China)
OSS – (United States) Office of Strategic Services
OWI – (United States) Office of War Information
PLA – People's Liberation Army
PUMC – Peking Union Medical College
SCM – Student Christian Movement
SPG – Society for the Propagation of the Gospel
UNRRA – United Nations Relief and Rehabilitation Administration
YWCA – Young Women's Christian Association

Bibliography

Interviews

Courtney Archer, October 1985.
James Bertram, 19 October 1985.
Nancy Jansen, 10 November 1985.
H.B. Turbott, 16 November 1985.
Brian Low, 18 November 1985.
Agnes Moncrieff, 5 December 1985.
Alice Cook, 16 December 1985.
Colin Morrison, 7 January 1986.
Graham Milne, 12 January 1986.
Marjorie Southward, 17 February 1986.
Ron Malcolm, 19 May 1986.
Lindsay Crozier, 6 January 1987.
Max Wilkinson, 9 September 2015.

Newspapers and journals

Auckland Star
China's Millions
Dominion
Evening Post
Evening Star
Journal of the West China Border Research Society
National Geographic
New Zealand Journal of East Asian Studies
New Zealand Listener
North China Daily News
Otago Daily Times
Saturday Evening Post
The Reaper
Time
YWCA Review

Unpublished

(Much of the material contained in the drafts by Condliffe and Holland has now been brought together in Paul F. Hooper (ed.), *Remembering the Institute of Pacific Relations: The Memoirs of William L. Holland* (Tokyo: Ryukei Shyosha, 1995)

ABCFM: papers of candidates – George W. Shepherd

Alley, Rewi, Memorial Cooperative Foundation, brochure

Condliffe, J.B., autobiography, typescript, ATL qMS-0511-0513

Crozier, Lindsay, 'Pieces of String', typescript for private circulation

Crozier, Mary, 'More Pieces of String', typescript for private circulation

Edgar, James Huston, 'From Trapper to Missionary in China', unpublished manuscript

Holland, William L., 'IPR Activities 1930–1933', typescript

Holland, William L., 'IPR Activities 1934–1939', typescript

Holland, William L., 'IPR Memories 1939–1946', typescript

Holland, William L., 'India–China Trip 1943', typescript

Holland, William L., 'The IPR: A Historical Sketch', typescript

Morrison, Colin W., 'Report from China, 1947', typescript

Yuan, Silvia Yang, '"Kiwis" in the Middle Kingdom: A Sociological Interpretation of the History of New Zealand Missionaries in China from 1877 to 1953 and beyond', PhD thesis, Massey University, 2013

Article

Kano, Fujio & Maurice Ward, 'Socialism is a Mission: Max Bickerton's Involvement with the Japanese Communist Party and Translation of Japanese Proletarian Literature in the 1930s', *NZ Journal of Asian Studies* vol. 16, no. 2 (December 2014), pp. 104–06.

Books and book chapters

Alanbrooke, Field Marshall Lord, *War Diaries 1939–1945* (London: Weidenfeld & Nicholson, 2001)

Alley, Rewi, *Fruition: The Story of George Alwen Hogg* (Christchurch: Caxton Press, 1967)

Alley, Rewi, *Rewi Alley on Gung Ho* (Beijing: Beijing Review Press, 1989)

Alley, Rewi, *Rewi Alley: An Autobiography* (Beijing: New World Press, 1987)

Alley, Rewi, *Sandan: An Adventure in Creative Education* (Christchurch: Caxton Press, 1959)

Alley, Rewi, *Shantan Bailie School, 1949* (Hong Kong: Tai Wah Press, n.d. (1950?))

Alley, Rewi, *Yo Banfa!* (Shanghai: China Monthly Review, 1952)

Auden, W.H. & Christopher Isherwood, *Journey to a War* (New York: Random House, 1939)

Bailey, Lt-Col F.M., *China – Tibet – Assam (A Journey, 1911)* (London: Jonathan Cape, 1945)

Barton, Henry H., *George Hunter McNeur: A Pioneer Missionary in South China* (Christchurch: Presbyterian Bookroom, 1955)

Bell, Sir Charles, *Tibet Past and Present* (Oxford: Clarendon Press, 1924)

Belmer, Roy, *The Teeth of the Dragon* (London: Epworth Press, 1964)

Bertram, James M., *Crisis in China* (London: Macmillan, 1937)

Bertram, James, 'Fifty Years of China: A Personal View', in Ann Trotter (ed.), *New Zealand and China: The Papers of the 21st Foreign Policy School, 1986*

Bertram, James, *Capes of China Slide Away: A Memoir of Peace and War 1910–1980* (Auckland: Auckland University Press, 1993)

Bertram, James, *North China Front* (London: Macmillan, 1939)

Bertram, James, *The Shadow of a War: A New Zealander in the Far East 1939–1946* (London: Gollancz, 1947)

Boddy, Gillian & Jacqueline Matthews (eds), *Disputed Ground: Robin Hyde, Journalist* (Wellington: Victoria University Press, 1991)

Brady, Anne-Marie, *Friend of China: The Myth of Rewi Alley* (London: RoutledgeCurzon, 2003)

Brasch, Charles, *Indirections: A Memoir 1909–1947* (Wellington: Oxford University Press, 1980)

Buck, John Lossing, *Land Utilization in China* (Taipei: Southern Materials Center Inc (reprint), 1986)

Buck, Pearl S., *My Several Worlds: A Personal Record* (London: Methuen, 1955)

Cameron, Catriona, *Go Anywhere, Do Anything* (Wellington: Beechtree Press, 1996)

Carlson, E.F., *Twin Stars of China* (New York: Dodd, Mead, 1940)

Challis, Derek & Gloria Rawlinson, *The Book of Iris: A Life of Robin Hyde* (Auckland: Auckland University Press, 2002)

Chapple, Geoff, *Rewi Alley of China*, Auckland: Hodder and Stoughton, 1980.

Chiang, Mayling Soong, *Sian: A Coup d'*État (Shanghai: China Publishing Company, 1937)

China Proper (2 vols), Geographical Handbook Series (London: Naval Intelligence Division, 1944)

Church of Christ, *Let Us Unite: The Church of Christ in China* (Shanghai: Willow Pattern Press, n.d.)

Coates, P.D., *The China Consuls* (Hong Kong: Oxford University Press, 1988)

Condliffe, J.B., *China Today: Economic* (Boston: World Peace Foundation, 1932)

Cox, E.H.M., *Plant Hunting in China* (London: Collins, 1945)

Dalzell, Matthew, *New Zealanders in Republican China 1912–1949*, University of Auckland/NZ Asia Institute Resource Paper no. 4, 1995.

Edgar, J.H., *The Land of Mystery: Tibet* (Melbourne: China Inland Mission, 1927)

Edgar, J.H., *The Marches of the Mantze* (London: China Inland Mission, n.d. [1908])

Elder, C.J. & M.F. Green, 'New Zealand and China, 1792–1972', in Ann Trotter (ed.), *New Zealand and China: The Papers of the 21st Otago Foreign Policy School, 1986*

Farmer, Rhodes, *Shanghai Harvest: A Diary of Three Years in the China War* (London: Museum Press, 1945)

Farnsworth, Robert M., *From Vagabond to Journalist: Edgar Snow in Asia 1928–1941* (Beijing: Foreign Languages Press, 2003)

Fenby, Jonathan, *Generalissimo Chiang Kai-shek and the China He Lost* (London: Simon & Schuster, 2003)

Fitch, George A., *My Eighty Years in China* (Taipei: Mei Ya Publications, 1974)

Fitzgerald, C.P., The *Birth of Communist China* (Harmondsworth: Pelican, 1966)

Ford, Daniel, *Flying Tigers: Claire Chennault and the American Volunteer*

Group (Washington & London: Smithsonian Institution Press, 1991)
Francis, Barbara (ed.), *You Do Not Travel in China at the Full Moon: Agnes Moncrieff's Letters from China 1930–1945* (Wellington: Victoria University Press, 2017)
Frillman, Paul & Graham Peck, *China: The Remembered Life* (Boston: Houghton Mifflin, 1968)
Gilkey, Langdon, *Shantung Compound* (London: Anthony Blond, 1966)
Goodwin, R.B., *Hong Kong Escape* (London: Arthur Barker, 1953)
Gordon, Sydney & Ted Allan, *The Scalpel, the Sword: The Story of Doctor Norman Bethune* (London: Robert Hale, 1954)
Gunther, John, *Inside Asia* (New York: Harper & Brothers, 1942)
Hahn, Emily, *China to Me* (New York: Garden City Publishing, 1946)
Hahn, Emily, *The Soong Sisters* (London: Robert Hale, 1943)
Hall, Kathleen, 'Recollections of the Days of Bitter Struggle', in *The Twenty Years of the China Welfare Institute* (Shanghai: China Welfare Institute, 1958)
Hao Hu, Funing Zhong & Calum G. Turvey (eds), *Chinese Agriculture in the 1930s* (Palgrave Macmillan, 2019)
Hensley, Gerald, *Beyond the Battlefield: New Zealand and its Allies 1939–45* (Auckland: Penguin/Viking, 2009)
Hogg, George, *I See a New China* (Boston: Little, Brown, 1944)
Hyde, Robin, *Dragon Rampant* (London: Hurst & Blackett, 1939)
Isherwood, Christopher, *Christopher and His Kind* (London: Eyre Methuen, 1977)
James, Annie, *I Was in Prison* (Christchurch: Presbyterian Bookroom, 1952)
Jansen, E.G., *Jade Engraved* (Christchurch: Presbyterian Bookroom, 1948)
Kahn, E.J., *The China Hands: America's Foreign Service Officers and What Befell Them* (New York: Penguin, 1976)
Li, Laura Tyson, *Madame Chiang Kai-shek: China's Eternal First Lady* (New York: Atlantic Monthly Press, 2006)
Lindsay, Michael, *The Unknown War: North China 1937–1945* (London: Bergström & Boyle, 1975)
MacDiarmid, D.N., *Tse Koo: A Heroine of China* (Dunedin: Missions Cttee of the Presbyterian Church of NZ, 1945)
MacKinnon, Janice R. & Stephen R., *Agnes Smedley: The Life and Times*

of an American Radical (Berkeley: University of California Press, 1988)

MacManus, James, *Ocean Devil: The Life and Legend of George Hogg* (London: Harper Perennial, 2008)

Marcuse, Jacques, *The Peking Papers* (London: Arthur Barker, 1968)

Mawson, Rev. William (ed.), *The Story of the Canton Villages Mission of the Presbyterian Church of New Zealand*, Dunedin: Foreign Missions Cttee, 1926)

May, Rachel & John Minford (eds), *A Birthday Book for Brother Stone* (Hong Kong: Chinese University Press, 2003)

McGregor, Rae, *Shrewd Sanctity: The Story of Kathleen Hall, Missionary Nurse in China, 1896–1970* (Auckland: Polygraphia, 2006)

McHugh, J.M., *Introductory Mandarin Lessons* (Shanghai: Kelly & Walsh, 1931)

McNeish, James, *Dance of the Peacocks* (Auckland: Random House, 2003)

McNeur, George Hunter, *New Zealand and China* (Dunedin: W.H. Adams, 1926)

McNeur, George Hunter, *The Missionary in Changing China* (Dunedin: Foreign Missions Cttee, 1935)

Milner, Ian F.G., *New Zealand's Interests and Policies in the Far East*, IPR Inquiry Series (New York: Institute of Pacific Relations, 1939)

Molloy, Bob, *Colossus Unsung* (Milton Keynes: Xlibris Corp, 2011)

Murray, J.S., *A Century of Growth: Presbyterian Overseas Mission Work 1869–1969* (Christchurch: Presbyterian Bookroom, n.d.)

Needham, Joseph & Dorothy (eds), *Science Outpost: Papers of the Sino–British Science Co-operation Office 1942–1946* (London: Pilot Press, 1948)

Newnham, Tom, *He Mingqing: The Life of Kathleen Hall* (Beijing: New World Press, 1992)

Ogilvie, Gordon, *Little Feet in a Big Room: Frances Ogilvie of China* (Christchurch: Shoal Bay Press, 1994)

Pakula, Hannah, *The Last Empress: Madame Chiang Kai-shek and the Birth of Modern China* (London: Phoenix, 2010)

Peck, Graham, *Through China's Wall* (London: Collins, 1941)

Peck, Graham, *Two Kinds of Time* (Boston: Houghton Mifflin, 1967)

Pennell, Wilfred V., *A Lifetime with the Chinese* (Hong Kong: South

China Morning Post, 1974)
Sandys, Elspeth, *A Communist in the Family: Searching for Rewi Alley* (Dunedin, Otago University Press, 2019)
Scott, Monroe, *McClure: The China Years* (Toronto: Canec Publishing, 1977)
Service, John S., *Lost Chance in China* (New York: Vintage, 1975)
Service, John S., *The Amerasia Papers: Some Problems in the History of US–China Relations* (Berkeley: University of California, 1971)
Smedley, Agnes, *Battle Hymn of China* (London: Gollancz, 1944)
Smedley, Agnes, *China Fights Back* (London: Gollancz, 1938)
Snow, Edgar, *Journey to the Beginning* (London: Gollancz, 1959)
Snow, Edgar, *Red Star Over China* (London: Gollancz, 1937)
Snow, Edgar, *Scorched Earth* (2 vols) (London: Gollancz, 1941)
Snow, Helen Foster, *My China Years* (London: Harrap, 1984)
Snowden, Rita, *Never a Dull Moment: Life and Letters of Annie James* (Christchurch: Presbyterian Bookroom, 1948)
Spence, Jonathan D., *The Search for Modern China* (New York, W.W. Norton, 1991)
Spencer, Barbara, *China Thirty Years On* (Whanganui: Advocate, n.d.)
Spencer, Barbara, *Desert Hospital in China* (London: Jarrolds, 1954)
Stericker, John, *A Tear for the Dragon* (London: Arthur Barker, 1958)
Stewart, Roderick: *The Mind of Norman Bethune* Ontario: Fitzhenry & Whiteside, 1977)
Sues, Ilona Ralf, *Shark's Fins and Millet* (Boston: Little, Brown, 1944)
Tawney, R.H., *Land and Labour in China* (London: Allen & Unwin, 1964 [1932])
Teichman, Eric, *Travels of a Consular Officer in Eastern Tibet* (Cambridge, Cambridge University Press, 1922)
The Twenty Years of the China Welfare Institute (Shanghai: China Welfare Institute, 1958)
Thomson, James C. Jr, *While China Faced West: American Reformers in Nationalist China 1928–1937* (Cambridge, Mass.: Harvard University Press, 1969)
Training Rural Leaders: Shanton Bailie School, Kansu Province, China (Washington: Food and Agriculture Organization of the United Nations, 1949)
Wickert, Erwin (ed.), *The Good German of Nanking: The Diaries of John*

Rabe (London: Little, Brown, 1999)

Wilson, Ernest Henry, *A Naturalist in Western China, with Vasculum, Camera and Gun* (2 vols) (London: Methuen, 1913)

Winchester, Simon, *Bomb, Book and Compass: Joseph Needham and the Great Secrets of China* (Camberwell: Penguin, 2009)

Yule, Jean, *About Face in China* (Melbourne: Joint Board of Christian Education, 1995)

Index

D